THE
BROWN BULLET

THE
BROWN BULLET

★∴ *Rajo Jack's* ∴★

DRIVE TO INTEGRATE AUTO RACING

BILL POEHLER

Lawrence Hill Books

Chicago

Copyright © 2020 by Bill Poehler
All rights reserved
Published by Lawrence Hill Books
An imprint of Chicago Review Press Incorporated
814 North Franklin Street
Chicago, Illinois 60610
ISBN 978-1-64160-229-7

Library of Congress Cataloging-in-Publication Data
Is available from the Library of Congress.

Interior design: Nord Compo

Printed in the United States of America
5 4 3 2 1

CONTENTS

Introduction

THE UNLIKELY HERO

THE SPEEDWAY WAS an embarrassment to the racing world, but to the pesky seven-year-old boy with a mop of curly dark hair it was an oasis in a world that disappointed him at every opportunity.

The kid, large for his age and with a slight southern twang in his voice, landed in California after his family fled Oklahoma during the worst of the Great Depression. His family settled in the Lynwood neighborhood of Los Angeles in 1936, a short walk from the new yet already decrepit Southern Ascot Speedway in the Southgate neighborhood. The kid had no money to pay the steep thirty-five cents for a ticket to the races, but the sound of engines growling at full throat and tires squealing for mercy from his backyard was too much for a speed-obsessed kid to resist.

All the kid knew of racing before arriving in California was the tales his father—a middle-aged man everyone called "Pops"—told of racing at fairground ovals in Dust Bowl states like Oklahoma, Kansas, and Texas in the years before the family went broke. To the kid, those were stories; this was *real*.

He got his first view of the racing at Southern Ascot Speedway from the active railroad trestle high over the Los Angeles River just beyond turns three and four. From that height—provided the trains were not running—he could see over the wood fence onto the rented, hastily-constructed wood grandstand, built to hold five thousand souls. The paying fans packed in to watch a dozen race cars rip around the oil-drenched dirt constituting the half-mile oval for a few hours and forget how poor they were. The infield of the track was neglected: dead, overgrown grass, flattened in places by street-driven sedans used to tow race cars to the track. The only thing that protected the street cars and crew members from the race cars on the track was a white crash wall, something considered a luxury. The only thing protecting the fans on the other side of the front stretch from the race cars was a thin fence of chicken wire. Nothing protected them from the dust the cars kicked up. Each fan went home with a fine coating of brown grit from the track. The track appropriated the name "Ascot" from two previous racetracks in Los Angeles but shared none of their elegance. Unlike the other Ascot speedways, with movie stars hanging around the pits and acting as trophy girls, Southern Ascot was populated by dreamers and the working poor.

The train trestle wasn't close enough for the kid, so he figured out how to sneak in by climbing under the wood fence surrounding the oval. He had to try it multiple times each race because policemen inevitably caught him and threw him out. When the kid finally made it into the pits in the infield of the track, he pestered the drivers with questions. For men racing at Southern Ascot Speedway, making time for little boys who snuck into the pit area—the rules strictly prohibited children and women—was not a priority. The boy quickly learned which ones were the best drivers and sought them out. These men had the ambition, desire, and talent to win the biggest races in the world, and they didn't have time for a child who barraged them with questions in the few minutes they had between races.

Rajo Jack was different.

Rajo was the first black man the little boy knew. Rajo cut an imposing figure with his chiseled six-foot-two, 235-pound frame earned through days of backbreaking labor as a mechanic in the heat of southern California. When prompted, he would pick the front end of his fifteen-hundred-pound race car off the ground with no assistance.

Rajo Jack had style. He always wore immaculate white coveralls with "Rajo Jack California" embroidered in red lettering across the chest to race, while other drivers wore whatever grease-stained clothes they had. Rajo's pencil-thin mustache recalled the style of movie stars like Errol

Rajo Jack, Bud Rose, Shorty Scovell, Spider Webb, and other Southern California drivers are joined by George Robson (far right) at a gathering. *Ted Wilson photo, Bruce R. Craig Photograph Collection, Revs Institute*

Flynn, but Rajo never carried himself like he was better than anyone else. He aspired to be like the other drivers. But he wanted to beat them on the track.

Rajo Jack was emerging as a star race car driver in California by the time the kid showed up at Southern Ascot. Rajo became a larger-than-life figure, earning attention wherever he raced for his exploits on the track and the social prejudices he overcame to get on it.

To those in the rest of the racing world, the drivers at Southern Ascot Speedway were nobodies in inferior equipment at a far-off outpost, as far as possible from the temple of speed that was the Indianapolis Motor Speedway. Indy was a grand two-and-a-half-mile oval paved with bricks that played to sold-out crowds of over 150,000 in its covered grandstands each May as the world's greatest race car drivers tested themselves for five hundred miles. The racing elite did not consider drivers like George Robson, Hal Robson, Travis "Spider" Webb, Jimmy Wilburn, and Swede Lindskog to be the quality of those who drove in races sanctioned by the Contest Board of the American Automobile Association (AAA)—the organization designed to lobby for better roads, which branched into automotive services like towing passenger cars— such as the Indianapolis 500. And Indy was strictly off limits to a black man like Rajo Jack.

Of the grown men engaging in the most dangerous activity of 1936, Rajo Jack was a rare figure. The frequency with which he won races at tracks like Southern Ascot—and the fact he was the one black man racing against fields of white drivers—was what made Rajo well known. But that wasn't what made him a hero to the young boy.

"There were a few who had the patience to at least answer some of my endless questions. One of those, whom I'll never forget, was Rajo Jack. Classed as the greatest Negro driver in the history of auto racing, Rajo was a mighty patient guy. He'd answer my questions, each and every one I'd throw at him," Troy Ruttman wrote in 1952, the same year he won the Indy 500.

To Ruttman, his favorite driver at Southern Ascot Speedway was Rajo Jack, one of the many names appropriated by Dewey Gatson. Rajo was different because he was black, but he also stood out because he won big races with style. Every race car driver in 1936—and little boys like Ruttman who held them up as heroes—dreamed of one day racing in the Indianapolis 500. An unusually large number of drivers, car owners, and little boys hanging around Southern Ascot would race at Indy; some would win it. Rajo Jack possessed the same dream of racing the Indy 500 as the other Southern Ascot drivers.

The reason Rajo Jack never raced at Indy wasn't a lack of skill; it was the color of his skin.

1

LONGING FOR THE ROAD

THERE WAS SOMETHING UNIQUE about the first-born child of Noah and Frances Gatson.

The skinny boy had a wide nose and dark hair like his father, but his complexion was light, so light many white people in the East Texas town of Tyler couldn't tell what race he was. The black people of Tyler knew him as the son of Noah and Frances, the best-looking couple on their side of town. When Dewey Gatson was born in 1905, the area had been difficult for black people for the better part of a century and wasn't improving.

When the Emancipation Proclamation took effect in most of the United States on January 1, 1863, the former slaves in Texas were not notified. They wouldn't learn they were free until June 19, 1865. Abraham Lincoln's executive order did little else to benefit former slaves. The largest industry in east Texas was farming, especially cotton, which was why the landowners brought the slaves in the first place. The land was almost exclusively owned by white men. Most of the former slaves were granted only their freedom and had few prospects for their future. For many of the formerly enslaved, their former masters gave them an option: live in the accommodations they already occupied and continue to farm the land. They could work a portion of the land with an option to purchase it after a few years. With no education and few skills, many of the former slaves agreed to the arrangement, though it was heavily weighted to the benefit of the white landowners.

The Gaston family rose to prominence before the Civil War by buying up large swaths of land previously thought unfarmable in East Texas and turning it into a booming agricultural operation. They made what seemed unattainable amounts of money off the backbreaking labor of their slaves on the plantations. The Gastons—French by origin, South Carolinians by emigration, and Texans by choice—were a well-to-do family before the Civil War. Robert Gaston moved his family and twenty slaves to Texas in 1849 and bought 320 acres along the Trinity River, followed soon by other branches of the family. Many of the slaves died along the way, but Robert prospered and served two terms in the Texas legislature. During the Civil War, many farmers in the area went broke as their family members went off to fight, but the Gastons prospered with their large workforce of slaves. After the Civil War, in which many Gaston men were killed or gravely injured, their farming operation continued to grow.

A young girl named Quilla was working as a domestic servant in the house of one of the Gaston families at a plantation outside Mount Enterprise in rural Rusk County, Texas. During the Civil War, she had been one of the family's slaves. When she was freed, she stayed on in the same position, only this time for meager pay. One of the Gaston men—Quilla wouldn't tell anyone who until much later—found the girl attractive.

When she found out she was pregnant, she dared not tell anyone. The other former slaves still working at the plantation said nothing; she was unmarried and feared what would happen should someone in the Gaston family learn the truth.

Noah Gatson—the Gaston family bestowed on their former slaves the bastardized last name Gatson as a courtesy—was born in 1877. Noah would never know his father, and his mother did not tell him his father was named Anderson until later in life. As Noah grew, people on the farm began to remark on the striking similarity between the light-skinned black boy and the Gaston men. The questions grew frequent, and Quilla opted to leave the farm to protect her child.

When Noah and his mother moved west from rural Rusk County to the town of Tyler—the seat of Smith County—there was a large and growing population of black people in the north part of town. In the late 1890s Tyler was booming, its population to 6,908 from 2,023 in the span of a decade. Tyler became the distribution hub for the massive amounts of cotton and other crops grown in the area. Bigger buildings appeared every year, and it quickly became a metropolis compared with the farming communities surrounding it. The roads of Tyler, however, were still dirt.

The city of Tyler was a departure from life on the farm for Noah and Quilla. Noah was seven years old when he first enrolled in school, a school specifically for black children. The benefit of moving to Tyler was more opportunities for black people to find work, but there wasn't much diversity in the jobs available. Quilla found a job as a domestic worker for a wealthy white family, the best job for which she could hope, but the work was degrading.

Life in Tyler was still rough for black people. Every aspect of the town was segregated. Vast swaths of property on the south side of town were owned by white people, and large numbers of stately houses were constructed there. The north side became home to the black population and was made up of poorly constructed, high-density housing. Noah Gatson dropped out of the "coloreds only" school in Tyler at age twelve and found work in what odd jobs he could find. He cleaned horse stables and worked as a janitor. When Noah was fifteen, Quilla suddenly grew ill and died. She had been religious and took her son to church, but when she died, he stopped going.

Noah had first met Mattie Anderson at church, however. She was short and had a darker complexion than him. She was older and exotic to young Noah. In 1894, seventeen-year-old Noah and twenty-two-year-old Mattie married in what everyone referred to as Tyler's "colored" Baptist church, the Jackson Spring Hill Baptist Church. They rented a room in a building at 1103 West Ferguson Street and made it home.

The building was technically on the white side of town—and in the same block as the all-white Oakwood Cemetery—but was so derelict and close to the town's unofficial racial border of the railroad tracks that black people were allowed to occupy it. Though at the time the Ku Klux Klan was dissipating in the area and its influence was waning, racial tensions hadn't improved since the Civil War: black men were lynched in Tyler in 1897 and 1898.

Noah wanted to start a family immediately; Mattie couldn't conceive a child. Mattie found work as a housekeeper. Noah sought a job where he could make more money than he could earn as a menial laborer.

Tyler was the main hub of the St. Louis Southwest Railroad, known as the "Cotton Belt Railroad," with its general office, round houses, and machine shop in its depot on the north side of town. Its business of moving goods to Arkansas, Tennessee, and Louisiana boomed with the growth of agriculture in Smith County in the 1890s. Many industries in town excluded black workers, but railroads were an exception. Top jobs like conductor went to white men, but jobs were available to black men, especially ones with light skin. On passenger trains, light-skin black men could find work as porters or mechanics. When it came to the freight trains moored in Tyler, there was constant need for men to work.

Through friends, Noah Gatson learned of the lucrative jobs on the railroad. He had no technical skills but showed up at the railroad's shop every day until he was finally given a job sweeping floors. He progressed to machinist assistant and eventually to machinist. With his lofty and lucrative position, Noah became the envy of many. Most jobs in the area for black people at the time involved growing and picking cotton, something he despised. And the perk was Noah could ride the railroad.

Mattie's job with a prominent white family often took her on trips far from home. In late 1903, she joined the family for a trip south to the state capital of Austin. On January 5, 1904, Mattie was admitted, barely conscious, to the black hospital in Austin and died of exhaustion. Noah was devastated.

The funeral for Mattie at the Baptist church in Tyler lasted days. The women of the town looked after the handsome twenty-six-year-old widower, bringing him food and caring for him while he grieved.

It wasn't long before they introduced him to eligible women in town. The black community wasn't large, so he thought he already knew all the available women. Noah begged off invitations, but it didn't stop the women from trying.

One woman caught Noah's eye. Her name was Frances Scott, and she was striking. Frances was born in the rural Texas town of Lampasas to Mimi Scott in 1888. Like Noah, she never knew her father, also a white man. Frances had a similar fair complexion as Noah and came from similar heritage. Frances was sixteen years old and new to town when she first met Noah, and he was an intriguing twenty-seven years old. He had a good job, was handsome, and seemed to live a good life. On September 28, 1904, ten months after his first wife died, Noah Gatson married Frances Scott.

Ten months later, on July 28, 1905, Dewey Gatson was born. It would be another fifteen years before he would become Rajo Jack.

Born in the family's apartment in the derelict two-story building on Ferguson Street in Tyler, Dewey was a tall child. As soon as he could walk, he was a tornado of motion and a challenge for anyone to keep up with. Dewey was affectionate with his mother; Noah Gatson didn't return his son's affection. Noah had always been a casual drinker, but he drank more and started smoking cigars while working long days for the railroad.

Noah's lofty position with the railroad paid well—so well Frances wouldn't have to work and could take care of her new son, a rarity in the black community. Frances took after her mother by keeping chickens in a coop outside their rented building, as much for something to do as for the food. Having money gave the Gatson family comfort, but it didn't buy them acceptance.

In the summer of 1907, the Ringling Brothers Circus came to Tyler and set up downtown, a short walk from the Gatson family home. For the people of Tyler, it was the event of a lifetime. There was a plethora of attractions, many off limits to black people like the Gatson family. The attraction Noah wanted to see most was a car, an attraction open to everyone. It wasn't much compared to most of the cars of the day, but it was the first car to come to Tyler. Though Noah was mechanically inclined and spent long days working on train engines, this was amazing. When the car's engine stumbled to life, it gave off a great roar. Some of the crowd backed away due to the noise and smoke. But two-year-old Dewey was fascinated and went in for a closer look. He desperately wanted to climb into the car, but Noah was left to explain why a black person couldn't get in a white man's car.

On August 18, 1907, Lindsey Gatson was born, giving Dewey a little brother. Another brother, Sydney, was born in 1908, but died days later. Frances was crushed.

Frances Gatson was religious and read the Bible to her sons daily. Every Sunday, Frances would gather her children—but not Noah—to attend church. When he was sober, Noah was a hard-working, diligent man, but those times were becoming rare.

In 1909 Jim Hodge of Tyler—a black man the Gastons knew in passing—was accused by a white woman of rape. He was arrested and taken to the Smith County Jail in downtown Tyler. A mob of white men wanted justice and weren't willing to wait for the court to decide his fate. The men gathered sledgehammers, broke down the door to the jail, stole Hodge out of his cell, and lynched him at the site where the new courthouse was under construction. The white woman later gave statements that made people believe Hodge was innocent, but he was already dead. It sent ripples through the black community. There was still a small presence of Ku Klux Klan in the area, but this wasn't its doing. Average white people in the community had done it.

———————

Dewey Gatson was a five-year-old boy who wanted only to play with his new sibling in the dirt outside their house and hear Bible stories read by his mother when a series of events that would shape the course of his life took place.

A fellow Texan, Galveston-born Jack Johnson—the child of former slaves who grew up a frail boy—rose to prominence in the boxing world. During an apprenticeship with a painter and boxing fan, Johnson first tried the sport and showed an aptitude almost immediately. His ascension in that world was astounding. In February of 1903, Johnson defeated Ed Martin to win the World Colored Heavyweight Championship.

Johnson hungered for a shot at the World Heavyweight Championship, a realm reserved exclusively for white fighters. Jim Jeffries, a white man from Ohio, won the World Heavyweight Championship in 1899, but he avoided Johnson at every turn and eventually retired in 1905.

When Johnson knocked out former World Heavyweight Champion Bob Fitzsimmons in 1907, he was finally considered a contender for the title. World Heavyweight Champion Tommy Burns agreed to fight Johnson for the championship on December 26, 1908. After fourteen rounds, police stopped the fight and Johnson was declared the winner, making him the first black man to hold the belt. It was the first time a black athlete had proven himself greater than a white man at such an athletic pursuit. In response, Jeffries came out of retirement in 1910 to fight Johnson in an eagerly anticipated July 4 bout in Reno, Nevada. The press dubbed Jeffries "The Great White Hope."

"I am going into this fight for the sole purpose of proving that a white man is better than a negro," Jeffries said.

Billed as the "Fight of the Century," the match ended when Johnson won by technical knockout after fifteen rounds. And he earned a fortune of $60,000. Around the United States, race riots broke out in New York, Pennsylvania, Georgia, and Texas after the fight. At least twenty people died in the riots.

The anger white people felt wasn't just about a black man defeating a white man in the boxing ring, but also the brash manner with which Johnson presented himself. He wore fur coats and dated—and eventually married—white women. Transporting white women across state lines was a violation of the Mann Act and would land him in prison later in life. Johnson was unapologetic in how he carried himself, especially to the press. Outside the ring, Johnson spent money on whatever caught his fancy, and the newest and fastest cars were among his splurges. In his grand motor cars, Johnson sped constantly on public roads—many times while drunk—and often attracted the attention of police.

After beating Jeffries, Johnson declared himself the greatest athlete in the world and stated he could defeat any athlete in any sport. Most athletes wanted nothing to do with him.

But one man desperately wanted to take part in such an event and craved the publicity from such a competition: Barney Oldfield.

Barney Oldfield, a cigar always in the corner of his mouth, was one of the first professional race car drivers and cemented a reputation as the world's greatest race car driver after winning the inaugural national championship awarded by the American Automobile Association in 1905. Oldfield decided he could capitalize on a match race with Johnson with the help of agent Will Pickens. Oldfield, through the press, was quick to accept Johnson's challenge. Johnson drove flashy cars fast on the street, but racing against Oldfield was something at which even the best race car drivers struggled.

As soon as Johnson signed to race Oldfield, Pickens and manager Ernest Morass started a publicity war with Johnson and played up the race as a black vs. white competition in the vein of "The Fight of the Century." Few in the press believed it would be anywhere near the spectacle as the Johnson-Jeffries fight, but the idea of black vs. white made a compelling storyline.

The match race was scheduled for September 1910, and Pickens secured a one-mile dirt oval primarily used for horse racing at Sheepshead Bay, New York, not far from Coney Island. Rain postponed the race to October 20, and more rain forced it to be pushed to October 25. Since no one was willing to put up money to sponsor the race, the drivers placed a wager of $5,000 to be paid to the winner. They commissioned a film crew from Hollywood to record it. Oldfield and Johnson envisioned the match race would provide such drama they would reproduce it as a stage show with which they would tour the country and play to sold-out theaters.

This was Oldfield's perfect type of race: a match race for money with guaranteed nation-wide publicity.

The attention they got was from the wrong people.

The American Automobile Association was formed in Chicago, Illinois, in March 1902 by nine motor clubs to advocate for better roads. Three months later, the AAA established its Racing Board to sanction races, but didn't sanction its first race until the Vanderbilt Cup in 1904. The AAA dissolved its Racing Board and started the Contest Board on the same day in 1908 and began an autocratic rule over racing in the United States. The AAA wanted control over all aspects of automobiles.

Licenses for drivers, mechanics, and car owners—available only to white men—could only be granted with approval of regional supervisors and taken away at any time for any reason. The men who promoted the biggest AAA races and owned its most well-known racetracks earned the highest seats of power. Becoming part of the leadership of the AAA Contest Board was about money.

"Of course the contest board will not register a negro driver, much less sanction such a meet, and the white man in question probably will not care to participate in an outlaw meet, which is the only sort of contest in which the two principals could be brought together," the *Horseless Age* wrote.

Johnson sent in his American Automobile Association driver's application and the required fee of one dollar for his race with Oldfield. Without realizing who he was, the AAA office granted a license to Johnson. As soon as the Contest Board found out about the Oldfield-Johnson race, its displeasure was made known. AAA Contest Board chairman Sam Butler convened a special meeting of the board, and they voted to revoke the licenses of all participants—including Oldfield and Pickens—if the race took place. The organization immediately revoked Johnson's license.

"You are in error when you state that I obtained the license by trickery or misrepresentation," Johnson wrote to the AAA. "You cannot blame me for your lack of office system. I will go to the courts if necessary to secure my rights and privileges."

The threat of his license being revoked enthused Oldfield. He was certain he was more important than the AAA.

When the Johnson-Oldfield race finally took place October 25, 1910—a drizzly, cool Tuesday morning—a meager crowd of six thousand appeared. But enough members of the press were on hand to satiate Oldfield's thirst for notoriety. The match was scheduled to be a series of three five-lap races, with the driver winning two races to be declared the winner. Oldfield, driving an underpowered Knox, demonstrated he was the world's greatest race car driver in the first race by speeding away from Johnson's more powerful Thomas Flyer to win by a huge margin. In the break between races, Pickens insisted Oldfield let Johnson win the second heat race to build drama for the third race. When Johnson and Oldfield took off in the second race, Oldfield started slowly and gave Johnson every opportunity to win. But Oldfield was so competitive he couldn't let anyone beat him, even if it was only for show. Johnson kept to the inside rail and Oldfield flew around him on the outside of the second turn of the last lap and won by fifty yards.

But Jack Johnson became the first black man to drive in an automobile race, thirteen years before Dewey Gatson would make a lap.

"I raced Jack Johnson for neither money nor glory but to eliminate from my profession an invader who would have to be reckoned with sooner or later," Oldfield boasted. "If Jeffries had fought Johnson five years ago and the white man had won he would never have had to fight him again. If I had ignored Johnson for a year or so he probably would have gained much experience on the tracks and bought a high-powered car."

Oldfield stuck his neck out competing against Johnson, and it was immediately chopped off. Oldfield was suspended by the AAA, and the AAA Contest Board determined the suspension was to run through January 1912, an unusually long suspension. The first Indianapolis 500 was run in 1911 under the sanction of the AAA, and though Oldfield was the most well-known race car driver in the world, he wasn't allowed to race.

And it set a precedent which would haunt Dewey Gatson the rest of his life: no black man—or any man who wasn't white—would be allowed to drive in a AAA-sanctioned race, especially the Indianapolis 500. It was never written in any rule book, but it became a gentlemen's agreement much like the segregation of Major League Baseball.

At the time, the five-year-old Dewey Gatson was more concerned about his new sister, Katie. She was born on December 5, 1910. Frances doted on her children, and Dewey followed her lead with his siblings.

They didn't have much room in their apartment to play, but Dewey could always come up with a game to entertain his siblings. Frances loved how Dewey, Lindsey, and Katie were carefree in their play, not burdened by worries as she had been during her childhood.

Between rising racial tensions in Tyler and the strain caused by Noah's growing drinking problem, Frances decided the family needed a fresh start.

Frances Gatson lived in Texas and Oklahoma her entire life but had distant family in California. She imagined a fresh start would be the solution to her family's problems and orchestrated a move. In a short time, Noah had become an experienced machinist, and Frances thought he could find work in California. The stories of the state she heard made it sound like a utopia for black people. It was—just not for the Gatson family.

In 1911 the family took a series of trains to reach Los Angeles, and the city was a welcome change from the desolation of Texas. There were many black people in Los Angeles—the same percentage as Tyler, but from a significantly larger population. The black community was largely self-sufficient, with its own grocery stores, restaurants, and medical professionals. In Tyler, the only black-owned businesses were services like barbershops.

The Gatson family found a two-bedroom apartment on the outskirts of Los Angeles. While Noah had been leery of the move, young Dewey was excited about the change, especially to an area with so many cars. The Gatson children attended school—a significantly better one than in Tyler—and Frances found work as a housekeeper for several well-to-do families. Noah, however, failed to find a job. Machinist jobs were plentiful in Los Angeles, but not for black men. The only work Noah could find was low-paying menial labor in Bakersfield, a city about a hundred miles north of Los Angeles. The Gatson family moved to Bakersfield to attempt to improve their situation.

When the family moved to Bakersfield, Frances Gatson sought out photo studios, but only one would accept the business of black people.

Frances valued photographs of her family. There was a mysterious man in Bakersfield who went by the name of M. B. Marcell. He owned a photography studio and did brisk business. The white man's prices were steep—$3.50 for a full sepia portrait—but the photography wasn't how he made his fortune. Frances didn't have money to spend on items that weren't necessities, but photos of her children were critical. Frances took her three children to Marcell's studio for a sitting, but Noah wanted no part of it. To him it was a foolish waste, and his shyness in front of cameras would later rub off on his oldest son.

Marcell—born Marcus Belmont Marcell in 1869—was a strange man, quiet in one moment, a burst of energy the next. Marcell earned a reputation as a photographer for the *New York Journal*—including a stint in Cuba during which he reported on Theodore Roosevelt's Rough Riders—and for death-defying assignments at rodeos like the Calgary Stampede. When he met the Gatson family in 1911, Marcell also was running the "Mr. Raffles" scam. He would sell raffle tickets under the premise one person would win a large cash prize. After convincing locals to buy tickets, Marcell would gather them for the drawing. A few locals would have their numbers drawn and receive prizes of five or ten dollars while a mysterious stranger would win the largest prize of hundreds of dollars. The stranger was in on the scam. A few days later Marcell would skip town, rendezvous with the stranger, and split the profits. Marcell cleared $750,000 at one point.

He was also one of the few photographers around. After his first sitting at Marcell's studio, young Dewey Gatson became a frequent visitor. Dewey was curious how cameras worked and bombarded him with questions, and Marcell answered every question he could. Marcell told the six-year-old Dewey that when he was old enough, he'd hire him as his assistant. He didn't mean it—Marcell was hard to find as he frequently skipped town as he moved from one scam to the next—but a young Dewey Gatson took him seriously. For years, Dewey would declare that, when he grew up, he would become the world's greatest photographer.

Most of the Gatson family enjoyed the California life. But Noah Gatson was miserable. Being away from his native Texas for the first time in his life, he struggled to make friends and find work. Frances deplored the idea, but Noah made up his mind the Gatson family was moving back to Texas after less than a year.

As soon as they returned to Texas, Noah's mood improved somewhat as he got his old job back at the railroad machine shop, and the family moved back into their former accommodations on Ferguson Street. The family settled back in Tyler as quickly as they left. But the idea of California never left Dewey's mind. He dreamed of living in a magical city he had only heard of: San Francisco.

Dewey Gatson went back to the segregated school in Tyler but had lost interest in his classes. He spent as much time as possible hanging around his father at the machine shop, though Noah didn't want him there. Dewey was a quick study and showed an aptitude for working with machines. He found a couple photographers around Tyler, but none took to him as Marcell had. When Dewey was in school, he daydreamed about how one day he would drop out and run off to California to work as a photographer. Dewey idealized California. He grew restless and yearned to hit the road again.

Dewey's family grew again when sister Jennie was born in 1916. Unlike the other Gatson siblings, Jennie was a difficult child. She cried constantly and was a challenge for her parents. The only person in the family who could calm her was her eleven-year-old big brother Dewey. Even Frances couldn't calm the child as well as Dewey.

Though the family lacked space in their apartment, they always managed to find room for animals. At times the family raised pigs and goats along with chickens, all destined to become food. And they often had a dog or cat, though Noah insisted the animals be kept outside. As the oldest of the Gatson children, caring for the animals often fell on Dewey. He enjoyed the responsibility and formed bonds with the animals.

Dewey did well in the few classes in school in which he tried, but his mind was elsewhere much of the time. He was poor at history, but in subjects like science, he excelled. He had nearly perfect penmanship, even when he wrote in all capital letters, and Dewey could always invent a grand story that would impress his English teachers.

While much of the United States developed fast, Tyler didn't. It wasn't until the late 1910s the first passenger cars showed up in the area. And when they did, they were found exclusively on the white side of town. Tyler was stuck in time. The roads were still dirt, not an inch of pavement in sight.

Dewey's prospects in Tyler were poor. At the best, he could follow his father into a job with the railroad. At worst, he would end up working in the fields. He longed for the haven of California.

Dewey Gatson completed the eighth grade in 1920 at the age of fifteen and decided he was done with school. He had more schooling than any previous member of his family. He had a job offer in California—or so he thought—and the spirit of adventure. Dewey packed his few possessions, walked out the front door of the Gatson house unannounced early one morning in the summer of 1920, caught a train heading west, and set off to live his dream.

2

BECOMING RAJO JACK

THERE WAS NO SIGN OF M. B. MARCELL when fifteen-year-old Dewey Gatson stepped off the train in Bakersfield, California, in 1920. After one of his many schemes took a bad turn, Marcell had skipped town and left the state. When Dewey asked around, people claimed either not to know who Marcell was or expressed contempt for the man. It wasn't until Dewey happened upon a homeless man that he found his needed information. The last the man had heard, Marcell had moved to Washington.

Dewey spent his last dollar getting to California. To get to Washington would have been impossible for most, but Dewey Gatson knew how to ride the rails after a childhood spent around train yards. Dewey hopped a train to Los Angeles and found a train heading to San Francisco. In San Francisco, he hopped another bound for Washington. When he disembarked in Seattle days later, he learned Marcell moved again to Portland, Oregon, and Dewey found another train bound for Oregon.

After weeks of traveling, Dewey landed in Portland with the idea Marcell was in town. But he was immediately struck by the landscape. Tall fir trees were everywhere, and huge swaths of green grass made a remarkable landscape compared with the desolation of Texas. Finding Marcell in Portland wasn't as hard as he feared, either. Marcell— now calling himself Doc Marcell—had a new scam he was preparing to unleash upon the public, and he needed help to accomplish it. Marcell's photography was now a side business, but it was paying the bills until he could get a new scheme off the ground—one on a level Marcell had not previously attempted.

Marcell obtained a medical degree from American University of Sanipractic in Seattle in miraculous fashion: he never attended a class. Instead, he paid thousands of dollars and was given a worthless doctorate degree. Marcell devised an elixir of rare minerals he purported would cure all types of illnesses, even cancer. A glass of water worked as well.

Marcell figured the best way to sell his miraculous product was to draw in customers with a grand medicine show. He decided to assemble all manner of attractions and put on a show unlike anything else. Marcell went on a hiring spree: he wanted acrobats, vaudeville-style comedians, and anyone who could entertain the public. But trained performers were few and far between in Portland.

Marcell bought a block of land on the outskirts of Portland in the St. Johns neighborhood. He decided to use the block as an occasional venue and a base of operations from which he would launch extensive tours of the country. He would need lots of trucks to transport the menagerie. Finding trucks for sale was difficult, so he bought them in whatever condition he could find them. Some of the trucks ran, some didn't. Marcell needed a mechanic.

When Dewey found Marcell, he proclaimed he was ready to start his photography apprenticeship. Marcell didn't recognize him at first. Dewey had sprouted to six feet tall, rail thin at 165 pounds. Marcell tried to balk at his previous offer, but Dewey was persistent. He convinced Marcell he could do any job necessary. Marcell desperately needed a mechanic and Dewey had rudimentary mechanical skills from his days helping his father on the railroad. More than that, Dewey was a problem solver who could figure out how to repair things.

After Dewey fixed the first broken truck he was assigned, Marcell hired him as a general hand or "roustabout." It was the lowest job possible and, in some areas, roustabouts were shunned by the black community, not that there was much of one in Portland. But the position offered Dewey the adventure he desired. Dewey's first test drive after fixing a truck was the first time he drove a vehicle. A large part of Dewey's new job was driving one of the trucks to whatever town the medicine show was visiting, where he would set up tents and attractions.

Oregon in 1920 was far from a utopia for black people. The Ku Klux Klan had a large presence in Oregon's political system, and the organizations' largest presence in the state was in Portland. Of the 275,000 people living in the city, more than 10,000 identified as Klan members.

When Oregon was established in 1843, the state government set a ban on slavery, but also required all black and mulatto settlers to leave the Oregon territory within three years or be whipped. More laws forbidding black people from living in Oregon were passed in the following years and become known as the "Negro Exclusion Laws." The reason given for an 1849 law was if free black people were to mix with American Indians, it could incite antiwhite sentiment. Sections of the laws were repealed, and most were ignored by 1920, but they were still on the books. In the 1920 census, 1,627 who identified as Negro lived in Multnomah County, which was mostly made up of Portland.

Living in Portland was a risk for Dewey Gatson, but in the confines of Marcell's insular community, he was relatively safe. Marcell's main concern about the kid, though, was the name Dewey Gatson. Marcell had been through many names and knew the importance of a person's name to their status in society. On the spot, he decided this kid would be known as Jack DeSoto. The kid had an adventurous streak and loved to explore, so DeSoto—from Spanish explorer Hernando de Soto—was appropriate. Marcell thought the name Dewey sounded childish, so he anointed him Jack.

Dewey Gatson effortlessly shed his former persona. For the rest of his life when someone asked his real name, he would offer Jack DeSoto. Mostly. A new life was what Dewey wanted. Noah Gatson had been hard on his children—and the rest of his family—and Dewey had long dreamed of leaving Texas. Jack DeSoto wrote a few letters to his mother after moving to Portland, but otherwise cut ties with his family.

At the Marcell property in St. Johns, Jack DeSoto's accommodations were meager. The property had few buildings, and sleeping in the cab of a truck or under its flatbed was a luxury. But Jack DeSoto loved the independence. One of his first jobs—when he wasn't on the road—was constructing permanent buildings on the property. By the early fall, he and a few workers erected two buildings as dormitories, each large enough to hold a dozen people.

Photographers were in short supply, and Marcell didn't want to spend the money he'd grifted in his previous cons to get his medicine show started, so he took photography assignments when they were offered. Wealthy families frequently engaged Marcell for portraits. Marcell would take assignments for the largest Portland newspaper, the *Morning Oregonian*. Most were in Vancouver, Washington, which required a ferry ride or a short drive over a toll bridge. Marcell needed an assistant and DeSoto quickly volunteered. His main duty was carrying cumbersome photography equipment.

In October 1920, M. B. Marcell took on a job which would change the life of Jack DeSoto. And his name. Again.

In early October each year, the Multnomah County Fair was held at the fairgrounds in Gresham, a few miles east of Portland. Construction of a five-eighths-mile dirt oval was completed in time for the 1920 fair, and to show it off the fair board scheduled an inaugural auto race for the October 5 fair. To sanction the races, the fair board brought in the International Motor Contest Association.

J. Alex Sloan and Will Pickens—formerly Barney Oldfield's manager who was instrumental in his match race with Jack Johnson—founded the IMCA in 1915. Sloan and Pickens started the organization in part as a response to the autocratic rule of the AAA Contest Board. The IMCA focused on sanctioning fair races across the United States and would promote over one hundred races in some years. They brought consistent fields and steady purses without unrealistic rules. To fairs like the one in Gresham, the IMCA could offer significant car counts at a reasonable cost.

With his experience photographing wars and rodeos, an assignment of photographing a race seemed tame to Marcell. And Jack DeSoto was more interested in the photography than the racing.

The Oregon skies filled with rain in the days leading up to the race, but the promoters were determined to get the show in, as many racers had traveled to Oregon from across the country. Most notable among them was the Rajo Racing Team, owned and managed by Joe Jagersberger.

Born in Weiner Neustadt, Austria, in 1884, Jagersberger was a mechanical prodigy. At the age of fourteen in 1898, he began an engineering apprenticeship at the Daimler factory in Stuttgart, Germany. With Jagersberger's size and mechanical aptitude, the Daimler team found a greater use for him. In his first year on the job he was given the task as a riding mechanic in the Daimler racing car driven by Carmelle Janatzy in an endurance race from Vienna to Salzburg, Austria. With Janatzy's driving skill and Jagersberger's ability to keep the car running, they won the ninety-mile race at a blistering pace of fifteen miles per hour. Theirs was the only car to finish, but it was a monumental win for the Daimler factory. While working for Daimler, Jagersberger continued his schooling and finished the equivalent of high school.

At a race in Ireland in 1903, Jagersberger met a pair of wealthy Americans: Standard Oil vice president Harry Harkness and John Jacob Astor IV. Astor was so taken with Jagersberger he convinced him to move to New York and become his chauffeur. Once on American soil in 1903, Jagersberger also took on the job as Harkness's riding mechanic. They hit every race they could find, from a fairgrounds oval track in New Jersey to an endurance race from New York to Pasadena, California, and a hill climb up Mount Washington in New Hampshire.

The Case Thrashing Machine Company, known for building farm equipment like tractors, entered the automobile business through a marketing arrangement with the Pierce Motor Company. Case needed publicity. The best way to convince consumers to consider Case cars was to race them. Case hired Merrill Megis, also a former publicity man for Oldfield, as the racing team's manager. Megis had the responsibility of hiring drivers. The first he snagged was 1908 AAA National Champion Lewis Strang. Then he hired Jagersberger to be a mechanic and driver. The Case Company was based in Racine, Wisconsin, and Jagersberger relocated to the town with which he would be forever associated.

In the inaugural Indianapolis 500 in 1911, Jagersberger qualified eighth, but a steering knuckle broke on the 87th of two hundred laps. He tried to wrestle the car under control, but it veered across the track, hit the pit wall, and ricocheted back across the track. Jagersberger's riding mechanic, C. L. Anderson, fell out of the car and onto the track. Several drivers piled into each other trying to miss Jagersberger and his mechanic. Jagersberger finished thirty-first.

Jagersberger produced better results the rest of the summer, but in November 1911 while practicing for a race in Columbia, South Carolina, a tire went flat on his car, and it veered into the infield crash wall. Jagersberger was struck in the face by a wood board from the crash wall, damaging an eye, and his car rolled over and pinned his right leg. Doctors tried for five months to save the leg until they had no choice but to amputate. Case still valued Jagersberger's mechanical ability and employed him until 1914.

With the Ford Model T selling at an unheard-of pace since its introduction in 1909—and with the most underpowered engine on the market at twenty horsepower—Jagersberger saw an area on which he could capitalize. He left Case in 1914 and formed his own company, the Rajo Manufacturing Company. The name Rajo (pronounced "Ray-joe") was a combination of the place (Racine) and the man (Joe).

Jagersberger produced a few products to hop up the Model T, but his biggest breakthrough came in 1919: an overhead valve conversion head. The racing version showed great promise and made twice as much horsepower as a stock Ford engine in early tests, so Jagersberger restructured his company and incorporated it as Rajo Motors. The Rajo was one of the first aftermarket heads on the market and earned a significant share of it. Since people potentially interested in purchasing the heads were race car drivers and race car owners, Jagersberger knew his best marketing route from experience: start a racing team. He formed a three-man racing team and entered them in an International Motor Contest Association competition.

For the Multnomah County Fair on October 5, 1920, in Gresham, Jagersberger accompanied his three cars to Oregon, two thousand miles from Wisconsin, along with his star driver, Jack Watters. But rain made the track a mess. The day before the race, drivers tentatively went out for practice, but the dirt was so sloppy the drivers succeeded only in getting stuck or breaking down. The race seemed doomed.

On the day of the race, Marcell arrived with his dusky new apprentice. As Marcell signed in for credentials at the fair office, he received a few curious looks from the fair's organizers because his assistant was a skinny black kid. Marcell explained the kid was Jack DeSoto, his new camera assistant from Portugal. Jack took on a vaguely Hispanic accent and greeted the officials. The track officials were wary, but they needed the money, so Marcell and Jack DeSoto were given credentials and sent into the pits. No one seemed to notice the most glaring violation: Jack DeSoto was only fifteen years old. At most races, men had to be at least twenty-one to go in the pits.

The rain wouldn't relent. The promoters said the speedway-type cars—big cars like the ones raced at the Indy 500—couldn't race because the track was so bad. They decided only the lighter cars like the Rajo team cars could try. But the track was such a mess not one lap was made in competition. The few fairgoers who ventured from the carnival games to watch were disappointed.

Marcell had his assignment, but the only way he could make money was to photograph something. He walked through the pits and struck up conversations with racers and team members in the constant drizzle. Marcell arranged to take portraits of many of the drivers with their cars. At best, he would make five dollars per portrait, but Marcell was going to make what he could. Jack DeSoto was interested in the race cars, as he had never seen one before, but he was more interested in photographing them.

As DeSoto sat on the pit wall waiting for Marcell to finish a conversation, Jagersberger sat down next to him. Between Jagersberger's thick German drawl and Jack DeSoto's subtle southern accent, they found common ground. Jagersberger quickly realized how much mechanical aptitude the kid had. When Jagersberger asked his age, DeSoto was truthful for one of the few times in his life and said he was fifteen. Jagersberger recognized a familiar spirit.

Jagersberger had a superior product to the other aftermarket heads slowly reaching the market, but he needed a distribution network. He proposed a deal to young Jack DeSoto: he would become the exclusive Rajo salesman for the Portland area. The street version of the Rajo head cost $60 and the racing version was $78.75. Jack DeSoto could keep ten dollars per head sold. And, Jagersberger explained, Jack could charge ten dollars to install each head on a customer's car. As he only earned a few dollars a week on top of room and board from Marcell, DeSoto accepted the deal.

Jagersberger understood marketing. He insisted his salesmen use Rajo as their first name in public. Jagersberger tried to go by Rajo Joe, but it was unnecessary as he still had name recognition from the Indianapolis 500.

This skinny kid, however, was branded Rajo Jack. It was the only time Jagersberger's idea stuck.

A skinny, fifteen-year-old black kid was an unlikely salesperson for performance engine parts. When Marcell found his assistant talking with the strange European man, Jagersberger introduced himself and asked Marcell if his young charge would be allowed to take on such a job in addition to his position for Marcell. Marcell wasn't going to hold anyone back from making money. In fact, Marcell had a suggestion: take a picture of the kid as proof of his position. Jagersberger's cars weren't going to make any money racing, but they could generate income by helping this kid sell equipment. Rajo borrowed a helmet from one of the team's drivers and sat in car number 88. For years that photo was pulled out of Rajo's pocket and showed to each potential customer.

The most important thing that happened that gloomy, miserable day in Gresham was the invention of Rajo Jack. Rajo went from a runaway child to having two jobs in a matter of months, and soon was earning more money than he had ever dreamed. He marketed the full line of Rajo products and sold so much he had difficulty keeping parts in stock. Rajo figured he would only sell the heads between Marcell's shows, but soon he was outselling all other distributors in the company. Most buyers required installation, and Rajo quickly accumulated a small fortune.

Rajo pondered leaving Marcell's medicine show but still held the dream of becoming a photographer. Marcell was constantly buying cameras, so Rajo always had equipment with which he could practice for his dream job. And Marcell was taking fewer photos so Rajo picked up a few photography assignments.

Rajo Jack stands by his roadster with a Rajo head, "Sally," in Portland. *Kem Robertson Collection*

Rajo Jack went to every race he could around the Portland area to market his namesake heads to racers running a Ford engine. The first few times Rajo arrived at races, suspicious officials tried to turn him away because he looked different, but he had learned from Marcell. The fair-skinned Rajo Jack used his new purported Portuguese lineage to gain entry. His skin was a slight shade darker than most white people at the races, so it seemed plausible. Rajo soon became so well known and well liked at the tracks that officials and racers accepted him as they would anyone else.

The Portuguese line worked so well Marcell decided to build on it. Rajo became proficient as a general mechanic, but Marcell also saw the makings of a showman in his young charge, so much so he decided he would become an attraction of his own. Marcell played up the Portuguese heritage and decided to craft yet another persona. When show time came, Rajo would become Rajah del Ramascus, the great Portuguese fortune-teller. Marcell's wife had a silk robe from her travels in Asia and draped it over Rajo's shoulders. Rajo fashioned a turban and put a peacock feather in it. A crystal ball—it was cheap glass but looked real enough—finished out the gimmick. Few people knew where Portugal was, let alone had met someone from the country, so Rajo's fake Portuguese accent seemed authentic. Marcell gave Rajo a raise.

Taking on the persona of Rajah del Ramascus brought him a new way to pronounce his name. While the Rajo head was pronounced "Ray-joe," Rajo started pronouncing his name "Rah-joe."

Even though Rajo Jack was spending an increasing amount of time at racetracks and was interested in cars, he was content to be another one of the guys in the pits, assisting customers and making money. Even when racers asked Rajo to drive their cars, he declined.

On July 4, 1922, Rajo's perspective changed.

The Tacoma Speedway, a two-mile, high-banked oval constructed of wood, was putting on a grand reopening after the grandstands were rebuilt following a fire. The American Automobile Association agreed to sanction a national championship race at the track with an advertised $10,500 purse.

Rajo Jack was interested in traveling to the race to sell parts, but his plan wasn't realistic. A company started by Harry Miller was producing a line of complete engines superior to any stock-block engine on the market. Despite the Miller engine being more expensive than an overhead conversion like a Rajo, the nation's top racers bought Millers as quick as they could be produced and found immediate success with them.

The drive from Portland to Tacoma was a route of 150 miles but would take eight hours. With national AAA races few and far between, several hundred Portlanders made the trek north into Washington along winding back roads—some paved and some not—to Tacoma. Though Rajo didn't own a car, he borrowed a Ford sedan from Marcell's growing stable and set out July 3. Rajo had grown accustomed to the way people in Portland—primarily around the St. Johns neighborhood—accepted him despite the state's laws. There were businesses in Portland friendly to black people and Rajo frequented them. But when he stopped at a service station for gasoline near Centralia, Washington, the attendant informed him they didn't sell fuel to black people. The attendant displayed his gun to prove his point. Even when Rajo claimed he was Portuguese, the attendant told him to leave. Rajo was forced to soldier on until he found a gas station near Tenino, Washington, which would sell him gasoline so he could make it to Tacoma.

When he arrived, Rajo Jack found the AAA took its segregation seriously. He first tried to purchase a pit pass but was rejected. He purchased a ticket to sit in the massive grandstands and found a seat in turn four, well away from the rest of the crowd. The only bathrooms at the track were reserved exclusively for white people, though never marked as such. The only time Rajo could go to the bathroom was when the race was taking place and no white people were there.

Walking to the grandstand, Rajo Jack was amazed by the size of the massive facility. Compared with the dirt tracks he had previous visited, this wood superspeedway was awe inspiring. The turns looked impossibly banked, as if the cars would inevitably slide down. The spectacle of the venue was mesmerizing. Rajo Jack sat in silence at the spectacle.

The officials for the race included Eddie Rickenbacker and Barney Oldfield, both of whom would make huge impacts on Rajo Jack's life.

Oldfield had retired from his career as a driver with the mantle as the greatest race car driver of his time intact. It took time and consolation on his part, but Oldfield crawled back into good terms with the AAA and completed his driving career in good standing. As soon as Oldfield retired from driving, he tried to cash in on his name, as it was all he had left. The Marmon dealer in Portland retained his services for the Tacoma Speedway race, paying Oldfield to drive the pace car.

Eddie Rickenbacker was born in Ohio in 1890 and, after showing mechanical aptitude at an early age, got a job as a riding mechanic for Lee Frayer in the inaugural Indianapolis 500 in 1911. Rickenbacker drove at Indy in 1912, 1914, 1915, and 1916 with a best finish of tenth in 1914. He didn't race at Indy in 1913, as he had been suspended by the AAA Contest Board for racing in outlaw races.

Rickenbacker built the first part of his legend as a race car driver by winning races throughout the United States. But when America entered World War I in 1917, Rickenbacker traveled to France with the desire to become a pilot. Once he managed to get in a plane, he quickly took to it. Rickenbacker shot down twenty-two enemy planes and four balloons to become the American Ace of Aces, rising to the rank of captain and earning fame throughout the world.

When he returned to the United States, Rickenbacker's desire to drive race cars was gone. He exploited his fame by going on a Liberty Bond tour and started the ill-fated Rickenbacker Motor Company in 1920. Rickenbacker came to races like Tacoma for promotional purposes, and his power in the racing world was about to grow.

The Tacoma race was a dud. Jimmy Murphy was the biggest name driver in the race, having won the Indy 500 a month earlier. Oldfield, chomping on his trademark cigar, drove the Marmon in the pace laps at such a fast pace people thought he might take off from the rest of the field and drive the full 125 laps. Oldfield eventually pulled off the track in time for the green flag, allowing Murphy and Tommy Milton to speed off from the rest of the field. Murphy won the race and the $7,500 top prize. As the prize winnings were announced over the public address system after the race, Rajo Jack could hardly believe what he was hearing. Even the last-place money was more than he could earn if he sold dozens of Rajo heads each year for the next decade.

After the race, Rajo Jack and a throng of spectators gathered around Oldfield, who loved the attention. He told the fans stories about his glory days as a driver. Some things were true, some weren't. But Oldfield took time with each fan, signed autographs, and treated each as if they were important. When Rajo Jack finally got close enough to meet Oldfield, Oldfield told the story of his 1910 match race with Jack Johnson. Rajo had no previous knowledge of the race and for the first time realized a black man could be a race car driver.

Three things stuck with Rajo Jack from his encounter with Oldfield: he was going to become a race car driver, he was a fan of Oldfield, and when he became a race car driver, he would treat each fan like they were important.

During his ten-hour drive home to Portland, Rajo Jack devised a plan of how he was going to build his own race car. There were few race car manufacturers, and the cars they produced were impossibly expensive except for all but the few richest race car drivers and owners. For someone like Rajo Jack to race, he was going to have to build a car.

Days after returning he collected a cache of parts he imagined could be used in constructing a race car. He found a frame from a wrecked and abandoned Model T, wheels and tires from junkyards, and a Ford engine in need of rebuilding. The easy part was getting a Rajo head; he only had to write a letter to Jagersberger explaining his plans for racing a car with a Rajo head and Jagersberger sent him a racing version for free. Even with the parts Rajo collected for the car, he still needed money to finish it. The only person with money he knew was Marcell, and he needed Marcell's permission to keep the car at the St. Johns property.

When Rajo showed his collection of parts to Marcell and gave his pitch, Marcell was quick to acquiesce. What Marcell saw was the potential for a new attraction for his medicine show. If Marcell could gather a couple race cars and drivers, he could set out a course—not a big one—and put on races at his medicine shows. Marcell was happy to loan Rajo the hundred dollars he needed to finish the car.

Rajo decided he would build the lightest, most nimble racer possible. With little engineering knowledge and no training, he designed the car as a bobtail, with no tail tank and the back of the car ending just behind the seat. The leaf springs most race cars utilized were stiff, so he figured if he cut them in half and attached them perpendicularly to the front end— contrary to how most race cars had their springs oriented—he could have a smoother ride through the rutted dirt tracks that dotted the northwest.

It took time to complete the car, as Rajo Jack was traveling across the western states with Marcell's medicine show every few weeks, so his progress was slow. Rajo hoped to finish the car for the May 20, 1923, race at the five-eighths-mile dirt oval at the Clarke County Fair Grounds in nearby Vancouver, Washington, but between the rush to finish the car and setting up the medicine show a mile away on a block of property Marcell had purchased, Rajo postponed his debut. Rajo came to the race, but he sat in the grandstands, well away from the white fans. Watching the twenty-five cars and motorcycles fly around the oval and delight the fans, Rajo Jack grew more determined to have his new car ready for the next race.

Now eighteen years old and standing six-foot-two, Rajo had bulked up to 215 pounds. Rajo painted his new speedster a stark white. With no tail tank on which to affix a number—and a seat that rose inches up his back—Rajo had "Jack 13" stitched on the back of his white driving uniform for identification.

Rajo knew the Clarke County Fair Grounds races were AAA-sanctioned, but as June 24, 1923, dawned, he was determined to enter the day's race. Though his previous dealings with the organization weren't great, he had a plan. This was to be a regional AAA race, not national. On regional tours, rules were more flexible, as promoters couldn't rely on big fields of race cars. Only ten drivers pre-entered the race in Vancouver. And most of the race officials already knew Rajo from his years of hanging around the tracks and generally accepted him.

Rajo Jack and two of Marcell's workers loaded the race car on one of Marcell's flatbed trucks and headed north to Vancouver the morning of race. The car was a rickety machine, hastily assembled by someone with no experience, but it was his.

When he arrived at the Columbia River Interstate Bridge at 10 AM, Rajo was shocked to see a lineup of cars waiting to pay the steep thirty-five-cent toll and cross into Washington. A huge group of Portlanders were heading to watch the race. It took Rajo and his helpers from Marcell's show a half hour to get across and on their way. When they arrived at the humble fairground oval in north Vancouver, Rajo Jack entered the race under the name Jack DeSoto.

When Rajo went to sign in for the race, he produced a full complement of paperwork under the name Jack DeSoto proclaiming he was from Portugal. It was forged, courtesy of a man Marcell knew. The AAA's unwritten rules prohibiting black men from driving race cars weren't known to all regional supervisors, but the officials were skeptical. There was a bigger problem: to drive in a AAA race, drivers were required to be twenty-one years old; Rajo was eighteen.

But when a scant field of eleven cars showed up, the AAA officials desperately needed every race car they could get, and they gave him a provisional license for the day. It allowed him to race but required him to get a real AAA license to race again. It was good enough for Rajo. Since he lacked experience, he was allowed to enter the five-mile race for non-stock cars of 220 cubic inches or less.

As he crossed the track in Marcell's truck and pulled into the pits, the officials sent him to the north end of the pits, before the start-finish line, where he would be the farthest from the rest of the drivers and isolated from the bigger, faster race cars and their crews. They didn't do it to keep him away from the fast cars, though, they did it to keep him away from the white drivers and crew members. Rajo Jack, the same kid who grew up in segregated Texas, wasn't surprised at this kind of treatment. He didn't fight it because the race was too important. From then on, he decided a pit spot before the start-finish line was lucky.

In hot laps around the five-eighths-mile dirt oval, Rajo Jack was slow. To an ignorant watcher, he was simply struggling to keep control of the car, but this was the first time he had driven on a racetrack. The rains from the previous few days had made the dirt surface soft and rutted, and the soft springs on his race car were a disadvantage. The heavier-sprung cars skipped over the ruts while Rajo's car bounded and jerked around. The best he could do was hang on. It didn't help the few other cars at the track were battle tested and his wasn't. He struggled to place last in the second race.

By the time the finale Free For All race—the main event for all remaining cars—of thirteen laps got underway, only eight of the twelve cars remained. The fans were not happy, but Rajo was. The track was horrible, and the racing was bad. Gus Duray, behind the wheel of his Stutz-powered speedster, had built a reputation as the top driver in the northwest in the previous years and lived up to that by speeding out to the lead of the main event. Rajo Jack was proving a slow learner. His car got out of shape, nearly stuck in a rut at one point, and was lapped by Duray a few laps into the main event; Duray would lap him again four laps later. Duray streaked under the checkered flag to win while Rajo Jack finished seventh out of eight cars, his only improvement coming when another car broke.

Rajo Jack accomplished one thing that day in 1923: he became a race car driver. Dusty, dirty, and exhausted after the race, he wanted more.

As Rajo Jack and his two helpers pushed his race car onto Marcell's truck for the ride home, AAA official Frank Watkins approached. Watkins first got into racing promotion in 1922 and quickly became the

AAA representative for Portland and the surrounding area. He admitted Rajo had done a reasonable job driving on the track considering his lack of experience but warned him not to return. The other drivers had been fine with Rajo, but Watkins had realized Rajo was black and not Portuguese. Watkins was afraid for Rajo's sake if he came back to race again—it could be disastrous for all involved. Watkins badly needed race cars to make his series of races in Oregon and Washington work that summer, but he couldn't risk a race riot breaking out. If anyone in the AAA found out Watkins had let a black man race, he would lose his license to promote races.

Promoting a AAA-sanctioned race was a risky proposition. The promoter would have to pay AAA a large fee and a cut of the profits from the race, pay the AAA's officials to operate the race, abide by their rules, and hope the AAA's drivers showed up to race. But the racers who did show up were guaranteed a payout and a professionally-run race.

Then there was another class of racers: the outlaws. Almost as a response to the control of the AAA—and the exorbitant cost of putting on a AAA race—promoters increasingly put on races independently. Promoters like Watkins were already doing most of the work to put on races and were fortunate to eke out small profits. If a promoter put on their own race, they could keep all profits. Any race not sanctioned by AAA was dubbed an outlaw race; anyone who competed in such a race was labelled an outlaw. If someone from the AAA found out a driver or car owner had an involvement in an outlaw race, they would immediately be suspended from the organization.

But aspiring promoters viewed outlaw races as potential gold mines. Some outlaw races were wildly successful; other outlaw races in the 1920s played to scant crowds due to limited promotion. In some cases, the results of outlaw races were predetermined, and when they weren't, the quality of race cars was suspect. Drivers who participated in these races also faced the prospect of racing without getting paid. On many occasions, unscrupulous promoters absconded with the prize money before the races would finish. A race held one week after Rajo's debut—July 1 in Centralia, Washington—was typical of many outlaw races. Six cars raced in front of two thousand spectators at a hastily-built, half-mile dirt oval for a brief program. Everyone involved left disappointed.

But becoming an outlaw was Rajo's only option to keep racing. And Rajo's job with Marcell seemed to grow shaky. Marcell was putting on a performance of the medicine show in August 1923 at his St. Johns property—this time under the billing "Marcell's Great Medicine Exhibition." Lance Seward came from his Portland home on August 12 to witness the show. During a break between performers, Marcell was on stage extolling the miraculous properties of his elixir. Seward stood up in the audience and called Marcell a fake. He said Marcell's medicine was no better than anyone else's and cost three times as much as what could be bought at a drugstore. Marcell was furious. Anyone coming to his show, Marcell reasoned, should be grateful and shell out any price he asked for his fake elixir.

"I'll bet fifty dollars with that faker!" Seward yelled.

"Come up and put up your money!" Marcell shouted back.

Seward angrily approached Marcell. Without Seward noticing, Rajo Jack and another worker sidled up alongside him. Rajo watched as Marcell's other worker delivered a devastating punch to Seward's jaw, knocking him to the ground. Seward never saw it coming. A small scuffle in the crowd ensued and Seward retreated. Marcell didn't let the distraction stop him from shilling his medicine and telling the crowd what Seward offered was not as effective.

Three Portland policemen arrived and squelched the near riot in the aftermath. The following day Seward went to Portland police headquarters and sought to press criminal charges against Rajo Jack and the other member of Marcell's troupe. The problem the police faced was that Rajo and the other worker had left Marcell's property immediately after the punch, and Seward couldn't identify them. When police arrived at the St. Johns property, Marcell claimed the two men had been fired and left town. Rajo quietly returned to Marcell's operation a few weeks later. It was as close as he got to a vacation for some time.

It was the first of many holes poked in Marcell's latest scheme, and it got worse. In 1924 Marcell pled guilty in district court to practicing medicine without a license and was fined fifty dollars. Mrs. Ollie

Alstad had come to Marcell seeking treatment for cancer. He gave her bath salts.

The Oregon State Board of Medical Examiners built a case against Marcell, and at trial jurors voted five to one to convict Marcell, but without a unanimous verdict he escaped conviction. Instead of going through a retrial, Marcell pled guilty. The American University of Sanipractic had been sued for being a diploma mill in November 1923, and Marcell's medical license in Oregon was revoked. Marcell changed the name of his medicine show again to Marcell's Miracle Medicine Show. The show had become popular enough that most people didn't care it wasn't a doctor selling them medicine. Not many bought it anyway.

———

Rajo Jack was determined to race again, but he knew his days of racing in Vancouver, as well as in Oregon, were over with the AAA in charge.

California was a hotbed of racing in the United States from the beginning of the sport. With its warm climate and land available at reasonable prices, new racetracks seemed a sure bet for aspiring promoters and drivers. In 1923 a mile dirt oval was constructed for horse racing in Culver City—not far from Los Angeles. But California law prohibited gambling on horse racing. A horse-racing track without gambling was a quick way for a promoter to go broke, and the Culver City track initially failed spectacularly.

The promoters elected to schedule an auto race on June 8, 1924. It was an outlaw race, but garnered attention up and down the West Coast, more than most of the AAA races that year. The first race had a rodeo and boxing matches on the same program. The twenty-five-lap race was won by Babe Stapp. It went well enough to warrant a second race.

When Rajo Jack found out about the planned July 4 race at Culver City, his mind raced more than he had.

It was a lonely three-day haul to Culver City from Portland in one of Marcell's trucks. When he arrived after nights of sleeping in the cab of the truck, the pits were filled with cars. A $2,000 purse for a hundred-mile race was significant. As he gazed over the oval, Rajo Jack determined this facility—and this quality of drivers—was what he needed. That year in California, the AAA had offered a lean racing season for big cars—a style of large, dedicated racing cars so named to distinguish them from midgets, Indianapolis-type cars, and stock cars. Many of the local AAA big car racers had few options for where to race. The purse advertised for the race at Culver City was so significant that many notable AAA drivers opted to go outlaw. Among the AAA drivers who risked their careers to race were Ed Winfield, Cliff Begere, Fred Frame, Pop Evans, and John Kay. Some didn't care if the AAA welcomed them back.

It was the last time Rajo would drive a race car under the name Jack DeSoto.

When the field of twenty cars lined up for the hundred-lap race, billed the Independence Sweepstakes by promoter William A. Reid, Rajo Jack lined up in the final starting spot. He was significantly slower than the rest of the drivers. But the nineteen-year-old had a spot in the pits between two racers who would play significant roles in his life: Ed Winfield and Pop Evans. After his experience in Vancouver, Rajo was surprised how his competitors were willing to help him at this race. The Californians saw his humble car as far inferior to their sterling machines. They wanted him to get faster so he would stay out of their way.

By the time R. B. Raymond lost a wheel on the thirty-third lap, Rajo had already been lapped by leading Ed Winfield. Winfield continued to drive a blistering pace to win the race with Fred Frame second. Rajo finished sixteenth, respectable considering his lack of experience. Even after he returned to Oregon, he remained in touch with Evans and Winfield for years, writing letters more frequently than he did to his beloved mother. From that day forward, Rajo Jack would be an "outlaw."

It was in California that Rajo Jack would make his name as a race car driver, but it was almost another decade until he raced in the state again.

Neither Winfield nor Rajo nor any of the drivers from the race were paid their winnings, however. On July 31, 1924, Reid—originally from the East Coast—told friends he was going to Omaha, Nebraska, to work and wasn't seen again. The race at Culver City was disastrous financially and Reid didn't have the money to pay anyone. It was truly an outlaw race.

Rajo hoped to return to the Culver City track to race again, but the next race, planned for August 17, was being promoted by the Western Racing Association under AAA sanction. Winfield, Evans, Stapp, and Frame were forgiven by AAA for their transgressions of running the outlaw race, but Rajo wasn't. And the race was boosted when 1915 Indy 500 winner Ralph DePalma was reinstated after running a separate outlaw race. A crowd of eighteen thousand showed up and DePalma won.

The race under AAA sanction had been such a success it garnered the attention of Art Pillsbury, the regional supervisor of the contest board of AAA. Pillsbury was a native of Massachusetts who graduated with an engineering degree from Massachusetts Institute of Technology before heading to Alaska to hunt for gold. When his gambling in Alaska got out of control, Pillsbury moved to California for a new start and became involved in developing real estate in Beverly Hills. Pillsbury put his engineering education to use, associating with people of great wealth to build some whoppers of speedways such as the Beverly Hills Speedway, a one-and-one-quarter-mile palace that featured seventy thousand seats on land too expensive to justify being occupied by a racetrack.

After that track Pillsbury specialized in wresting control over operation of the tracks with which he would become involved. He developed a foolproof way of getting the wood speedways built: Pillsbury would find a location near a railroad line and have a spur built to the track's future location. He would bring in dozens of craftsmen who would first build a wooden fence around the location and then build barracks to house workers on site. He would sequester his hundreds of workers for months while they built the track. And every Saturday afternoon he would bring in a trainload of prostitutes; they would stay until Sunday afternoon. The workers were properly motivated for the following week.

Despite no prior knowledge or experience in racing, Pillsbury rose to the position of the supervisor over all AAA racing in California. Pillsbury found a new group of investors he could bilk into converting the Culver City oval into a board speedway. On December 14, 1924, seventy thousand fans showed up to watch Bennett Hill beat out Harry Hartz in a

AAA-sanctioned race on the new board track. When the race in Culver City took place, Rajo was in Oregon. Art Pillsbury influenced Rajo Jack's career for the first time, taking a venue that had once accepted Rajo and turning it into a true AAA track—and yet another place he could not race.

Still, when Rajo Jack lived in Los Angeles later in life, he would drive by the former site of the Culver City Speedway—by then occupied by television studios—and remember his first race in the big time.

Marcell refused to let the loss of his medical license slow his show. In late 1924, he applied to the City of Portland to hold a parade with a calliope automobile, a unique vehicle with all sorts of gadgets. It was a Cord Rajo Jack had modified to play music as it drove through the streets. Rajo had festooned the car with spinners and lights designed to draw attention. Marcell envisioned it as a grand promotional gimmick and planned to arrive in towns in which he was setting up a show and drive the calliope around to herald the medicine show's performances. Marcell appeared before Portland's city council in January 1925 requesting permission to drive the car around Portland for fourteen days. The council rejected the request. Marcell was so disliked they passed an ordinance against the car. Marcell's reputation in Portland was as a nuisance.

The calliope wasn't Marcell's only vehicle Rajo spent an extraordinary amount of time converting for a new purpose. He took one of Marcell's trucks and converted it into a motor home for Marcell and his wife. By the time Rajo was done, the truck had a bed, kitchenette, and bathroom. When the medicine show hit the road, Marcell and his wife would sleep in the relative luxury of the motor home. Rajo Jack would sleep across the bench seat—or under the bed—of whatever truck was around.

Rajo Jack tried to enter another race at the speedway in Vancouver—now being called Bagley Track after new owner B. A. Bagley—on May 31, 1925. When he entered the pits with his car on the flatbed, AAA head judge L. C. Eastman was called forward and declared that Rajo couldn't race. Any other driver who showed up, regardless of skill level, was granted a temporary license. Rajo Jack's identity and race were well known around the area by that time, and Eastman denied him the opportunity to race because he was black.

But Rajo convinced Eastman to let him find another driver to put in his car for the race. There were no AAA rules, written or not, prohibiting black people from being car owners in their races because none had tried. Eastman needed the car count. Rajo found Bill Reuter, an aspiring driver with a few starts under his belt, and agreed to split any prize money with him fifty-fifty. Rajo entered his car as the Rajah Special, playing up his alter ego. Reuter placed second in the auto speed trials. In the three-mile auto race, Reuter won in four minutes, twenty seconds and earned twenty dollars. For the first time, Rajo Jack made money on a race. Rajo Jack liked making money, but he wanted to drive.

Rajo's business of selling Rajo heads was shrinking due to the growing number of aftermarket engines and heads on the market and his lagging interest in the proposition.

By the summer of 1925, Marcell's medicine show had grown stale and needed a new attraction. Circuses were featuring animals performing tricks. Marcell had no experience training animals but decided he would be good at it.

Marcell, Rajo Jack, and several other workers from the troupe set off for southern Oregon in one of the company trucks. Marcell had learned of a man who trapped bears in the remote mountains of southern Oregon, and after two days of driving they met him outside of Medford. Once Marcell paid the man to help him find a bear, it was another three days until they came upon a 300-pound brown bear. The trapper captured the bear, put him in a crate, and Marcell and his men brought the bear to Portland. Even to Rajo Jack, who kept pets throughout his youth, this seemed dangerous.

They built a large cage in a barn on Marcell's St. Johns property and kept the bear in it on a long chain. Marcell didn't seem to realize that wild bears don't make good candidates for performers.

The day before Thanksgiving 1925, while Marcell was attempting to train the bear—specifically, hitting it with a whip—the bear snapped. It jumped on Marcell and mauled him. Edward Marcell, M. B.'s son, had to club the bear to get him off his father. When the bear released

Marcell, Rajo dragged his near-lifeless body out of the cage. Rajo loaded Marcell in the back seat of a car and sped to a nearby hospital. Marcell spent Thanksgiving in the hospital. He instructed Rajo to get rid of the bear before he left the hospital. Rajo managed to lure the bear back into a cage and drove it back to the trapper to be released again into the wild. Marcell's injuries healed in time—and they didn't prevent him from dreaming up new schemes.

———————

Rajo Jack's racing career got a boost in 1926. The Clarke County Fairgrounds oval wasn't renewing its AAA sanctioning, and the track was going outlaw with a full schedule of races.

Rajo Jack was ecstatic for the April 5 race at Bagley Track, the first of its 1926 season. When he showed up, for once, no one protested his entry. No one belittled his race. No one questioned his lineage. The track workers only wanted his entry fee.

For the first day of Bagley's 1926 season, Rajo Jack entered only the two-mile race. He reasoned that racing against less experienced drivers would be his best chance to win. The track was significantly faster than it had been when Rajo raced on it in 1923 because the dirt had since been hardened by thick coats of used motor oil. Rajo was no match and placed a distant third in the four-lap race. But he was improving and wanted to race again.

Rajo challenged for the lead early in the second ten-lap race at the May 2 event, but he spun out of control in the far turn in the fourth lap, slid into the outside fence, and took out a fifty-foot section of wood planks. He managed to back his car up, continue on, and place third.

And, despite rough races and mishaps, Rajo would make a new friend and powerful ally as the 1926 season at Bagley progressed.

Francis Quinn was far different from other race car drivers. As a youngster in Washougal, Washington, Quinn had been to a few races. Being from a relatively wealthy family, Quinn would have been ostracized had he opted to become a race car driver, so he went to college. Quinn enrolled at the University of Oregon, played football, and was in the leadership of his fraternity. In 1925 the prematurely balding Quinn graduated from Oregon at age twenty-one. Instead of seeking a career as a white-collar worker like most graduates, Quinn decided to chase his dream.

Quinn became a formidable race car driver in a short span. He left the northwest for the promise of California and ended up at Legion Ascot Speedway in Los Angeles in 1925. Legion Ascot had developed a reputation of a racetrack like no other since it opened in 1924. At five-eighths of a mile in length, the dirt oval was one of the first in the United States built specifically for automobile racing. It was a perfect, high-banked oval, hard packed with thousands of gallons of motor oil, making the dirt hard as pavement. It made for fast and intense racing. Los Angeles was a town full of movie stars but was light on live sporting events, as there were no major professional baseball, basketball, or football teams. Hollywood stars frequented races at Legion Ascot to witness the thrills and to be seen. The reputation of the track built fast, and the best upcoming drivers in the United States left home to race there. This quality of racing accelerated Quinn's driving ability.

Quinn returned to his home state of Washington and Bagley Track and on July 18, 1926, placed second to Guy Deulin in the main event, demonstrating how far he had come in a small amount of time. Rajo's rickety speedster broke a rear axle warming up for the race, but they pitted next to each other and became fast friends. Francis Quinn, a twenty-two year-old white man with a college degree, and Rajo Jack, a twenty-one-year-old black man who dropped out of school after the eighth grade, seemed an unlikely pair. But their bond as race car drivers formed.

For the next race at Bagley on August 1, Rajo and Quinn decided to put on a show. Rajo came up with the idea of a match race and envisioned it as a grand exhibition like the Barney Oldfield–Jack Johnson race of 1910. Rajo had learned a great deal about driving race cars and was improving each race, but he was still far behind Quinn.

They decided Rajo and Quinn would drive in a series of ten-lap match races in a best-of-three format, copying the format of the Oldfield-Johnson match race. Rajo's car was no match for Quinn's Miller-engine speedster, but they wanted to put on a show for the crowd and still drive in that night's main event. Quinn and Rajo attempted to hype the match race, but the local newspaper would only dedicate a few paragraphs to the best-of-three. Though Quinn was earning a reputation at Legion Ascot, both men were relative unknowns in the northwest.

As the two lined up on the front straightaway for the first race, few fans understood what they were watching. In the first race, Rajo sped out to a fast start from the pole position—the favorable starting placement at the inside of the front row of cars. Quinn trailed him closely and had the superior car, but Rajo was determined. The pair came around on the ninth of ten laps with Rajo in the lead and Quinn on his tail, but as they came through the second turn, Rajo's car slowed; Quinn sped by and easily won. Rajo had run out of fuel. His car had just enough momentum to make it into the pits. Quinn lent Rajo his extra can of gasoline so he could continue in the next match race.

In the second race, they lined up with Quinn on the pole and Rajo outside. Quinn bolted out into the lead with Rajo determined to not let him get away. Two laps into the race, Rajo pulled inside Quinn and they raced side by side. Coming into the third turn, Rajo hit a bump. His car briefly caught air, and when it came down the seat fell out and Rajo went tumbling along with it onto the track. The fans roared with laughter. His car glanced off the outside guard rail before gently coasting to a stop on the front stretch. But he had to live with the embarrassment.

After the race was over, Quinn consoled Rajo and encouraged him to keep racing. He told Rajo about greener pastures of racing in southern California and how great life was there. Quinn explained how many opportunities there were for an aspiring race car driver around Los Angeles. But Rajo Jack was still making money working for Marcell and selling Rajo parts and he couldn't justify taking a gamble on California with the hope of finding work. Rajo wasn't just done racing for the day; he was done driving for the next six years.

Before the 1926 racing season ended, Quinn moved permanently to Pasadena, California. He won his first Legion Ascot Speedway main event on January 9, 1927, when it was still so cold and wet in Oregon that racing was the farthest thing from the minds of everyone except Rajo. Quinn and Rajo stayed in communication by mail, and Quinn wouldn't give up on trying to convince his friend to leave Oregon. The AAA racing in California was the best in the country, and the outlaw racing was improving. With the outlaws, experience as a driver was unnecessary and no one cared what color a driver's skin was, as Rajo had learned.

There were a few outlaw races in the northwest in 1927—Barney Oldfield appeared at one in May at Bagley Track—but Rajo's racing career was put on hold. The outlaw racing in the Portland area was unprofitable and dried up. Rajo wanted to race, but with no venues, he sold his race car. He got $500 and split the proceeds with Marcell. Marcell needed his share of the money but would never admit it.

Marcell paid $40,000 in cash for a fleet of vehicles in 1928 from the REO company: four Flying Cloud passenger cars, one Wolverine passenger car, seven Heavy-Duty Speed Wagons, and a locomotive built on a special chassis. Those were in addition to his previous fleet. But Marcell extended himself beyond his means, and some of his workers started leaving when they didn't get paid.

Even when Marcell struggled to sell any of his medicine, he still spent money as if he was loaded. In one instance, Marcell sent his daughter on the first transcontinental flight out of Oregon, costing hundreds of dollars. But by 1928 the medicine show performed only a few times a year.

When Marcell stopped paying Rajo Jack, Rajo took the little money he had remaining and a well-used Ford Model T with a Rajo head he called "Sally," and he headed for California in October 1928.

3

TAKING A STEP BACK
TO MOVE FORWARD

THE WAY FRANCIS QUINN HAD MADE IT SOUND, there was a racetrack on every block in California. Rajo Jack believed all he needed to do was arrive in California and he would become a star race car driver. He found a far different world.

In 1928 Rajo moved to San Jose and rented a room from an older couple. The only work he could find was as a car washer. It was a step back.

Rajo heard tales of San Jose Speedway, a five-eighths-mile dirt oval built in 1923 that went outlaw in 1925. Once it went outlaw, San Jose became known as a track where more cars would show up for races than drivers. But when Rajo first tried to wrangle a ride at San Jose in 1928, car owners turned him away. Unproven young white drivers like Ted Horn could get rides, but no one in California had heard of Rajo Jack, and no one was willing to take a chance on an unproven black driver.

Rajo thought he had found an opportunity as a driver for 1929 at San Jose, but the AAA, in desperate need of regaining footing in California, took over sanctioning the track. The AAA declared an amnesty for all outlaw drivers on the West Coast. But when Rajo applied for a AAA driver's license and was rejected, he took Quinn's advice and moved to Los Angeles. At least there he had a friend.

In August 1929, Rajo packed up his Ford and headed south. It was the best—yet most frustrating—move he ever made. When he arrived in Los Angeles, he accepted Quinn's invitation to sleep in the back room of Quinn's house in nearby Pasadena. Quinn was happy to have his friend around, but Quinn's white neighbors didn't want a black man living in the neighborhood. Rajo moved out weeks later when he found a room to rent in the more diverse Watts neighborhood of Los Angeles.

Watts had been annexed into Los Angeles in 1926 and had some black residents and a few black-owned businesses. There was a significant population of white people and Mexicans in the neighborhood, but there was enough of a mix Rajo wouldn't stand out. He felt like a minority, except in one aspect: many in the neighborhood worked on the railroad or at the station in town. Having a railroad as a major economic driving force was familiar.

Rajo had no interest in working on a railroad, though, and found a mechanic job at a garage near his new accommodations in Watts. There were few black mechanics, and many white mechanics wouldn't take work from black customers, so he was busy immediately. He gave up selling Rajo heads.

———————

Francis Quinn had promising results early in his career and decided to try to land a ride in the 1928 Indianapolis 500. Quinn hustled throughout Gasoline Alley—the garage area at the Indianapolis Motor Speedway—but couldn't find a ride for the 500. Two teams did engage him as a relief driver, though, something frequently necessary for the 500-mile race. When Quinn took the required medical examination, however, doctors found what they described as an enlarged heart. The AAA barred him from long distance races, especially the Indy 500. Quinn left Indianapolis determined to prove the AAA wrong.

Quinn could still race on dirt, but he didn't enjoy hustling for rides and often grew frustrated having to hunt for competitive cars to race. Quinn was thrifty and saved winnings to buy his own race car, which he dubbed the Dayton Thorobred Special. It was complete with a state-of-the-art Miller engine.

Quinn had gained such popularity and had such success at the California tracks he figured he had the pull to start getting Rajo Jack rides at Legion Ascot. When Rajo showed up to the track for the first time in 1929, officials were wary. They were dubious of the Portuguese heritage he claimed, though he was still unknown in Los Angeles. The track officials, who were part of the American Legion post who operated the speedway, brought in AAA's western zone director, Art Pillsbury. Pillsbury immediately told Rajo to leave, but Quinn interrupted and explained how he had known Rajo for years, that Rajo was an established race car driver and now his mechanic. Pillsbury was skeptical, but he also knew Quinn was one of the most bankable drivers at the track. Pillsbury agreed to allow Rajo to come in the pits to crew for Quinn, but it was all he would allow.

Rajo was so pleased with himself for making it to the big-time of Legion Ascot he lit up a cigar, something he had been doing at races since meeting Barney Oldfield, legendary for cigar smoking while driving race cars. Prior to the night's main event, while the regular crew of the Dayton Thorobred Special buttoned up Quinn's big car, Rajo couldn't wipe the smile off his face. This was where he needed to be. As soon as Rajo started wrenching on the car, Quinn's performances improved. Quinn proved he belonged with the AAA by winning two races and placing seventh in points in the AAA Pacific Southwest Championship.

It was easy for outsiders to take note of the work Quinn's new mechanic was performing. And it was apparent Rajo wasn't going away anytime soon. Pillsbury began to soften on the issue and issued Rajo a AAA mechanic's license for the 1930 season. It was a monumental step for the AAA: it was the first time a black man received a legitimate AAA license of any kind—not counting Jack Johnson's short-lived driver's license. The mechanic's license allowed Rajo to drive Quinn's car in practice around the five-eighths mile at Legion Ascot as well as other AAA-sanctioned tracks. Rajo struggled at first driving such an advanced car but improved with each lap around the track. Driving his own speedster was significantly harder than driving a proper race car like the Dayton Thorobred Special.

Rajo hoped his performances in warm-up sessions would convince Pillsbury and other AAA officials that he should be allowed to be race.

Rajo got up to speed quickly, and on one occasion was so fast in Quinn's car he could have qualified for the pole position for the main event. Even though Pillsbury saw Rajo's talent and was a huge proponent of Quinn, he still denied Rajo permission. Pillsbury claimed Rajo didn't have the experience to race at this level, which wasn't untrue.

Finding a race car driver or car owner who didn't hate Pillsbury was difficult. Pillsbury was a stickler for rules, even ones not written in the rule books, and he was adamant that his lower officials should let nothing get by them. If Pillsbury thought there might be an impropriety in a race, he would quickly suspend the driver, car owner, and anyone else in question. If a driver was thought to have run an outlaw race, they would immediately be suspended without proof. Pillsbury ran his section of the AAA with an iron fist.

After being consistently confronted by Rajo, Quinn, and other drivers and car owners about letting Rajo race, Pillsbury finally put his foot down: it was a AAA rule that black drivers couldn't race. That rule had been honored by the AAA since the Barney Oldfield–Jack Johnson match race in 1910, and few black drivers challenged it. Rajo feared if he told Pillsbury about driving in a AAA race in 1923, things would only get worse. He opted to gain acceptance one day at a time.

———————

Hastily built oval tracks were popping up all over the Los Angeles area. The dry lakes at El Mirage and Rogers, along with dirt tracks at the Riverside Fairgrounds and dirt ovals in places like Chowchilla, Santa Maria, Colton, Huntington Beach, and Jeffries Ranch in Burbank, were regularly hosting circle track races for slightly modified street cars, ones cruder than Rajo's "Sally." Racers would take Model T's, remove the fenders and install a performance head—such as a Rajo—and race. But if Rajo raced as an outlaw, his AAA mechanic's license would have been immediately revoked and with it, his hope of ever receiving a AAA driver's license.

With Legion Ascot Speedway on the schedule, the AAA Pacific Southwest tour became a marquee series. Quinn's best chance of getting back in the good graces of the AAA—and to finally get his shot at racing in the Indianapolis 500—was to win the Pacific Southwest championship.

At one time in 1930, Quinn placed in the top three in seven consecutive races, including winning a race at Bakersfield and two more at Legion Ascot. He was so far in the lead of the points chase in the summer that he even took time away to race in Texas. Rajo served as Quinn's guide in Texas. When Quinn won in Abilene, Texas, on July 4, Rajo sat in a segregated grandstand because the track officials wouldn't let him in the pits, despite his AAA license. The racism Rajo experienced growing up in Texas hadn't changed.

With Quinn distracted in early August, Jimmy Sharp reeled off five straight wins to take the lead of the Pacific Southwest series and eventually won eight straight. Quinn's performances fell off because the engine in his race car needed a major overhaul. But a surprise offer arrived from Russ Garnant to drive his Frontenac. The combination of Quinn and Garnant was odd, as they were former rivals, but it was the boost Quinn needed. Quinn won the next five races, took the point lead for good and won the 1930 AAA Pacific Southwest championship at the age of twenty-seven with ten wins in fifty-one races.

Others took notice of Quinn's improved success since the backing of his new mechanic. Rajo Jack became such a popular force in such a short span at Legion Ascot that the top drivers would come to him for advice about their cars.

The driver who pestered him most was Kelly Petillo. A transplant from Pennsylvania, Petillo had learned to drive at the wheel of a fruit truck, making deliveries for his family's grocery store. He started racing in outlaw races and, at the relatively late age of twenty-six, made his first race at Legion Ascot in 1929. Though he was fast immediately, he was also hard on equipment and frequently wrecked. Petillo was frequently in trouble, quick to anger and often involved in fights. He also felt a kinship with Rajo. But the budding friendship between Rajo and Petillo wasn't enough for Rajo to leave Quinn's team.

Not everyone at Legion Ascot was a fan, however. Drivers Nick Martino and Byron "Speed" Hinkley tied a rope from the tow truck around Rajo's waist and pulled him by his hands and feet in opposite

Rajo Jack, with rope around his waist, is pulled by Nick Martino and Byron "Speed" Hinkley at Legion Ascot Speedway in 1930. *Bruce R. Craig Photograph Collection, Revs Institute*

directions in front of a photographer. When Petillo saw this going on, he stepped in and gave them a tongue lashing. Kelly Petillo was always up for fun, but he also was protective of his few friends.

Quinn sold his championship car after the 1930 season and decided to build a new car for the 1931 season. He and Rajo spent late nights building it in Quinn's garage. When the car wasn't ready for the beginning of the 1931 season, Quinn resigned himself to picking up rides from car owners he barely knew.

Quinn purchased a new Miller marine engine for the new car. At 183 cubic inches, it was smaller than most Miller engines on the circuit, but it was less expensive and allowed Quinn to spend more on the chassis and other components. This wasn't a standard Miller engine, though. It had a lightweight crank made of a special metal that allowed it to accelerate quicker than other similar engines. And the valves were cut in a special way to improve air flow and produce more horsepower than bigger engines.

By the time the new car was finished and ready to race, the season was well under way. But there was something else on Quinn's to-do list: the Indianapolis 500.

After Quinn won the 1930 AAA Pacific Southwest championship, Pillsbury and other AAA officials could no longer deny he was healthy enough to compete in the greatest race in the world. Quinn convinced car owner James Wade to give him a chance in his Tucker Tappett Special for the 1931 Indy 500.

Francis Quinn left California in early May for the three-day drive to Indiana and brought Rajo Jack with him. It was a long journey and they slept most nights in Quinn's Model A roadster, one man lying across the front seat and the other across the back. In many areas of the country, it was frowned upon for a white man and a black man to be seen riding together, so Rajo learned to duck when a car was coming in the opposite direction.

There was a major change at the Indianapolis 500 in 1930: the riding mechanic position was being resurrected for the race. In the early days of racing, the riding mechanic was necessary as cars didn't have things like mechanical fuel pumps and oil pumps. Keeping fuel and oil pressure by pumping valves became the duties of riding mechanics. By 1930, the cars had the technology to eliminate the need for the riding mechanic. With the race declining in popularity, AAA officials decided to revive the tradition of the riding mechanic to try to reclaim its past glory, though it was unnecessary. And the field was expanded to forty cars from its traditional thirty-three to encourage more entrants.

When Quinn and Rajo arrived in Indianapolis in early May, they were ready to get to work. From the time Rajo met Barney Oldfield in 1922, the Indianapolis 500 had been Rajo's obsession, but this was his first time seeing the spectacle. But when Rajo and Quinn tried to enter Gasoline Alley, AAA officials working the gate told them Rajo was not allowed. Rajo produced his valid AAA mechanic's license, but the Indianapolis Motor Speedway officials informed him they didn't care what some person in California said. They were the arbiters of who could come in the pits at the Indianapolis Motor Speedway. The AAA officials said the only way a black man would be allowed in the garage was as a janitor after everyone else left for the day. Quinn was upset, but Rajo assured him the situation would be fine.

Quinn first sought out Pillsbury. He was the big man in the Pacific Southwest, but at Indy Pillsbury was a low-level official. Pillsbury said the decision was up to the track officials. Quinn decided to seek out the ultimate authority on the matter: Eddie Rickenbacker.

After failing as a manufacturer of automobiles, Rickenbacker bought the Indianapolis Motor Speedway in 1927 for $750,000, most of it borrowed. As he was the owner of the most important speedway in the nation—and one of the most well-known racing personalities—Rickenbacker was installed as president of the AAA Contest Board. Immediately after purchasing the track, Rickenbacker sent several new employees to make a series of improvements to the aging facility. But one area remained the same: the section of seating marked "coloreds only." It was a section of grandstands between turns one and two and the only section from which Rajo Jack could watch.

During the run-up to World War II, Rickenbacker supported black people becoming pilots, though in segregated squadrons. But he also worried about the influence of black people on society in the United States. Though the rules against black drivers in the Indy 500—and the AAA as a whole—existed long before Rickenbacker took power, he did nothing to change them.

"Although I see no hope for the pockets of whites in the areas dominated by the nonwhite races, I believe that here in the United States people of color will remain loyal to their mother country, the United States. Negro Americans, Japanese Americans, and Chinese Americans, in short, will continue to be Americans like the rest of us in this melting pot. A possible alternative could conceivably come about if the Negros within our boundaries continue to proliferate to the extent that they outnumber the whites," Rickenbacker wrote.

Every time Quinn asked AAA officials to talk with Rickenbacker, he was informed Rickenbacker was unavailable. Only a few officials knew Rickenbacker's actual location in the aircraft division of General Motors.

Despite owning the Indianapolis Motor Speedway, Rickenbacker spent a scant few weeks a year there. He left daily operations of the track to T. E. "Pop" Myers. Quinn found Myers, but Myers said the decision was over his head and only Rickenbacker could make such a decision. Quinn was upset he could not get a straight answer from the AAA, but Rajo assured Quinn he had a more important job to do. Quinn wanted Rajo Jack to be his riding mechanic, but he eventually settled on Dave Frank, a white man inferior to his friend.

On May 25, the third day of qualifying, Quinn qualified with an average speed of 111.321 miles per hour around the two-and-one-half-mile brick oval for the twenty-sixth starting spot in the race. Had Quinn's car been ready on the first day of qualifying, he would have earned the fifth starting spot. But on the last practice day he had a problem with the rear end—a stripped ring gear—and it took two days to fix. While he was supposed to be sweeping the garage floor in the late-night hours of May 24, Rajo meticulously disassembled the rear end, put it back together, and returned it to working order. Rajo Jack had a knack for fixing hopeless causes. The rear end was inadequate for the powerful Miller engine in the car, Rajo assured the crew, but it was all car owner James Wade had. He had overextended himself financially by fielding the car in the Indy 500 and didn't have the money to buy a stronger rear axle. Rajo instructed Quinn to baby the car and hope the rear end would last through the race.

When May 30, 1931, arrived—the day of the Indy 500—every seat in the speedway was filled. Rajo Jack was disappointed to watch the race from the "coloreds only" section in turn one, but he was excited to watch the race for the first time. As the green flag fell and the forty cars entered the first turn, Rajo Jack finally understood the majesty of the Indy 500. Reading and hearing about the race hadn't prepared him for what he was seeing. Rajo grew determined he would become the first black driver to race in the Indy 500 as he watched the cars streak past. When the field came by on the fourth lap, though, he couldn't see Quinn's car. On the third lap, the rear end in Quinn's car had snapped under the pressure. He finished fortieth of forty cars. Five hours after the race started, Louis Schneider won.

Even after being at the speedway the entirety of May, Rajo was in for another shock: the official starter for the Indy 500 was his hero, Barney Oldfield. Rajo patiently waited through the race to meet Oldfield again. By the time Rajo managed to make his way from the "coloreds only" seating section and through the crowd after the race, Oldfield was gone. Rajo finally made his way into Gasoline Alley to help Quinn's other pit men load up the last of their equipment. The duo then quietly climbed into Quinn's Ford and started the three-day journey home to Los Angeles.

As soon as they returned to California, Quinn resolved to do two things: finish building his race car and win the Pacific Southwest championship again. To build the car, Quinn spent $6,000—a fortune. But when he finally got it on the track, it wasn't nearly the rocket he envisioned. There were myriad mechanical problems. And there was an influx of successful national AAA drivers into Legion Ascot and the other Pacific Southwest races. Drivers like Kelly Petillo, Fred Frame, Louis Schneider, Mauri Rose, Bill Cummings, Louis Meyer, and Floyd Roberts—all of whom had won or would win the Indy 500—were now competing with the local California boys, as was Ernie Triplett, Quinn's greatest rival.

For the final race of the 1931 season, Quinn towed north on December 13 for a race scheduled for the next day at the new mile dirt oval at Oakland Speedway, a traditional track designed by Art Pillsbury. For once, Rajo Jack didn't go with him. Instead another mechanic, Claude French, rode with Quinn. The route from Los Angeles to Oakland was a dangerous one for a black man.

The decision saved Rajo Jack's life.

It was miserably raining in California and the chances of the Oakland track being ready for the race were slim, but Quinn was willing to risk it. He made it a hundred miles south of Oakland when a violent rainstorm hit, and they had to pull into a service station near Madera. While waiting for the weather to break, Art Pillsbury pulled in to the same gas station to seek shelter. Pillsbury called to Oakland and learned the race had been cancelled. Quinn was not surprised. In California, there was always another race.

When the worst of the storm passed, Quinn turned his Model A roadster around and headed south toward Los Angeles with the race car on the trailer behind it. Pillsbury left shortly after. Five miles north of Fresno on Highway 99, Russel Frasher—a twenty-eight-year-old truck driver from San Jose—veered between the lanes and hit Quinn's Model A roadster head on. Frasher's truck struck with such force that Quinn was thrown out of the car and died in seconds. French was also injured. The race car was completely unharmed. Pillsbury arrived minutes after the crash, and he was devastated to see his young star dead.

Pillsbury urged prosecutors to go after Frasher, but Frasher was charged with manslaughter. The prosecution argued that Frasher was drunk when he hit Quinn. But in Superior Court in Fresno on January 29, 1932, Frasher was acquitted on the manslaughter charge after thirty minutes of jury deliberation. French filed a civil suit against Frasher asking for $10,675. He later settled for less.

Though Quinn died before the 1931 season ended, he still finished fourth in the AAA Pacific Southwest championship with six wins, all in other people's cars. His car hadn't yet reached its potential.

Quinn had put so much time, money, and energy into building the car that his family wanted to continue in his honor and make back the money it cost to build the car. Neither Quinn's fiancée, Gertrude Allen, nor Quinn's brother, Les, knew much about racing, but they convinced Rajo to stay on as mechanic on the car. It became Rajo's responsibility to get the car to the track, line up drivers, and make sure the car was ready to race. They made a deal that when the car had earned back the $6,000 Francis spent building it, Rajo would be given the Miller engine.

Babe Stapp placed third in a main event at Legion Ascot on December 20 in the car, and on January 1, 1932, the rained-out Oakland Speedway race was finally made up. Stapp led after fifty-one of the scheduled hundred laps, but the rain started, and the race was declared official with Stapp awarded the win. The first win for Quinn's beloved car was at the race the car's creator died trying to reach. Later in 1932, Bob Carey won two more hundred-mile races at Oakland in the car.

Rajo Jack's greatest hope was that he would be allowed to race the car in which he and Quinn had invested so much time and energy. But Rajo knew well he was going to be told he couldn't race. He had been rejected so many times because he was black, it became normal.

Rajo wanted to honor the memory of his friend, but he still wanted to race. He was working on the car week after week, essentially as a volunteer mechanic, with the vague promise of an eventual reward.

4

THE OUTLAW EMERGES

GETTING AND MAINTAINING A STANDING with the AAA Contest Board was a tricky thing for anyone—white men had their licenses revoked for any perceived slight. Rajo Jack didn't want to risk getting caught racing as an outlaw in California for fear of never being accepted by the AAA. In his four years since moving back to the California, he didn't race at all despite ample opportunities.

The only way he could race without the AAA finding out was to race somewhere in the United States where no one knew him. A late-summer gap in the 1932 AAA Pacific Southwest schedule gave him a chance to travel in search of a chance.

He spent five days on the road in his Ford to visit racetracks throughout Oklahoma, Texas, and Kansas, where Rajo Jack was unknown. He met a man named Johnny Berger in Kansas who had a rarely-used speedster on his farm. Rajo exaggerated when he told Berger he was a race car driver of the first order in California. The only thing most Plains States car owners knew of Californian race car drivers was they were rumored to be the fastest in the nation.

Before Rajo and Berger could take the race car to the track, they had to evict the chickens that had taken up residence in the car.

A dirt oval outside of Wichita, Kansas, called Bo Stearns Speedway was having a race on August 7, 1932. Berger's car had a Miller engine and potential. But Rajo quickly discovered this car wasn't near

Rajo Jack is handed a rag by wife, Ruth, after placing second in the 1938 Gold Trophy 500 at Oakland Speedway. *Bruce R. Craig Photograph Collection, Revs Institute*

the capability of Quinn's beloved mount or any of the California cars. Rajo qualified in fifteenth place in the poor-handling car and finished a disappointing twelfth place in the main event, a lap behind winning local driver Pat Cunningham in the ten-lap main event.

The best thing to happen to Rajo Jack that day, however, didn't come on the track. After the race, a pretty woman came out of the crowd with a group of friends. Her name was Ruth Grace. To Rajo, it was love at first sight.

After the race, Rajo collected the few dollars he was due for driving the car and took Ruth to an all-night diner in Wichita. As they ate and talked into the night, the seventeen-year-old Ruth explained she was born in Oklahoma and had dreamed of seeing an ocean. She also was of mixed heritage, as her mother was American Indian, giving Ruth a light complexion like Rajo's mother, Frances. Rajo told her his real name was Jack DeSoto and explained how he came to be Rajo Jack. She wouldn't learn his real name for months.

Their courtship was fast. Since Rajo Jack had ties to California, he decided he could live in the Plains long enough to get the consent of Ruth's parents to marry him. He moved to Oklahoma City and found a job as a mechanic at a garage in a matter of days, as well as a room to rent in a house on Laird Avenue. Though there was a large age difference—Rajo was twenty-seven years old—Ruth's parents consented to the marriage. On August 31, 1932, Jack DeSoto married Ruth Grace.

By late in 1932, their lives in Oklahoma had already stagnated. Rajo Jack and his new bride took a vacation to California, a place Ruth desperately wanted to visit after hearing Rajo's grand tales of the West Coast paradise compared with the Depression-ravaged Plains. The trip was supposed to be a vacation for the newlyweds, but racing never left Rajo Jack's consciousness.

AAA races in southern California were struggling as only the top few drivers dominated the races. The Miller racing engine had taken over as the dominant power plant, and the rest of the drivers—piloting stock-block cars with overhead conversions like the Rajo heads—were the back markers finishing last. In a promoter's worst nightmare, the back markers stopped coming altogether. Placing eighteenth in a main event and not getting paid wasn't fun. The AAA decided to start a class for the stock-block cars to run as companion races to the Pacific Southwest races. It worked, as the underpowered cars started coming back. But those same drivers were jealous about not being part of the big show.

When a group including Lee Conti and Joe Neil built the Silvergate Speedway on a marsh in San Diego in 1932, they carved out a five-eighths-mile dirt oval on a piece of land previously thought unusable. They initially called the track Neil's Speedway, but that name wouldn't stick—nor would their plans for the speedway to be host to top-level racing, as the track soon became a major venue for the new stock-block races. They outfitted Silvergate with a large, elevated grandstand big

Rajo Jack receives a trophy from Gus Schrader (wearing hat) after a race at Southern Ascot Speedway. *Podurgiel Collection*

enough to seat four thousand souls. To gain AAA sanctioning, the promoters needed to prove they could draw a crowd.

After the first race at the new Silvergate Speedway on New Year's Day 1933 drew few fans, they set a race for January 8. This race they dubbed Mexico Day, and they desperately wanted drivers who didn't look white. They found an Italian, Albert Spencer—who they promoted as Alberto Spencero from Old Mexico—and, on the recommendation of IMCA champion Gus Schrader, Rajo Jack.

In his early days of racing, Gus Schrader had raced AAA circuits around the United States. During one of Schrader's early appearances at Legion Ascot Speedway, he met and befriended Rajo Jack. Schrader had given up racing with the stuffy AAA and moved over to race with the International Motor Contest Association and became a star.

For the race at Silvergate, Rajo landed a ride in the number 11 car of Pop Evans, who had abandoned his AAA leanings for the less-restrictive realm of the outlaw tracks. Rajo first met Evans in the 1924 race at Culver City, and they had remained friends. Evans had decided to step out of the driver's seat, and Rajo yearned to drive his car for years. This was Rajo's opportunity.

For Rajo Jack, this was his best shot as a race car driver. But he also knew the minute he took a lap in the competition, the AAA would brand him an outlaw and no longer grant him a mechanic's license, let alone the driver's license he so desired. This opportunity was worth it. Rajo decided to give up his AAA standing and become an outlaw. He needed to race.

But the only thing Rajo displayed to thirty-one hundred fans at Silvergate was that he had much to learn about driving a race car. He qualified poorly, drove poorly in the heat race, and barely made the fifteen-lap qualifying race. Everett Balmer drove away from the field and Rajo hung on to second but didn't advance to the feature. He sat in the pits and watched Earl Mansell win the fifty-lap race.

Francis Quinn's car managed to place eighth in the 1932 AAA Pacific Southwest owner's points as his family slowly recouped Quinn's investment. One week after Rajo's California debut, on January 15, 1933, Al Theisen won a main event in Quinn's car, and the car placed eleventh in series points again in the 1933 season. Rajo had been shocked that his mechanic's license was renewed after his race in San Diego. Most important for Rajo, Quinn's family finally earned back his investment. The family gifted the Miller engine to Rajo and sold the rest of the car. An engine, no matter how good, wasn't worth much without a car. It would be years until Rajo finished building his own car, but he had the most important—and expensive—component.

After the first few AAA races of 1933, Rajo and Ruth returned to Oklahoma City. It was worse than when they left. The economy hadn't improved, and they each struggled to find work. In desperation Rajo took Ruth to his family home in Tyler, Texas, and they moved in with the rest of the Gatson family in the already-cramped apartment at 1615 West Claude. It was Rajo's first chance to meet some of his new siblings, including brothers Warren and Gerald. And it was the first time Ruth learned that her husband was really Dewey Gatson. The economy in Tyler was better than in most areas of the United States because of booming industries in cotton and oil. But there was no racing in Tyler, and Rajo longed to return to California.

After the first few races of 1933, Silvergate Speedway earned AAA sanctioning. The first AAA race was run with the Class A cars of the AAA Pacific Southwest series, but the sanctioning fee made it unprofitable. The owners of the track opted to bring in the Class B cars of AAA, but they also were unprofitable. The track was going outlaw for 1934.

Charlie Curryer seized the opportunity. Curryer, nicknamed "The Thin Man," was a tall man with a wide view of the racing landscape. Curryer started in the 1920s as a motorcycle racer. He began racing on road courses but quickly figured out the money was on oval tracks. Among the tracks at which Curryer raced was Silvergate Speedway. The immaculately styled Curryer, with a thin mustache and wide-brim hat, decided in his early thirties the real money in racing was as a promoter.

Curryer lived in San Diego, opened an office in centrally-located Sacramento, and started his promotional career on June 4, 1933. Curryer promoted the first modern race for midget-class cars on the cinder running track at Sacramento Junior College with a field of twelve cars. The fans for the race were happy with the field, but Curryer wasn't. He realized that to promote consistent racing programs, he needed a steady group of cars.

Curryer saw promoting races under AAA sanction was a tough way to make money. But prospects for promoting true outlaw races were dim, as few cars and fans showed up to those races. Curryer decided his best option was to start his own racing organization. If he awarded a season champion and paid winners well, Curryer would be assured consistent fields for his races.

Curryer formed the American Racing Association (ARA). His new association would be an outlaw organization, but it would become the premiere outlaw racing association on the West Coast.

Curryer decided a key in making his new racing association work was having a showplace track to stage most races. And he'd gamble on tracks in towns where other promoters never would have tried. If there was a fairground with a grandstand and a rodeo arena, Curryer would convince the fair board to turn it into a racetrack. He'd employ the wives of racers to sell tickets. He'd print up posters advertising the race and drive kids around to hang them up on fences and light poles.

Sometimes Curryer would make money, sometimes he didn't. Curryer never got rich promoting races, but he maintained his image by always driving a new car. Curryer carried an air about him that made people—especially his racers—believe in him and his races.

With outlaw racing picking up in southern California and prospects of finding work improving, Rajo Jack and Ruth elected to move to California for good. Rajo bought a house in the Watts neighborhood of Los Angeles for just over $1,000 late in 1933. The house was built in the 1920s and needed work, but it had a two-car garage out back: the most important component he needed to build his new race car. The neighborhood was still diverse, and there was a larger concentration of black people than anywhere else in Los Angeles. Rajo still had friends living in the neighborhood. Watts would become home.

Rajo found a stall in a complex of storage garages not far away in which he could start his own business as a mechanic. For once he wouldn't have to work for someone else. Rajo found a niche and earned the reputation as the man who could fix any car.

Rajo Jack's name still held weight in the racing community. The AAA wouldn't have him—he tried repeatedly to get rides at Legion Ascot Speedway late in 1933 but was denied each time by Art Pillsbury. Rajo was now an outlaw, and Pillsbury had more justification to keep him out. But Rajo refused to give up the hope that came with his AAA mechanic's license.

At Silvergate Speedway, however, Rajo had an opportunity he couldn't pass up. To start the 1934 season, Evans decided Rajo would drive his number 11 big car full time.

In the first race of the 1934 season at Silvergate Speedway on February 11, Rajo turned his reputation as a race car driver—built mostly on conjecture—into fact. With thirty-five hundred fans cramming into the stands, Curly Mills swept the program by setting fast time, winning the heat race and main event, but Rajo Jack finished second place in the main event, his best result yet in his career. In newspaper stories about the race, however, he was listed as "Rajo Jacks."

While the AAA promoters in California wanted Rajo Jack to go away, Charlie Curryer saw an opportunity. The kid could drive, but he also was a driver who could deliver a more diverse audience. And Rajo showed promise of becoming a marketable star.

When Rajo raced Silvergate the first time in 1933, Pop Evans shielded him from most of the verbal taunts from other drivers and crew members, not that most of them paid much attention to him. Now that Rajo was showing he was a legitimate driver, some of the white drivers resented him and feared he could beat them. Where most drivers received congratulations from such a showing, Rajo got a steady stream of insults and derogatory terms aimed his way. Only the intervening of Charlie Curryer kept some of the negative racers at bay.

Rajo was never one to fight. When someone insulted him, he would crack a joke. Where many in Rajo's situation could have been angered by the hostility, Rajo invited them to his house for a drink. Thirty-year-old driver Ed Levens died from massive injuries after a crash at Silvergate when his car hit the inside guard rail and he was flung from the vehicle. Though Rajo had little money and was barely scraping by in the Depression, he donated more money than he could afford so Levens could have a funeral. Even when other drivers didn't want him around, Rajo was trying to be one of the guys.

In the next three races at Silvergate—March 4, 11, and 18—Rajo's only notable finish was a heat race win. There were problems with Evans's car, and Rajo decided if Pop wasn't going to fix it, he would. He couldn't spend large amounts of money improving the car, but he knew how to make a race car work after his time on Quinn's cars. He spent every available moment after the March 18 race working on the yellow number 11. He found that dozens of small things needed help—brakes, springs, steering, and a couple bent wheels.

When Evans and Rajo showed up to San Diego for the March 25 race at Silvergate, the track was rough. At a dirt track like Silvergate, it wasn't a surprising condition. Even though rain was scarce in southern

California that year, the track workers feared the forecasted rain and put off the preparation of the track until it was too late to make a difference. A new promoter, J. F. McIntosh, had taken over the racing—though Curryer was still sanctioning the racing under the ARA banner—and McIntosh's workers were as inexperienced as he was. They watered the dirt too much. But the track played into Rajo Jack's hands.

Rajo found that his work on Evans's car made a dramatic improvement as he placed third in his heat race. Rajo had a plan for the thirty-five-lap main event. For the first eleven laps, Curly Mills, Earl Mansell, Bayless Levrett, and Rajo ran close together up front. Rajo didn't have the power to get around the leaders, but he could hang with them. The worst-case scenario for Mills happened when his right rear wheel broke and he was barely able to limp his car back to the pits. Mansell assumed the lead, but nine laps later the right rear wheel of his car also broke, and he pulled off. Levrett inherited the lead, but five laps later his engine misfired and slowed dramatically. Realizing Levrett's misfortune, Rajo capitalized and took the lead. By that point, he had such an advantage over second-place Carl Duncan he could have taken it easy and coasted to the finish, but that wasn't Rajo Jack's style. He pushed the pace during the final laps, and for once fortune was on his side.

Rajo Jack won a main event for the first time in his career. Rajo had been trying to win for over a decade so he could validate his existence. Pop Evans was elated too. He had been the only car owner who had believed in Rajo Jack, and his faith was rewarded.

While those in the racing community in Los Angeles knew Rajo was a black man, most fans at Silvergate still didn't know what race he was. His complexion had darkened since 1926 through long days in the California sun, but he was still obfuscating his race. After the race, he pulled off his helmet and his skin wasn't noticeably darker than the other drivers with the dirt and grease smeared over his face.

But the white trophy girl refused to kiss a black man in victory lane. Ruth rushed from the grandstands and gave him the traditional victory lane kiss. It would be her job for the rest of his career.

It was one win, but it validated Rajo Jack. In newspapers across southern California, the win was widely reported. Word also traveled

fast outside of the state to friends in the racing world. In the following weeks, he received calls and letters from scores of drivers and crew
members from around the country. Rajo Jack finally was the winner
many people thought he could be.

Even in victory, Rajo didn't proclaim his win as a triumph for his race;
it was a triumph for him alone. And he finally felt like one of the boys.

"He was not a pushy person or trouble maker, he just wanted to get
along with people," fellow driver Johnny Klann said.

Rajo's fortunes soon reversed. A week later at Silvergate, Rajo was well
back in the pack in the main event when a stray dog squeezed through the
fence and ran onto the backstretch. When Rajo came out of turn two,
he was shocked to see the dog. At the last second, he noticed the mutt
and managed to put his car into a slide to avoid him. He barely clipped
the dog and hit the wall. The dog hopped up and was shooed away from
the track by a pair of officials. Rajo felt terrible about hurting the dog,
but worse, he had wrecked Pop Evans's car and was out of the race.

Rajo was running a close second to Bud Maehnel in the main event
on April 8 when on the thirty-second lap Maehnel's car went into a spin
and Rajo had nowhere to go, crashing into him. Rajo's front teeth were
broken in the crash, and he had them replaced with false teeth. But it
made for another story with which he could regale people.

Rajo was already a distant third in points on the ARA championship
trail, behind Curly Mills and Bayless Levrett, but he got back into the hunt
on April 22 when he and Hal Cole waged a furious battle for second place.
For twenty laps, they passed each other lap after lap. With one lap to go,
Rajo overdrove his car coming out of turn two and got sideways, allowing
Cole to take the position at the finish. The fans talked incessantly about
the race between Rajo and Cole. Mickey Cooper's win was an afterthought.

Rajo Jack wasn't embarrassed by his race, and he could only hide it
so long. A black man finding success as a race car driver was not popular
with everyone. In between the day's races, a rival car owner was upset
that Rajo had beaten his driver.

"I could beat that nigger any day," the man said.

Rajo challenged the man to a grudge race. Rajo and the car owner
brought their street cars onto the track. The twist, Rajo declared at the last

minute, was that the race was to be run in reverse. The car owner didn't protest. Rajo won the one-lap race so handily the crowd was on its feet.

"Now you can call me Mr. Nigger," Rajo told the man after the race, one of the few times he proclaimed his race.

Rajo placed second in the thirty-five-lap main event April 29, but at the May 20 race, Rajo overdrove the number 11 car in qualifying, got sideways, and skidded to a stop in the murky pond in the infield. Rajo was up to his neck in muck. The story he would tell for decades was he wasn't sure the track workers would find him in the mud. By the time they got Rajo out and Pop Evans's car freed, they were both caked in mud. The fans loved it, but Rajo was done for the day. It took days of washing the car to clean out most of the mud and get the engine running again.

In the press coverage, his race was the center of attention. Being dubbed "the colored speed king" was a sign the press was building his image as a racer. But they didn't note the race of any of the other drivers. One writer wondered, "if he was trying to lighten his complexion or steal Johnny "Mudhen" Klann's nickname."

Rajo Jack quickly became mediocre. He placed a distant eighth on June 3 and on June 17 dropped out on the thirty-second of sixty laps in the main event. Pop Evans had enough. He knew Rajo could win races, but he couldn't afford the instances when he didn't win.

Rajo's younger brother, Lindsey Gatson, died three days later, June 20, 1934, at twenty-six years old. After finishing his job as a laborer in Tyler, Lindsey retreated to one of the many bars in town. After a few drinks, he got into a disagreement with another man. In the ensuing fight, Lindsey was stabbed with a shank and shot in the chest. Lindsey had a temper—and frequently drank, like all the Gatson men—so no one was surprised when he died in such a fashion. He was buried a day later. Rajo didn't find out his brother had died until a week later when a letter from his mother arrived.

Being out of a ride was not a comfortable position. Pop Evans's car had been Rajo's first steady ride in a competitive race car. Rajo had imagined he could rely on driving Evans's car, especially since he had been successful in it. But car owners were fickle and quick to exorcise themselves of anyone they thought would cost them more money than they won.

In the meantime, Rajo came back to Silvergate and picked up a ride in the low-level number 18 car. Rajo yearned to drive his own race car, but it was still a pile of parts. The best he could do in his first outing in the number 18 was a third-place finish in the fifteen-lap consolation race. Rajo transferred to the main event and placed sixth, far behind victorious Floyd Roberts.

Rajo picked up a different ride for the July 1 race, but it was lower quality.   The only saving grace was that promoter J. F. McIntosh decided the street car race in reverse went so well he wanted to put on another stock car race, this time with the cars going in the correct, counterclockwise direction. Rajo brought his Model T, "Sally," from the street and, with white mechanic Joe Ellis riding in the passenger seat, easily blew away the rest of the competition. People marveled at the way he drove the seemingly plain car so fast. Between the thousands of miles Rajo had driven it and the Rajo-head engine under the hood, his street car made more power than some of the race cars at Silvergate.

Rajo Jack was off the track for a month, but it wasn't because of a lack of finding rides. While he was earning fame and fortune in California, the rest of his family was struggling in Texas. His twenty-three-year-old sister, Katie, had been ill for a month and on July 8, 1934, went to a hospital in Tyler for treatment. She was diagnosed with an intestinal obstruction. On July 10, she had surgery to clear the obstruction. On July 13, Katie died from complications of the surgery.

Rajo and Ruth went to Texas for Katie's funeral. Under the weight of so much tragedy, Noah Gatson grew more distant, but Rajo felt it important to see his mother through this tragedy. He stayed in Texas for almost a week, but Noah was constantly drunk. Rajo never forgot why he left Tyler, and he and Ruth made a hasty departure.

Instead of returning to California immediately after the funeral, he and Ruth traveled to Detroit and Chicago to see some of Ruth's family members. As they were driving home on July 28, they happened by a speedway located outside of St. Louis, Missouri, named Creve Corner

Speedway. Rajo Jack couldn't pass a racetrack without stopping, especially if a race was going on.

At the pit gate, he used his story of being Portuguese to get in the pits. Once inside, he regaled car owners with stories about how he was the hottest race car driver in California. For once, he wasn't lying. A white car owner with a four-port Riley engine speedster needed a driver. Rajo talked his way into the ride. Despite never sitting in the car before, he qualified third out of thirty-seven drivers, won the second heat, and placed second in the main event to Red Bradley. The other drivers were impressed with the California hot shoe. And he earned enough money from the race to pay for their trip.

When Rajo returned to Silvergate to race, Lee Conti, a reporter from *Coast Auto Racing*—at that time the main source of racing news on the West Coast—interviewed Rajo. Rajo gave answers full of fabrications; he had learned the value of the press in the creation of an image from Marcell, who by then was living in Arizona and onto a new scam. Rajo told Conti he was born in San Francisco in 1905 and lost both parents in the earthquake and fires of 1906. He said he was taken to San Jose and lived with an aunt and grandmother until the age of eleven when he ran away, rode a fishing boat to Alaska and worked for nine months in a cannery. He said he returned to California two years later and won his 1926 match race with Francis Quinn. He also stated he had raced at nearly every track in the United States and had raced on more tracks than any other active driver.

The details Rajo imagined were so compelling that they seemed plausible. Little of Rajo's actual background was known in the southern California racing fraternity. Just as young Dewey Gatson had impressed his English teachers with colorful narratives, Rajo Jack dazzled his fellow racers with tall tales and legends. He always knew how to make up a good story.

After returning from Missouri with his new tales of his success, he found a decent ride for the Silvergate Speedway races in the George Sparks–owned number 2 car. It was an improvement, but the car had a reputation for being skittish and made some good drivers look mediocre. In the first heat race, Rajo skidded through the wall in the south turn and the car came to a rest over the embankment. He was done for the day.

In front of a record crowd of forty-five hundred on August 19, Rajo started out fast by winning the five-lap qualifying heat and was a close second in the early laps of the twenty-five-lap main event behind leading Mickey Cooper. But he hit a rut in the north turn and barely kept the car pointed forward. He struggled to place fourth while Cooper pulled away to win.

A new driver showed up on the racing scene in southern California with a name everyone in racing knew. And most spectators were confused.

A twenty-six-year-old man going by the name Barney Oldfield was turning heads racing big cars and garnering attention. When most people heard Barney Oldfield was racing at San Diego, they assumed the real Barney Oldfield was making a comeback. But the real Barney Oldfield was living not far away in Los Angeles, unsuccessfully trying his hand at owning and operating businesses, including a bar and a golf course.

The real name of this young man racing in big cars in southern California was Clarence Oldfield, or that's what he told people. Promoters latched onto him and entered him under the name of Barney Oldfield. Fans came to races expecting to see the real Barney Oldfield and nearly rioted over this man being passed off as the real thing. To satiate curious fans, promoters changed the billing to Barney Oldfield II and then back to Clarence Oldfield. At different times, he was purported to be the nephew, great nephew, and grandson of the real Barney Oldfield. Whether he was actually related to the great racer was never proven. He could definitely drive a race car well—just not as well as the real Barney Oldfield. Having met the real Barney Oldfield, Rajo Jack was dubious about this new man's lineage.

Rajo Jack had performed valiantly in the number 2 Sparks Special, but in the August 26, 1934, race at Silvergate he placed fourth in the first heat, engine problems hampering him. After the heat, Rajo dug into the engine and found the carburetor float was low, causing the engine to stumble in the sweeping corners.

Rajo Jack gave everybody a show in the fifty-lap main event. Rajo Jack and Clarence Oldfield flew away from the field in the top two positions. They set such a quick pace they were soon into lapped traffic. Rajo struggled every time he attempted to lap a car. When he was on

Rajo Jack in the number 3 Sparks Special at Oakland Speedway. *Tom Motter Collection*

the faster inside line, his car drove well. But when he got off line and attempted to pass someone around the outside, his car got loose, and he had to wrestle it back under control. By that time Oldfield had sped by into the lead. Rajo gave chase and took the lead back from Oldfield but got loose again in traffic and Oldfield got by.

The pattern repeated itself six times. On the forty-sixth of fifty laps, Rajo passed Oldfield for the lead and won, with Oldfield a car length back in second. Their finish was so good few fans cared there were four cars running at the finish. And Rajo's second win of the season moved him up to third in the points standings, not far behind leading Curly Mills.

The big car racing at Silvergate gained attention and other promoters wanted a piece of it. The fair board of the Coconino County Fairgrounds in Flagstaff, Arizona, had a dusty, D-shaped, half-mile dirt oval and offered a handful of the top Silvergate drivers guaranteed money to race in northern Arizona, Rajo among them. The fair board promoted Rajo Jack as an "Oklahoma Indian" in its advance press. He thought it sounded better than being branded as a Negro.

Rajo, Ruth, and a younger brother of Ruth's who was staying with them—one Rajo affectionately referred to as "boy"—arrived in Flagstaff wearing their finest clothes. When they tried to find a hotel in which to stay, they were rejected at first sight. After many tries, they finally found a room to rent miles outside of town. Despite slights against Rajo because of his ethnicity, he didn't complain.

Earl Mansell set the track record at Flagstaff and won the first sweepstakes race. In the second race, Curly Mills, now driving for Pop Evans, won with Rajo Jack second and local driver Bob Hornsbrook of Phoenix third. In the final race of the day, Hornsbrook won with Rajo second and Mills in third. Rajo earned enough prize money—supplemented with the appearance money, the first of his career—to make the trip worthwhile.

———————

Stock car racing was gaining popularity in 1934. Purpose-built, open-wheel race cars were thought to be the only type of cars capable of holding up on punishing dirt ovals for more than a few laps. After the success of stock car races as sideshows to the big cars at Silvergate, promoter J. F. MacIntosh opted to risk it and attempt a race with the stock cars as the main attraction.

MacIntosh established a $1,000 purse for a two-hundred-lap stock car race for September 16. Rajo had help in getting a ride. Months earlier Kelly Petillo drove the number 4 V-8 Ford in a AAA-sanctioned stock car race on the road course at Mines Field. When this stock car race was scheduled, Petillo nominated Rajo to drive the car. In qualifying on September 15 with Otto Sparks—a white man—serving as his riding mechanic, Rajo set fast time among the twenty cars with a lap of 35.32 seconds.

On race day, however, the track was a soup of mud due to heavy rain, and the race was postponed to September 23. When that day came another downpour made it look unlikely anyone would turn a lap. Pop Evans took over preparing the track, but the best he could do was make the track smooth.

Most of the twenty drivers entered for the race didn't return and nine cars lined up for the two-hundred-lapper. Otto Sparks couldn't make it for the race, so Rajo took on Al Hatton, another white man—one who didn't much like Rajo—as his riding mechanic.

Rajo and Curly Mills swapped the first and second positions early in front of a scant crowd and broke away from the rest of the field, which quickly thinned. After the first hundred laps, Rajo led with Mills second and all other drivers at least two laps behind. Rajo knew something Mills didn't: he didn't need to pit. Mills pitted for fuel on the 170th lap and dropped four laps back getting a few gallons. Even when Earl Mansell passed Rajo in the closing laps, Rajo wasn't worried; Rajo was still seven laps ahead of Mansell.

When Rajo took the checkered flag on the 200th lap for the $500 win, he still had one-and-three-quarters gallons of fuel left in his Ford. He was the only driver to go the whole way without a pit stop.

After the race, Rajo smoked a celebratory cigarette as officials and friends crowded around him in the impromptu victory lane. This was a big win for Rajo, and it was trumpeted in newspapers around southern California. There was one problem: in his hustle to make the race happen, MacIntosh failed to have a Gold Cup made. And the gate receipts were so poor he didn't have the money to pay Rajo.

It wasn't until the big car race September 30 at Silvergate that Rajo received his trophy and, more importantly, the $500 winner's check. Had Rajo cashed the check at that moment—which he might have, had a bank been open on a Saturday night—it would have bounced. The check only was good after thirty-five hundred fans paid admission to that night's race. And Rajo didn't do well in the big car, placing second in the consolation race. But at least he got paid.

A week later, Rajo was lapped traffic again. At the October 14 race at Silvergate, Oldfield easily won the race in front of four thousand fans, but the fans left the track talking about how Rajo narrowly beat out Earl Mansell to place second. After an October 21 race in which the most notable thing he did was win a three-lap qualifying heat race, Rajo placed third in the number 21 car in a four-lap big car race on October 28 behind Bayless Levrett and Mickey Cooper. Rajo placed fourth November 11 in the seventy-five-lap Armistice Sweepstakes and fifth November 25 in a forty-lap main event. The small results kept him in the points chase, something he valued above all. A championship, he reasoned, could lead to acceptance with the AAA, as it had for white drivers like Francis Quinn.

When Rajo Jack was first identified in the press as being black, he was concerned. The more his name was feted, the more his ability to obscure his race diminished. But it also served as an opening for aspiring race car drivers who weren't white.

A twenty-seven-year-old man by the name of Sey Sugi, born in Los Angeles of Japanese heritage, started racing during the second half of the 1934 season at Silvergate Speedway. He had met Rajo years earlier as they both worked as mechanics serving their respective communities in Los Angeles. Rajo brought Sugi to his first race, one at Legion Ascot Speedway, and Sugi was hooked. Seeing Rajo Jack's success early in 1934 bolstered his resolve. The first race car Sugi bought was among the worst ever to take to the track at Silvergate, but Sugi eventually improved it and his driving ability in the process.

And in the December 2 race—in which Rajo's only accomplishment was winning his qualifying heat race—Sugi was surprisingly competitive. Sugi came from seventh place to finish second, one spot ahead of points-leading Levrett. It was a step forward and one which he could have never taken in a race controlled by the racist AAA. To fans who watched him work his way through the pack, Sugi was now a real race car driver, too.

———

There was one race remaining in the Silvergate season on December 23, but Rajo had lost another ride. He wasn't close enough in points to have a shot at winning the Pacific Southwest Championship, but was high enough he could still win a portion of the points fund money. Many car owners still refused to let Rajo drive their race cars. He suspected it was because of his race, but his reputation as a driver who won races or broke cars also haunted him.

In a cartoon in *Coast Auto Racing* weeks earlier, a race car driver was shown going in front of a judge for speeding sixty miles per hour on a public road. It was speculated which driver was lampooned: Kelly Petillo, Floyd Roberts, or Rajo Jack. Petillo and Roberts had been ticketed for speeding on public streets, but Rajo outperformed them: he had been arrested for driving eighty-three miles per hour in a fifteen mile per hour zone.

Kelly Petillo had an occasional ride in Paul Weirick's Miller-powered, Indianapolis-type car. But Petillo also had another car in the back of his garage: an underpowered, Frontenac-powered, single-seat car with the number 63 on its tail, dubbed the "Lion Head Special" and sponsored by Gilmore Oil. It was a better car than any others racing at Silvergate. Petillo drove it in a few races when he could find no other ride, but mostly let it sit. Knowing the car was going to be idle, Rajo talked Petillo into letting him drive it in the final race of the season at Silvergate.

A baby-faced driver showed up late in the 1934 Silvergate season. The twenty-year-old with a shock of sandy-blond hair introduced himself as Jackie Dinsmore and told people how he had been racing in the Midwest. John Carlyle Dinsmoor was born in West Virginia, was raised in Ohio, and came to California with the same goal as many young men: to become a race car driver. And like many drivers, he raced under an assumed name to hide his racing career from his family. He soon became Rajo Jack's nemesis on the track.

The December 23 final race of the season, which was dedicated to a charity run by the Elks Club, was given a unique format with two twenty-lap main events. In the first main event, Rajo pulled off with a few laps to go because the fuel pump in Petillo's car failed. Rajo repaired it quickly. Fortunately for him, the field was inverted for the second race, meaning he would start up front.

Jackie Dinsmore took the initial lead of the second main event and was in front for the first thirteen laps. But the engine in Dinsmore's car soured, and Earl Mansell took the lead with Rajo close behind in second. When the white flag flew, Rajo pulled to the outside of Mansell coming out of turn two, and they raced side-by-side down the backstretch and into turn three. Coming out of the final turn, Rajo hammered on the throttle and narrowly passed Mansell as they passed under checkered flag for his fourth win of the season.

It wasn't until later the officials realized the checkered flag was flown a lap prematurely and Rajo's mighty effort to pass Mansell for the win came on the nineteenth lap.

The same day as the Silvergate race, the AAA was putting on a race for two-seat, Indianapolis-type big cars at Mines Field airport in Los Angeles and attracted attention from across the nation for it.

Petillo had a ride in Paul Weirick's big car for the Mines Field race, but he needed one thing for the race and found it in an unexpected place: a pep rally at Glendale High School. The first time Petillo laid eyes on Takeo "Chickie" Hirashima, he didn't care the upbeat seventeen-year-old was of Japanese ancestry. What Petillo saw was a skinny kid who could help him win a race.

Halfway through the race, Petillo's left elbow flew wild in the cockpit while trying to control his car and smacked Hirashima in the jaw. Hirashima's limp body slumped to the floor. Petillo was having none of it and repeatedly kicked the kid in the ribs until Hirashima woke up. Hirashima was groggy, but coherent enough to do some of his job as a riding mechanic the rest of the way.

Wilbur Shaw led by half a lap at one point, but Petillo was on a mission. He chased down Shaw on the east turn of the ninety-sixth lap, briefly gave up the lead to pit, passed him back and won his first AAA national event, pocketing a hefty $3,500 for the win. Hirashima got a few dollars for his work.

Petillo made a lot of money and risked his career that day by bringing a nonwhite contender to a AAA race.

"Takio [sic] Hirashima, riding mechanic for Kelly Petillo in that three-hundred-mile Mines Field auto race, isn't the only Japanese speed demon in the racket. Sey Ooly Sugi owns and drives his own racing car at San Diego. Only Caucasian drivers are allowed to pilot cars in the A.A.A., so Sugi performs in the outlaw tracks," columnist Bob Ray wrote in the January 3, 1935, edition of the Los Angeles Times.

Even in outlaw racing circles, nonwhite pilots were so rare as to be an oddity. But as Rajo Jack battled for wins through the year, he craved recognition for his racing, not his race. And his determination began to pay off. In the final Pacific Southwest points for the 1934 season, Rajo placed third with 151.88 points, with Bayless Levrett winning the championship. Rajo Jack finally mattered.

5

THE RISE TO PROMINENCE

SOME RACE CAR DRIVERS EXCEL AT DRIVING RACE CARS for other people. In theory, the car owner pays for everything, fixes the car when it's broken, and takes it to the races. The driver shows up and drives, receiving a percentage of prize winnings for his contribution.

Rajo Jack wanted to get his race car finished, but it was taking longer than he anticipated. Rajo saved every cent of prize money in 1934 and plowed it into building his new car. It became his obsession, so much so that he ignored his wife. He made little progress during the racing season as his schedule often included long days in his bustling auto repair business, followed by late nights at the garages of car owners for whom he was driving. He then spent every spare second of his weekends racing. After two years of working on the new car, he had scrounged together some important parts for the project—a fuel tank, a frame, some wheels, a steering gear, and a front end. But the pile of parts for the new car sat undisturbed in one bay on the dirt floor of his garage alongside "Sally," his beloved Rajo-headed Model T.

Racing with the AAA was as tricky a proposition as building a race car. Drivers like Ted Horn tried to join the AAA from the start of their careers but were turned away for not having enough experience.

And the only way drivers could get such experience was to race as outlaws. Once branded outlaws, they would have a hard time proving to AAA that they should be forgiven for racing as outlaws and deserved a AAA driver's license. It could take years for great drivers to navigate.

Rajo was determined to make the leap to the AAA as it was his only way to the Indy 500.

After his success at Silvergate Speedway in 1934, Rajo decided he would give his dream of racing at Legion Ascot Speedway another shot. He loaded up Petillo's Frontenac-engine big car and set out for the January 13, 1935, race at Legion Ascot. If the AAA was ever going to give him a shot, this was his chance. He had a AAA-licensed car owner in Petillo, his expired AAA mechanic's license, and proven ability with four main event wins in 1934 in San Diego; he was well known and respected by other Legion Ascot drivers.

When Rajo showed up at Legion Ascot—which was under a barrage of complaints from the media after many deaths at the track—Ed Martin, Legion Ascot's recording secretary, initially waved him through the entry gate to the infield pits. Rajo felt elation as never before. He was finally going to race at Legion Ascot.

But the chairman of the race committee, Henry Prussing, witnessed this and stopped Rajo before he got to the pits. Prussing said he had to confer with Art Pillsbury before Rajo could go any further. Rajo's heart sunk at the mention of Pillsbury. It was an hour until Pillsbury showed up to the track, and Rajo grew bored sitting on his trailer. When Pillsbury arrived and was informed by Prussing that Rajo wanted to race, Pillsbury called together the other AAA officials. They gathered in a circle and discussed the matter.

Rajo knew the answer before they delivered it. His hope was dying by the second. Some officials wanted Rajo to get his shot and voiced their desire. Pillsbury held veto power. Pillsbury left the officials and walked over to Rajo: he would not be racing at Legion Ascot that night or any other. Pillsbury, in his usual manner, passed the buck and said the officials had to abide by the AAA's rules on not allowing outlaw drivers. Rajo briefly pleaded his case, but with Pillsbury it was futile.

Rajo drove his Ford, with Petillo's race car on the trailer, on the track just enough to turn it around and leave.

———————

At least Rajo was wanted at Silvergate. Rajo won a heat race at the January 27 opening race at Silvergate, but struggled February 3, placing second in the ten-lap consolation race and recovering from a spin to place twelfth in the main event behind winning Bayless Levrett. After the race, the drivers were awarded their numbers based on their points finishes of the previous year. Levrett was given number 1 and was quick to apply it on his car. Mickey Cooper was given number 2 and took his time before painting it on. Rajo Jack was given number 3, but he was hesitant to paint the number on a car, especially as he was still driving for others.

A pair of promoters, Charles Feld and Herb Koenig, carved out a new half-mile dirt track between Colton and Redland about an hour from San Diego and sought out the best Silvergate drivers to race on February 17 at the facility they christened Tri-City Track. It wasn't much, but it was a race. And Rajo Jack was one of the first drivers to sign up. The problem for Feld and Koenig was few other cars showed.

Rajo placed sixth in the first heat race, fourth in the second heat, and won the third heat race when the cars of Jackie Dinsmore and Bob Frame—son of 1932 Indianapolis 500 winner Fred Frame—broke down. Rajo earned the sixth starting spot for the forty-lap main event and placed fifth despite a less-than stellar field. Feld and Koenig hoped to stretch out the show, so they cooked up a five-lap match race between Herb Kelley and Rajo. Rajo was always up for a match race. Rajo took the initial lead of the match race, but Kelley slid by on the second lap and won.

Rajo placed third in the February 24 race back at Silvergate. After the race, it was announced Charlie Curryer was returning as promoter of Silvergate and was also managing San Joaquin Valley Speedway in Goshen. His first race back as promoter at Silvergate on March 3 rained out, though.

Southern California's band of outlaw drivers, including Bayless Levrett and Rajo Jack, was receiving attention outside of the San Diego area as tales of their epic battles grew. Promoters found they could make more money bringing in a few big-name outlaws than by putting on a AAA race.

When San Jose Speedway opened in 1923, it was under the sanction of AAA. But after a few years of poor returns and multiple promoters running the track for short periods of time, Tommy Quinn (no relation to Francis Quinn) was brought in as the new track manager in 1935. He started his own sanctioning body, the California Auto Racing Association, for big cars. Quinn could put on races, but there weren't many big cars in the Bay Area, and the biggest name driver for the San Jose races was "Fat" Mario Branchero, a man known more for his girth than driving ability.

Since the early days of the track, the best battles had been compelling rivalries, most notably between the hometown northern California drivers and the invaders from southern California. The drivers from the south usually prevailed. Tommy Quinn was anxious to bring that rivalry back. Quinn arranged to pay Levrett and Rajo tow money of $100 on top of whatever prize money they earned to race. The tow money was more than Rajo or Levrett could earn by winning many of the races in which they competed. It was unheard of for a promoter to give that kind of guarantee to a black man. But Rajo and Levrett also had to agree to not tell the local drivers of the bonus money.

Levrett made Rajo an offer: the two would caravan for the day's tow north to San Jose. Rajo knew the roads between Los Angeles and San Jose, but there were many hazards for a black person driving a long distance on his own. California was progressive compared with much of the country, but that perception was based on what was happening in the big cities. Rural California was not as enlightened. Many gas stations and restaurants wouldn't serve black people. And it wasn't unusual under the strain of towing hundreds of miles for tow cars to break down. For the first time—and far from the last time—Rajo Jack and Bayless Levrett caravanned together from Los Angeles to San Jose for the March 17 race.

Rajo watched a few AAA races at the five-eighths-mile dirt oval in his brief time living in San Jose and while crewing for Francis Quinn.

He was in the pits for two of Quinn's wins at the track in 1930. Despite the track being reduced to a half-mile oval by the time Rajo came to race for the first time, he was confident he could get around the high-banked bowl. Rajo was piloting George Sparks's Sparks Special while Levrett was in his regular Frontenac-powered car.

An overflow crowd of ten thousand fans was busy jamming themselves into the grandstands by the time Rajo and Levrett arrived, a large crowd for a non-AAA-sanctioned race. The announcers played up the fact that Rajo was black, and it was the first time any of the fans had watched a black race car driver. Plenty of fans booed him, but many were curious to see if the southern California hot shoe was as good as advertised. Levrett won the five-lap heat race and Rajo was a close second. They would not only occupy the front row for the hundred-lap main event, but also show the rest of the drivers the southern California boys were the class of the field.

And from the start, Rajo and Levrett gave everyone their money's worth—especially Tommy Quinn. They leapt out front and took turns leading the opening laps; the northern California boys were no match. They quickly were so far in front they lapped most of the field. Even when Frank O'Neil went into a spin out of the far turn and nearly hit the inside wall or when Johnnie Fanucchi lost a wheel, most of the fans couldn't take their attention away from the battle between Rajo and Levrett.

On the seventy-eighth lap, however, the engine on Levrett's car blew up and his car slowed, giving the lead to Rajo. By that time Rajo and Levrett had lapped the entire field. Knowing he was far in front, Rajo slowed to conserve his car. A few laps later, Art Armstrong passed him, but Rajo was still ahead by nearly a lap. The rest of the way, the only time Rajo was near another car was when he was lapping one. He was a half lap in front of second-place Armstrong by the time he crossed the finish line after one-hundred laps. Mysteriously, though, most people in the pits congratulated Armstrong when the drivers pulled in the pits. They thought Armstrong's pass of Rajo had been for the lead, and Armstrong had won.

Rajo was incensed. He worked his way into the conversation with officials busy congratulating Armstrong. When he reached the officials, the most they would do was congratulate him for placing second. Aside from Tommy Quinn, the officials didn't like the southern California invaders.

Rajo tracked down Quinn and pleaded his case. Levrett, despite finishing a distant fourth, came to Rajo's defense. They both knew this type of scoring mix-up would have never happened at a AAA race. In many instances at poorly run tracks like San Jose Speedway, Rajo wouldn't have had a shot at an appeal. Quinn recognized his only hope that Rajo and Levrett—and in turn such a large crowd—might return was to placate the stars. While Armstrong celebrated his apparent win and signed autographs for the fans, Quinn brought the official scorekeepers together and had them review their scoring sheets.

Armstrong learned of the protest but wasn't concerned. He told everyone Rajo had never lapped him and third-place finishing Fanucchi backed him up. Tommy Quinn decided he wouldn't pay the drivers until a final decision was made. The first time the scorekeepers went through the scoring sheets, they found Armstrong was the winner. Rajo complained more, and finally Tommy Quinn declared he would go through the score sheets. It took so long most fans left convinced Armstrong was the winner and only a few drivers remained. Rajo, Levrett, Armstrong, and a few other drivers waited around the track patiently, their cars loaded up and ready to go home. They even started a game of poker on the hood of Rajo's car. They wanted to leave, but no one was going anywhere until they got paid.

Three hours after the race, Armstrong identified the mistake in the score sheets. Rajo had, in fact, lapped Armstrong while locked in his battle for the lead with Levrett. When Quinn made his way to pit road, he called the remaining drivers around. He apologized for taking so long but assured the drivers he needed to be accurate. Rajo Jack had indeed won the race. Armstrong was second.

The reaction to Rajo's win was mixed. Many fans and other drivers had never seen a black man drive a race car and assumed Rajo wouldn't be as good as the white drivers. They couldn't believe a black man had defeated the best drivers they had to offer.

The media took differing opinions about the decision. Some declared Rajo was the rightful winner. Some decided that, since Armstrong was flagged the winner, the result should never have been changed. "Rajo Jack, Negro Ace, Declared Official Winner" read one newspaper headline. At least, Rajo reasoned in talking with Levrett the next day, the papers called him an ace.

When Rajo returned to San Diego to race at Silvergate on March 31, he quickly found the competition was still significantly better back in southern California. He won his five-lap heat race but had nothing for the drivers in the forty-lap main, which Kenny Phillips—a complete unknown—dominated.

———————

Late April each year, racing shut down in many areas of the United States as the entire racing world focused on the Indianapolis Motor Speedway.

Kelly Petillo's success had grown, and he earned notice. Petillo's Indy 500 career had an inauspicious start, but in 1934, he got a ride in Joe Marks's Red Lion–sponsored car and earned the pole position. He led six laps, but a broken oil line relegated him to an eleventh-place finish.

Petillo's results on the track were solid, but his reputation was taking a beating from his off-track problems. He frequently won races for car owner Paul Weirick, but often took unnecessary chances and wrecked. And he was known to have a temper off the track. Car owners knew Petillo could win races but distanced themselves, and he couldn't find a ride for the 1935 Indianapolis 500.

Petillo had one remaining choice if he was going to race in the Indy 500: field a car for himself. Petillo took every cent he had, combined it with the money from his parents mortgaging their grocery store, and raised $5,000 to build a car to race at Indy. He engaged Curly Wetteroth to build a chassis and body and got parts from wherever else he could find them, including instruments from an airplane wrecking yard owned by racing fan and supporter Arrigo Balboni, a front axle from a Plymouth, and a transmission from a Studebaker.

Fred Offenhauser, a former employee of the Miller engine company, purchased the remains of Miller out of bankruptcy and produced the next evolution of the vaunted engines. Though Offenhauser was selling plenty of engines to the big car and midget markets, he wasn't making inroads with the Indy 500 bunch as Miller had. Petillo didn't have the $3,500 for a new engine, but Offenhauser offered to sell him one on credit. It was a huge gamble on Offenhauser's part; Petillo was a well-known risk.

The month of May at the Indianapolis Motor Speedway—with the only hope of a payday after the race—was an expensive undertaking. Petillo didn't have the money to make it through, and he knew it. But he needed a crew.

Guy Deulin had raced against Petillo at Legion Ascot but had also become a talented mechanic after frequently wrecking the race cars he drove. He agreed to help Petillo at Indy. And Petillo convinced Rajo Jack to accompany him to the Indy 500 as a mechanic. Petillo swore he was so well liked at Indy he could get the officials to allow Rajo in Gasoline Alley and to be his chief mechanic for the race. That position carried a perk, one Rajo coveted: the chief mechanic could drive the car in practice. But helping Petillo also meant Rajo would have to miss out on driving in races, and the money he could win in them, in California.

Rajo Jack still had stars in his eyes, though, and the Indianapolis 500—even if he wasn't to be racing in it—was too alluring to pass up.

Petillo loaded his wife, Val, and young son, Kelly Jr., into his car, put his race car on Rajo's trailer, and set out in late April for Indianapolis. Rajo followed a few days later in his Ford. Petillo promised to cover Rajo's expenses during the month. But when Rajo arrived in Indianapolis, the room Petillo had promised was rented out to someone else for the month. Rajo had to find a boarding house, and the best he could do was one far from the speedway. His drive to the track took a half hour each morning.

When Rajo Jack tried to enter Gasoline Alley his first day in Indianapolis in May 1935, he was turned away by the AAA officials. It was humbling, but not unexpected. When Petillo finally left Gasoline Alley that day and started to leave the track, Rajo spotted him from the infield and relayed how he was turned away. Petillo was quick to anger about many things, but this was a new level. To every AAA and Indianapolis Motor Speedway official he could find, Petillo argued Rajo was his mechanic and needed to be in Gasoline Alley. The officials swore there were rules prohibiting black men from entering and explained there was nothing they could do. The only thing they would allow Rajo Jack—the man who had become one of the hottest race car drivers in California—to be was a janitor for Petillo.

This time Rajo turned bitter at the rejection and immediately wanted to leave. Petillo pleaded for him to stay as he needed all the help he could get. At nights he worked on Petillo's car when he was supposed to be acting as a janitor, but Petillo's operation was on such a shoestring they only had basic tools to work on the car. And there were few spare parts. Rajo wanted to help but allowed himself to recognize that the snub was not about his credentials or character this time, but because he was black.

On the first day of qualifying, Petillo set a record with a speed of 121.687 miles per hour for the ten-lap average and was fast enough to earn the pole position. Even Petillo didn't expect that fast of a run. But the AAA officials had grown wary of Petillo and his attitude. After Petillo's qualifying run, they examined every inch of Petillo's car and decided the car had burned too much fuel. They disallowed the time, meaning he would have to qualify again later.

On Petillo's next qualifying attempt—two weeks before the race—he blew up the engine on the third lap of his four-lap qualifying run. It was so severe Rajo decided he couldn't help. Rajo had exhausted the little money he brought and was about to be evicted from the room he was renting. Rajo apologized, but informed Petillo he was returning to Los Angeles.

After Rajo left, Petillo and his scraped-together crew—along with Fred Offenhauser—removed the engine, and the damage was worse than they feared. The engine had thrown a rod and blew a hole in the side of the block. Offenhauser sent a telegram to his Los Angeles shop for the internal parts to be shipped to Indianapolis. There were few people capable of fixing the block in Indianapolis, one being engine-builder Karl Kizer. When Petillo first approached him, Kizer resisted as he had more work than he could manage, and Petillo had no money to pay him. It didn't stop Petillo from begging for fifteen minutes. Kizer gave him a list of other engine shops in Indianapolis to check out, so Petillo left.

Later that afternoon Petillo came back to Kizer's shop with his wife and son, nearly in tears. The other engine shops wouldn't take on the work because Petillo had developed a reputation for not paying his bills. Petillo told Kizer he had $18.26 to his name and began to cry. Kizer relented. He welded the block together and machined it for the pistons and rods that arrived from Los Angeles. The bill came to $800, and Kizer extended Petillo credit for the amount. It was a leap of faith on Keizer's part; Petillo had won $900 for the 1934 Indianapolis 500. Petillo expressed his gratitude and promised to pay Kizer the full amount. With the engine returned to Petillo's car, he qualified twenty-second for the 1935 Indy 500.

Rajo spoke to Petillo on the phone in the days leading up to the race and knew he was in far better spirits than when Rajo had left Indianapolis. Rajo regretted leaving. He would listen to the race on the radio.

The morning of the race, 1925 Indianapolis 500 winner Pete DePaolo was walking down pit road and recognized Petillo's predicament. He volunteered to be Petillo's pit manager if he would follow DePaolo's instructions.

"Just pay attention to the signals I give you from the pit," DePaolo told him. "If you don't do what I tell you, I'll hit you over the head with a hammer."

Petillo promised to do anything DePaolo wanted. Rex Mays sped out of the pole position to hold an early lead but Petillo was on an alternate strategy and steadily worked his way to the front. On the 120th lap, Mays's engine blew and Petillo inherited the lead. He briefly gave it up on the 140th lap when DePaolo called him in to pit. He took the lead back on lap 145 and lead the final 55 laps, even through drizzling rain that settled in late, to win by 40.02 seconds in front of second place Wilbur Shaw. Somehow, Kelly Petillo was the 1935 Indy 500 champion. AAA western regional director and Indy 500 official Art Pillsbury estimated in addition to the $32,000 for winning the Indianapolis 500, Petillo would pick up about $20,000 in lap and contingency money for the win. Petillo even paid Rajo Jack the money he promised him.

Four days after Indy, on June 2, Rajo towed back to San Jose Speedway, this time with more of the southern California drivers including Levrett, Art Scovell, Jackie Dinsmore, and Clarence Oldfield in a growing caravan. When the group of racers tried to rent rooms at the same hotel, the manager bluntly told them Rajo wasn't welcome. The entire group started to walk out of the office to find another hotel, but the manager backed down and offered to rent them all rooms. In the Depression, money was more important than societal norms.

The San Jose promoters were so taken with Rajo Jack and the attention he brought after his win in March they decided to advertise his coming appearance. They paid for a billboard along the highway in San Mateo and advertised in gigantic letters that Rajo Jack, who they labelled as the "Negro star," would be returning to race on June 2. When Rajo saw it, he was in disbelief. Rajo had been ejected from one speedway because he was black, but at this track he was being celebrated for it.

Rajo won the second ten-lap heat race to earn his way into the eleven-car main event. This created a problem. Ruth was traveling with him less frequently. She didn't appreciate being on the road like he did. When Rajo was feted for the win on the front stretch after the race, he couldn't give the traditional kiss to the white trophy girl. The newlywed bride of aspiring driver Fred Agabashian, Mable, was on hand and knew Rajo. She recognized the predicament and gave Rajo a handshake instead. It still caused a minor uproar—mostly from fellow racers giving him grief—but it passed.

Rajo, Dinsmore, and Levrett were the class of the field for the twenty laps of the main event, quickly breaking away from the field and swapping the lead back and forth between them. Rajo and Levrett banged their cars together and slowed but managed to continue. Dinsmore pulled away and won the race with Rajo second, nearly a lap back, and Levrett another half lap back in third.

San Diego had become a major hub for the military, and the June 16 race at Silvergate Speedway was designated to honor the armed forces. Rajo painted his car to honor the Marines, not that it improved his on-track performance. Jackie Dinsmore again won the forty-lap main event. The competition at Silvergate had grown exponentially with a new crop of young, aspiring race car drivers showing up in southern California.

Rajo Jack accepts a trophy from an unidentified white woman at Southern Ascot Speedway. *Podurgiel Collection*

The competition from locals at out-of-town races was not nearly as concentrated. On June 23, Rajo Jack headed to Goshen to race at what was then being called Valley Speedway. There weren't many cars, and Rajo was the class of the day, easily winning the thirty-lap main event.

Curryer's promotion of Silvergate suddenly ended, and he took the races scheduled at the track with him. It left a void in Rajo's racing, and his life, for a month. By late July, a new promoter, George Weber, took over Silvergate Speedway. He hastily assembled a schedule of races and on August 4 brought the big cars back for a forty-lap main event. A crowd of three thousand fans showed up to watch Jackie Dinsmore—now going by the name he would make famous, Duke Dinsmore—take the lead on the ninth lap and win by 150 yards. Rajo and Bud Bragdan fought for second place with Rajo nipping Bragdan at the finish line for second. A week later the best Rajo could do was win a five-lap qualifying heat. After a rainout the following week, he returned September 9 and placed third in a five-lap heat race. But Rajo rose to second place in the Pacific Southwest championship points chase. The championship was within reach.

As Curryer was no longer promoting Silvergate, he set up his southern California drivers to race at the Gresham Speed Bowl in Oregon for a September 8 race. Without consulting Rajo, Curryer signed him up.

Initially Rajo was excited. It would be the first time he would race at the track at which he first experienced racing in 1920. But there was a choice to be made. There was a race on the same day as a race at Silvergate. Rajo figured his best chance to earn his way into the good graces of the racing elite and prove himself finally worthy to the AAA was to win a championship, much as Francis Quinn did in 1930. The money to travel to the Portland area was enticing, but the chance at a championship was too important.

Rajo would have been better served traveling to Oregon. At Silvergate on September 8, he managed to win a heat race but was otherwise a non-factor, though he stayed in the points chase. The following week, September 15, there was to be a 175-lap stock car race at Silvergate, but after qualifying, Rajo and Oldfield got into an argument; Rajo qualified for the race and Oldfield didn't. Duke Dinsmore won the twelve-car main event in front of four thousand fans while Rajo struggled in a mediocre car to tenth place.

Weber caught wind of Rajo's argument with Oldfield and decided to play it up for the September 22 follow-up race. He scheduled a three-lap match race between the two as part of the program. But Oldfield's car broke during qualifying and instead Rajo had to settle for a match race against Art "Shorty" Scovell, who had nothing to do with the disagreement. Worse yet, Rajo placed second to Scovell. And then he placed second in the helmet dash to Bayless Levrett and third in his five-lap heat.

At another stock car race at Silvergate on October 6, Rajo took over the V-8 Ford Duke Dinsmore won in a month prior. With two laps to go in the 175-lap race, a head in the engine cracked and Rajo didn't finish while Wally Pankratz, driving a Ford Sedan Delivery truck, won. The match race from the previous race was so popular Weber lined up a race between Sey Sugi and Rajo in their regular big cars. In another humiliation Rajo placed second, and it was one of the few times Sugi ever won a race of any type.

In the October 13 big car race at Silvergate, Rajo took the lead on the thirteenth of fifty laps when Lou Salisbury spun out of the lead in the north turn. But one lap later, the engine in Rajo's car blew up. He raced once more at Goshen October 27, but after placing second in his heat race, he spun through the fence and was fortunate to get back on track to place fourth in the thirty-five-lap big car race. It was a humbling end to his season. Though he was still high in the points, Rajo couldn't find a ride for the rest of the season. He was burned out from racing all season, and he needed to spend time building his own car.

In the final points for 1935, Rajo placed third with 250.15, trailing Levrett and Cooper. Placing third in championships was already growing old.

6

THE FOLLY OF NEGRO LEAGUE MIDGET RACING

NEGRO LEAGUE BASEBALL STARTED DUE TO NECESSITY; midget racing happened because of convenience. The two sports were worlds apart.

Baseball teams composed solely of black players came about in the 1880s due to collusion among professional baseball owners to keep their teams solely white. Hundreds of all-black barnstorming teams were formed. If a black man wanted to play professional baseball, he had no choice but to play on an all-black team. In 1920, the first Negro league—the Negro National League—was formed. The leagues ebbed and flowed but gave organization to black professional baseball and legitimized it in the public.

With baseball, segregation was more overt than it was in racing. In 1887, a group of baseball team owners in the International League voted to ban signing black players to contracts. Owners of major league teams formed a gentlemen's agreement not to have black players on their teams from then on, much as the American Automobile Association would later do in the world of auto racing. The commissioner of baseball, Kenesaw Mountain Landis, who ruled the sport with an iron fist, lent his considerable might to keep black players out of professional baseball.

Racing cars was a costly undertaking. Not only were the cars prohibitively expensive, but it was costly to race them. When the economy was good, the biggest, most expensive classes drew a lot of cars but put on mediocre races because top car owners tried to outspend each other to win races. When the economy was down, racers and promoters sought affordable classes. When the Great Depression hammered the United States in 1929, many racers had to stop.

But an old idea gained new traction. The first race for the tiny cars that would become known as midgets occurred in 1910 in conjunction with a AAA race. (The star attraction of the big race that day was Barney Oldfield.) Races for the small cars continued until 1914, after which they disappeared. But in 1933, future automotive publisher Floyd Clymer came to California to promote motorcycle races and saw the potential of the midgets, if enough cars could be found. Midget racing became hugely popular in a short span.

The economics of the Depression were what gave midget racing life. In 1933 thirty percent of Americans were unemployed. Midget cars were small, though built to look like big cars. Their engines were small as well, so scaled-down racing was more affordable for car owners. And there was another aspect that made midgets popular among promoters: they could build a track as small as possible, or convert existing stadiums previously used for other sports like baseball and football into racetracks. Instead of building a five-eighths-mile oval, as had become standard, races could be held on the cinder running tracks around football fields at high schools and colleges, or on tracks built in baseball parks, which were plentiful. Promoters could rent venues, build racetracks (or use what was there) and move on to the next location. And they could charge admission as low as five cents.

At first most big car drivers wanted nothing to do with driving midgets, thinking they were second-rate. The midgets looked like toys compared to their big cars, and most drivers resisted racing midgets, even after it became more lucrative than big car racing.

———————

A baseball stadium in Los Angeles known as White Sox Park, previously used for Negro league teams, was struggling as a venue for baseball by 1935 and needed help. Built at the corner of 38th Street and Compton Avenue in 1924 with seven thousand seats, White Sox Park earned its name as the spring training home for the Chicago White Sox. The White Sox moved their spring training site after a few years, but the field caught on as a winter home for black teams. For a time, huge crowds came to the greatest Negro league players of their day. Fans were occasionally treated to seeing black teams play white major league teams such as the Kansas City Royals and Philadelphia Giants.

Holding a few exhibition games in the winter and a sparse schedule of pickup games between barnstorming teams wasn't a sustainable business model for the park. When minor league Pacific Coast League teams began to allow Negro league teams to play at their nicer parks, White Sox Park lost what made it unique.

The owners of the stadium needed revenue. Harry Levette and a group of businessmen from the east side of Los Angeles came up with a plan. They would build a temporary racetrack on the dilapidated baseball field. They hoped to recapture the audience of the black community that largely made up the neighborhoods surrounding the venue. To do so they envisioned holding a series of midget races featuring only black race car drivers.

A series of big car races solely for black drivers in the Midwest had been sanctioned by the Colored Speedway Association, with its biggest race of the season in Indiana—the Gold and Glory Sweepstakes—held yearly since 1924. Neither Rajo Jack nor any of those involved with White Sox Speedway knew that series existed. The Gold and Glory races drew large fields of cars, but the competition was poor and the crowds for its all-black races had waned; the races died out later in 1936.

The businessmen involved with White Sox Speedway were novices in racing and needed someone with connections to the racing world: William "Spider" Matlock was the man they needed. Best known as the charismatic flagman for midget races around the Los Angeles area, Matlock knew—and was universally liked by—everybody involved in racing. After the promoters hired Matlock to officiate the all-black midget races, he immediately went to work on the first task: gathering a group of willing car owners. What he found was a selection of owners of Class B cars, ones powered by motorcycle engines and outboard boat motors. Matlock easily rounded up a dozen such car owners. A large number of those cars were uncompetitive at most races and their owners could use the additional income. At the new venue, these cars would be stars.

There was a major problem with Matlock's next task. Finding black race car drivers in Los Angeles seemed impossible. There was one black race car driver in southern California at the time: Rajo Jack. Matlock knew Rajo Jack from their days at Legion Ascot—Matlock as a flagman and Rajo as a mechanic—but they were never close.

Without Rajo Jack, however, Matlock wouldn't have a driver capable of drawing any audience to White Sox Speedway, let alone the black audience the track owners coveted. Matlock hounded Rajo Jack at his auto repair shop in the Watts neighborhood for weeks. Matlock also canvassed other neighborhoods in Los Angeles in a constant search for drivers who might be able to drive a midget. He envisioned a field of twenty-four drivers on the quarter-mile dirt track he was tasked with promoting. Finding any black man capable of driving a midget proved difficult.

Rajo Jack had reservations about the operation. He also faced a physical challenge: he was six-foot-two and a muscular 235 pounds by 1936 and barely fit in a big car, let alone something half the size. He had never sat in a midget when Matlock first approached him, and Rajo expressed concern he wouldn't be able to fit. But Matlock promised to find him the biggest and best midget among the cars coming to race. And Matlock promised he would promote Rajo Jack as the star attraction.

There was an added benefit for Rajo: he would finally be known to a black audience. Until that point in his career, Rajo had been seen racing by audiences made up mostly of white fans. The black community of southern California generally ignored racing, and black newspapers paid Rajo no attention.

What clinched Rajo Jack's participation in the midget races at White Sox Speedway was Matlock arranging to have promoter Harry Levette pay Rajo a guarantee of one hundred dollars per race—more than the entire purse they were promising for the races. He was, after all, the star. Once Rajo signed on, the black newspapers—not only those in Los Angeles but also those in other cities—began mentioning him. Being known in his own community as something more than a mechanic was a new experience.

And Matlock had something on his résumé that appealed to Rajo Jack. Matlock wasn't just a flagman; he was also a riding mechanic. In 1930, Matlock was the riding mechanic for Billy Arnold when he won the Indy 500. Matlock had made more laps around the two-and-a-half-mile quad oval at Indianapolis than many of the drivers who actually drove in the race. And Matlock had a rare ability. The likeable, well-spoken, humorous, and tiny Matlock bounced effortlessly between competing in AAA races and his work with midget groups, which were considered outlaw organizations. He was one of few who bridged the opposing worlds.

Part of Rajo's deal was he was to help Matlock line up dozens of drivers for the inaugural February 2 race. Rajo had connections in the community of black mechanics and black men involved in other automotive-related businesses around Los Angeles. Rajo and Matlock took anyone they thought could drive a midget. These were delivery drivers, taxi drivers, and mechanics, but they were the best available. The most promising was a mechanic named Herman Giles, a friend of Rajo's who frequently worked on Rajo's race cars. Giles also owned the largest garage in Los Angeles' black community and frequently mentored young black people who sought to become mechanics. Like Giles, most of the drivers they found had at least some mechanical skill. The track owners lined up boxer "Baby" Joe Gans, a figure in the black community in Los Angeles, to be the official starter for the inaugural race.

After months of work by Spider Matlock to organize the races for the scheduled February opening race, it almost fell apart in a heartbeat. On January 25, 1936, Matlock was performing his duties as the riding mechanic for driver Al Gordon in a big car race at Legion Ascot Speedway. During the main event, the car got loose coming out of turn two and slid sideways. Gordon overcorrected the car. It shot to the right and went straight through the wood fence ringing the track. As the car cleared the fence, it leapt over the embankment, flipped in the air, and landed upside down. Gordon and Matlock were crushed by the car. Gordon was killed instantly. Matlock clung to life a few more days but also died from the injuries.

There had been many deaths at races and public uproar, led by the William Randolph Hearst–owned *Los Angeles Herald Examiner*, grew loud about the dangers of racing. The racing at Legion Ascot received the greatest amount of vitriol and was proclaimed to be a shining example of why racing needed to end.

"Automobile racing has outlived its usefulness. It has ceased to be racing and has become merely a morbid and brutal spectacle. Its carnage should end. Racing now is no more of a sport than hanging is a sport," Barney Oldfield said.

Glendale American Legion Post 127, which had been promoting the races at Legion Ascot, padlocked the gates to the track and closed it for good. Four months later the wooden grandstands burned down. The property was sold and subdivided for construction of houses. Seven years later, the track's janitor, Linden Emerson, admitted to burning down the grandstand, the fatal crash being the last straw.

"I saw Al Gordon and Spider Matlock killed out there and when the track closed, I thought maybe they might reopen it and kill some more of my friends," Emerson admitted.

It was the end of the Legion Ascot—the holy land of dirt track racing in southern California—and Rajo would never accomplish his goal of racing at the track. But it also changed racing in southern California over the next decade.

In large part due to the popularity boom of midget racing, big car racing waned in popularity in southern California the mid-1930s. The midgets played to unexpectedly large crowds. With the premiere track for the big cars gone and no suitable replacements available, Art Pillsbury, the regional director of the AAA Contest Board, essentially became a figurehead and was ultimately powerless. Outside of a couple races at El Centro, the AAA wouldn't sanction another big car race in southern California for over a decade. It wouldn't sanction any steady racing in California until 1939, and then it only sanctioned midgets.

Though the AAA stopped sanctioning big car racing in southern California, the area was still a popular destination for aspiring race car drivers. With the AAA ceding control of big car racing in the area, outlaw circuits such as the American Racing Association and the Western

Racing Association (WRA) received a major boost. Suddenly car owners didn't mind being outlaws.

But after the death of Matlock, Rajo and White Sox Speedway promoter Harry Levette were in a jam. They had days before the first scheduled race and the seemingly impossible task of putting on a midget race without their greatest ally and his connections in the racing world. They also needed someone who would officiate the races, someone the car owners trusted and who had a name in the southern California racing community. Fast.

The person they found was Mel Keneally. At the age of thirty-two, Keneally had a lengthy résumé as a driver. The highlight of his career as a driver was placing seventeenth at the 1930 Indy 500. But after his time as a AAA driver concluded, he sought out other avenues. He went outlaw and raced all over the West Coast, his best results coming in the Pacific Northwest. Up north he was a big shot and regularly won races. But southern California was where the money was. When Keneally agreed to officiate the races at White Sox Park, he had a lot of work to do. Fortunately, the first race was rained out and moved back to February 9.

The entry list for the first race was made up of drivers like Burke Johnson, Charley Moore, Herman Giles, John Barnes, Red Fredricks, George Gradham, Sunshine Prescott, Cleo Johnson, George Bradego, Harry Young, Joe Bailey, Buster Harrison, Elmore Templeton, Bill "Mouse" Fuller, William Foster, and a young mechanic Rajo had known for years, Bill Scott. Most had never been to a race. Rajo and Keneally had the tough task of teaching these men how to race midgets in a matter of days. Getting the cars started was challenging as they all had to be pull started behind street cars with tow ropes. Teaching the drivers what the flags meant required another significant session. It took every moment Rajo and Keneally could spare over the course of a week to teach each one of the novices how races were operated.

The crowd for the first race at White Sox Speedway wasn't large, but it wasn't because of the cost. Admission was twenty-five cents for adults, box seats were forty cents, and children were admitted for fifteen cents. For that first night's race, the largest group of fans were white.

The promotion of the race reached the black community, but it didn't make an impact. Few were interested.

And a problem arose because the midgets Matlock arranged weren't great. Midgets were graded into two classes. The cars that showed up to White Sox Speedway were the lower level. Eleven cars showed up for the first race and nine ran.

Rajo set a match race with a white driver who was supposed to have been a big car ace who had raced in the Indy 500 named Lester McMillian. (No one with that name ever competed at Indy.)

Bill Fuller won a trophy dash early in the program to win the Bill Robinson Trophy—named for the tap dancer and actor known as "Bojangles"—in the one race of the night that Rajo didn't drive.

By the time of the main event, seven cars still ran, and Keneally made the call to cut the race to ten laps. Even in those ten laps, it was painful for the crowd to watch Rajo Jack easily speed away to win, lapping every car except second-place Kenny Nelson.

A race with all black drivers had finally happened, and it wasn't a success. It showed promise, however, and the track promoters felt justified to schedule a second race.

Advertising the first race primarily in the black community hadn't worked, so Keneally decided he would try to draw from a wider base. Keneally came up with the concept of an international match race. He would have Rajo race against Sey Sugi—the big car driver of Japanese descent—and a Mexico-born driver named Celso Gomez. Gomez was known around Los Angeles for a successful bakery he owned downtown. Gomez owned and raced his own midget and had far more experience with the tiny cars than Rajo and Sugi. He would essentially be a ringer—an ace competing against relative novices.

Whereas much racing in southern California was controlled by the AAA, midgets were controlled largely by boxer-turned-racing-promoter Dominic Distarce, with help from brother Pedro "Pee Wee" Distarce. The Distarce brothers were originally from Mexico and welcomed all people, unlike the racist AAA. Dominic was the promoter and main figure in the Midget Auto Racing Association, which sanctioned most midget racing in the Los Angeles area, and Gomez had an open invitation to race with the MARA.

After a couple rainouts, Keneally's promotion finally came to fruition, but not before he put himself in a fourth midget for the match race. Gomez checked out to win with Rajo second, Keneally third, and Sugi fourth after breaking an oil line.

Instead of one main event, Keneally decided on staging a series of shorter races as most cars were not capable of lasting longer. In one, he pitted dancer Bill Robinson against movie and radio actor Clarence Muse, racing for a $50 bet. Muse took the early lead and won. After they took the checkered flag, they pulled their cars to a stop at the start-finish line and climbed out. They shook hands then performed a dance routine on the track as the crowd roared with approval. It was the most entertaining part of the night.

Rajo won the trophy dash with a newcomer who showed potential by placing second, Mel Leighton. Leighton was a skinny, industrious guy originally from Iowa who wanted to drive race cars long before he watched the first race of the season at White Sox Speedway. Now Leighton, one of the few black people employed by the city of Los Angeles, was part of the show.

In the six-car main event, Rajo again sped away from the field from the start and was clearly the driver to beat. But on the seventh lap an oil line in the engine broke, spitting hot oil over his legs and forcing him to pull off. It handed the win to Bill "Mouse" Fuller.

Every fear Rajo had about White Sox Speedway came true. Even the best cars were mediocre. And the black audience promoter Harry Levette had anticipated didn't materialize. Then Keneally walked away. Officiating racing wasn't for him; he wanted to drive. Levette tried to convince Rajo there would be more races at White Sox Speedway and the racing would improve, but Rajo was done. He detested midget racing more than before he raced one.

Rajo Jack wanted to get back to big cars where he was more comfortable and successful. He wrangled a ride in the number 56 Frontenac big car owned by Jack Taylor for the March 29 race at Silvergate Speedway.   It was his first race at Silvergate in six months, but when he arrived at the San Diego track, he saw the only things that had changed were that the crowd had dwindled to two thousand and a host of younger drivers was now showing up.

Rajo Jack was still the greatest driver at the track.

Earl Mansell led the first nine laps of the twenty-five-lap main event before engine trouble sidelined him and Rajo took the lead. Rajo struggled to maintain control of the number 56 car and led the race, but Duke Dinsmore caught up quickly. Rajo would pull out a comfortable lead, get loose, and allow Dinsmore to catch up, then gather the car back together, and pull away. But Rajo drove doggedly and streaked across the finish line to take the checkered flag for the win. Though Rajo had been relatively successful in his short stint at White Sox Speedway, the mainstream press ignored it. The races at Silvergate, though, brought him plenty of attention in the mainstream media.

Racing a big car was where Rajo Jack belonged.

Charlie Curryer was always on the lookout for a new track at which he could take over as promoter. The one-mile dirt oval of Oakland Speedway—designed by Art Pillsbury—was without a promoter to start the 1936 season, and Curryer snapped it up. Curryer had a knack for making money promoting races at hopeless small-town dirt tracks but had struggled with more prominent venues. Racers and car owners in the Bay Area agreed to compete under his sanctioning because it meant they would get paid, as opposed to other outlaw races. But Curryer had to convince his stars from down South—including Rajo Jack—to come north.

In the AAA days of the track, Francis Quinn and the rest of the Los Angeles drivers would be paid an advertised guarantee of twenty-five dollars, though many received larger amounts separate from the purse. It took months of negotiations by mail between Rajo in Los Angeles and Curryer in Sacramento for them to come to an agreement: Curryer would pay Rajo fifty dollars up front for every race at Oakland along with any winnings earned. It would, at least, cover Rajo's travel to and from the track.

After skipping the first two Oakland Speedway races while negotiating with Curryer, Rajo finally headed north April 19. Rajo had gone to one race at Oakland Speedway crewing for Francis Quinn, and he might have been concerned about making the trip, as the tow to Oakland for the 1931 race had been Quinn's last. But the lure of money eased any apprehension.

Curryer played up Rajo Jack in the press, billing him as "The Rajah" and calling him a veteran of twenty years of racing, one of many exaggerations. Curryer put the word out that Rajo was going to be racing the same number 56 Jack Taylor-owned Frontenac he raced at Silvergate. Taylor's ancestors in Virginia had been slave owners, and he hired Rajo partially to spite their memory.

"They would turn over in their graves if they knew I gave the driving job to a black race car driver," Taylor said.

Instead of holding the Oakland race on the mile oval, Curryer carved out a more manageable half-mile dirt oval inside of the big track. Rajo easily won his heat race in front of his largest crowd to date, seventy-five hundred fans. He clearly was the class of the field and lined up for the two-lap trophy dash. But Rajo sandbagged and let the other driver win. When Rajo pulled in, Taylor asked why he had obviously let the other driver win and kiss the white trophy girl.

"I wanted to save the lady the embarrassment of kissing a black man in front of a large crowd," Rajo said.

"When you race my car, I expect you to try and win the race," Taylor said.

Taylor's car was fast and Rajo pushed it as hard as he could in the main event, but the Frontenac engine went up in a cloud of blue smoke after a couple laps, and local driver Fred Agabashian made the race boring by winning the forty-lap main event by two laps.

Working long, hot days in the California sun as a mechanic had grown tiring for Rajo. Sweating while working under the hoods of cars in the heat of a San Fernando Valley summer was not fun. He started a side business buying used items and reselling them. Rajo received the unflattering label of junk dealer. One item he purchased was a thirty-foot-wide balloon used for advertising. When filled with hydrogen it could rise four hundred feet in the air. It had a blank sign hanging from the side. Curryer wanted to use it to promote his races—it was far cheaper than a billboard like the one San Jose Speedway promoters used—and paid Rajo to bring it to Oakland for the May 17 race. They made a sign advertising the race and moored it to a light post at the corner of 26th Street and Telegraph Avenue a few days before the race. Within hours of attaching it, the balloon became untied, drifted east, and was never seen again. Rajo's investment floated away.

On race day, Rajo was running close behind leader Duane Carter in his heat race, but the engine in his car began misfiring and slowed as the rest of the field sped past. Rajo made hasty repairs by removing a spark plug and managed to start the fifty-lap main event. Carter would win the main event, but Rajo managed to keep the car running long enough to place fifth. At least he would get paid for racing, even if he had lost money on the balloon.

Curryer arranged for Rajo and a group of Los Angeles drivers including Wally Schock and Orrie Bean to make a long tow to Aurora Speedway near Seattle, Washington, for the May 30 race. The publicity about how this was Seattle's first big car race was secondary to the publicity about Rajo. Billed as the "Brown Bullet," he was purported to be the only Negro racer on the Pacific Coast. No one in Seattle knew any different. Schock won with Washington driver Swede Lindskog second. Rajo, driving in one of Bayless Levrett's cars, crashed early in the program and didn't race in the main event.

Rajo's next race on June 1 at Oakland Speedway was more painful.

Stock car racing was gaining popularity in southern California, unlike most states, and proving profitable. Curryer lined up a Ford roadster for Rajo to drive in the two-hundred-lap race May 31, 1936, on the mile oval at Oakland, and Rajo enlisted Bill Walker, a white man, to be his riding mechanic. Rajo was respected by white mechanics, and always chose white men to ride with him. If black men couldn't be riding mechanics at Indianapolis, maybe white riding mechanics with a black driver could change things.

Rajo started second and passed Tex Peterson for the lead on the forty-eighth lap. Peterson took the lead back, and then the right rear axle of Rajo's Ford snapped while running second on the 100th lap. For 200 yards, he attempted to wrestle the car under control, but the right rear tire blew out in the struggle, and his car catapulted over the crash fence. The car flipped three times and landed upside down with a thud. The track officials feared Rajo was dead as there was no roof on the car. Rajo's foot and leg were jammed between the spokes of the steering wheel, and fans nearby jumped in to help free him. As Rajo and Walker crawled up the embankment, the track workers, including Pop Evans, asked the pair if they were all right. They responded by asking for cigarettes.

When Legion Ascot closed for good in January 1936, it left a void in racing. But it didn't benefit Silvergate Speedway as much as the track owners had hoped. Silvergate would close for good by the end of 1936. The land on which it was built wasn't good for much as it was a causeway and prone to flooding. A couple decades later it was bought by a consortium of businessmen who turned it into an aquatic theme park. They called it SeaWorld.

By 1931, boxer Jim Jeffries—the white man who was defeated by Jack Johnson in "The Fight of the Century" in 1910—had developed an affinity for racing, but he wasn't foolish enough to try driving himself. Instead, he had a five-eighths-mile dirt oval carved out of a field on his ranch in Burbank. It was the epitome of an outlaw track. There was only a small grandstand and a short length of wood crash wall on the front stretch. The track—alternately called Jeffries Ranch and Burbank Speedway— fostered competition between racers like Rex Mays, Floyd Roberts, and Bayless Levrett. It was also a training ground for new and interesting names in the racing word, such as the Robson brothers.

The Robson brothers—George, Harold (who would go by Hal), and Jimmy—were an anomaly among the outlaw racers. They were a refined, well-mannered bunch. Where many outlaws were crude and quick to

Rajo Jack drinks a beer after winning a stock car race at Oakland Speedway in 1937. *Tom Motter Collection*

fight, the Robsons were more genteel and refined. The Robson family lived in Newcastle upon Tyne, England, when oldest son George was born in 1909. The family immigrated to Mount Dennis, Ontario, Canada, where the next four sons were born, and moved again to Huntington Park, California, in 1923. Their father, also named George, set up a machine shop after moving to California and each of the sons received training as machinists. The brothers quickly earned a reputation as winners in the outlaw racing world.

Rajo Jack, however, never raced at Jeffries Ranch. Jim Jeffries appreciated the outlaw drivers, but his views on black people hadn't changed.

The cars that raced at Jeffries Ranch were different from those elsewhere. These were mostly Ford Model T's, channeled and sectioned with fenders removed and open wheels. Most had improved engines

but were low on horsepower compared with Class B cars. They became
the first roadster racers. There were few rules at tracks like Jeffries
Ranch, and there weren't many races. But the drivers could earn up
to sixty-five dollars at each race, significant amounts during the Great
Depression.

When racing ended at Jeffries Ranch in 1933, the roadsters needed
somewhere steady to race. Many of the outlaw tracks opened and closed
with regularity. Even racers weren't surprised when a new track would
close after a couple races. A group of the roadster racers formed the
California Roadster Racing Club in 1935 as they needed to band together
to get races. With no tracks in Los Angeles capable of hosting races on
a permanent basis, one of their own decided to build one.

Alex Podurgiel owned a crummy, undeveloped piece of low land
on the banks of the Los Angeles River at the intersection of Atlantic
Avenue and Tweedy Boulevard. His son, Vince, was an occasional
outlaw driver and saw the potential for a racetrack on the land. The
roadster club raised as much money as possible to fund construction,
but this outlaw track was set up for success by location more than
financial backing. Unlike most tracks, it was located close to a huge
population. For Rajo Jack it was even better, because the new track
was four miles from his house. For once he wouldn't have to travel
hours—or days—to race.

The group dug a half-mile dirt oval and rented a rickety wood
grandstand, the best they could afford. The first race at the track—
which was initially dubbed Southern Speedway—took place June 7,
1936. A robust group of thirty cars showed up accompanied by a
promising generation of drivers. In the first race at Southern Speedway, George Robson won the forty-lap main event, then—immediately after taking the checkered flag—flipped the car down the front
stretch. Rajo landed a ride in a poor car and finished back in the
pack. Travis "Spider" Webb, an outspoken transplant from Missouri,
placed second. He would soon become one of Rajo's best friends and
greatest allies.

Rajo's mind was elsewhere when he returned to Oakland Speedway on June 14, and he finished well back in the field. As soon as the race was over, he towed north to Portland, Oregon. Rajo was finally going to get to race in his former home.

A five-eighths-mile dirt oval was built in 1936 in north Portland and was so new it didn't yet have a name, though it would later be called Portland Speedway. The first race was set for June 21, 1936, and promoter Frank Nolan opted for the grandeur of a big car race. He grabbed up every big car driver from around the West Coast by offering them large amounts of money. Curryer was promoting an American Racing Association race at Goshen Speedway in Visalia that day, but the money offered to go to Portland was enticing. Nolan poached Duke Dinsmore, Rajo, and Jimmy Wilburn to come from California and brought in northwest-based drivers Art Scovell and Einar Theodore "Swede" Lindskog from Seattle to give himself a formidable field.

Wilburn won the twenty-five-lap main event with Frank Wearne second, Scovell third, and Rajo fourth.

"Rajo Jack, a colored driver from California, new to the northwest, gave indication in the fifth heat that he will make it tough for the leaders," the *Oregonian* reported, not acknowledging his history of racing in the Portland area dating back to 1923.

Curryer was upset with Rajo for forsaking the ARA to race in Portland and cancelled their previous agreement. When the June 28 race at Oakland Speedway was taking place, Rajo was home in Los Angeles. With the AAA gone, and a wealth of new outlaw racing promotions sprouting up around Los Angeles, Rajo had become a big enough attraction to have options.

Instead of going to Oakland, Rajo proceeded to race a dreaded midget June 28 at Southern Speedway for track owner Alex Podurgiel, followed by a big car race July 4 on a makeshift oval at Capitola Airport between two unpaved parallel runways, a fifty-mile race in Watsonville at a track called the Palm Beach Speed Bowl, and another midget race July 13 at Southern Speedway—by then known as Southgate Speedway. Rajo placed fifth in the midget main event at Southgate, but like every time he raced a midget, he swore it would be his last.

Then he raced in the July 19 race at Goshen Speedway on a hot and humid day. Most of the top southern California drivers had gone off to race in Oregon at Gresham Speed Bowl. Rajo showed up too late to qualify and struggled with persistent engine problems but was given the last starting spot for the race. In his haste to catch up with the leaders, he hit another car and crashed through the barbed wire fence in the west curve, scraping his chest and arm and damaging the number 28 car he was driving before coming to a stop on the road outside the track.

Rajo Jack had become so well-known and liked among the southern California car owners he had his pick of rides. He could drive in Alex Podurgiel's number C10 big car one week and the Famighetti brothers' beautiful machine the next. Rajo wanted to finish his own car but had built such a reputation he could find rides regularly and take his time with his machine.

Curryer was having a hard time drawing the southern California racers back up to Oakland so he included Rajo's name on the entry bill of every race—even though he wasn't coming. Rajo had become one of the biggest name drivers on the West Coast.

Where Rajo *did* go, instead, was back to Flagstaff, Arizona, on August 2. Rajo Jack gave the record crowd a show, winning a ten-lap trophy dash between the five fastest drivers in qualifying. Then he went out strong in the main event and passed Earl Mansell for the lead. After a brief stoppage due to a freak summer rain shower during the thirteenth lap, Rajo sped away to win. He followed that with a fifth-place finish in an August 9 roadster race at Southgate.

The name "Rajo Jack" was earning weight. Promoters all over the West Coast, advertised he would race, even though he had no intention of going near the track in question. A promoter in Yakima, Washington, advertised he would race there in September 1936 during the State Fair. Rajo didn't. He did, however, make an unscheduled race on September 17 on the freshly paved quarter-mile asphalt oval in Tacoma, Washington, in a midget at a track newly christened Athletic Park. Rajo didn't do well, but he did better than Sey Sugi, who wrecked his borrowed midget.

After months of disagreement, Curryer and Rajo resolved their conflict, mostly by Curryer opening his wallet. Curryer knew Rajo was the lynchpin of the southern California boys he desperately needed to legitimatize his races. Wherever Rajo raced, the rest inevitably followed. Curryer finally got Rajo back by agreeing to pay him $75 for each appearance. On September 20 Rajo entered a 250-mile race on the one-mile oval in the same Ford roadster that he flipped in June and had since been miraculously repaired. Rajo set fast time in practice without any warm up. He held a huge lead in the race until engine problems dropped him to seventh. On September 27, Rajo placed second behind Pat Cunningham at Southgate in the forty-lap main event for roadsters, then won the big car race October 4 at Southgate.

Winning races throughout the southwest earned Rajo Jack a reputation, though far less than that of the AAA stars. Many fans appreciated him and his breakneck style of driving. Plenty more disliked him because he was a black man racing against white men. Some saw him as a cocky driver who didn't belong. Whether they liked him or not, fans paid attention to Rajo Jack.

And he would soon become known throughout the country.

7

FROM OBSCURITY TO NATIONAL CHAMPION

THE POPULARITY AND CONCENTRATION of auto racing in Los Angeles was always ahead of other parts of the United States. From the early 1900s, drivers from around the country with dreams of making a living driving race cars realized two advantages the area had over everywhere else in the world: Los Angeles had warm weather year-round and a lot of racetracks.

But promoters were haunted by a persistent problem, no matter the location: to make money, they needed to get fans to pay admission to watch their races.

When the Los Angeles Motordrome opened in Playa Del Ray in 1910, the nearly perfectly circular, one-mile track made of wood boards—the first of the revolutionary board tracks—was built with seating for an optimistic twelve thousand spectators. It was regularly packed with fans until it burned down in January 1913. Also short-lived but packed, the one-and-one-quarter-mile oval known as Beverly Hills Speedway had seventy thousand seats that were full for most of its races between 1920 and 1924.

But in the 1930s, with most Los Angeles–area tracks just over a half-mile in length and offering a maximum seating capacity of a few thousand, promoters struggled to keep their racing programs afloat. And during the Great Depression, promoters couldn't charge much for admission. The days of fans paying two dollars each to watch a race were gone. They were fortunate when fans were willing to pay fifty cents.

Road racing offered an answer to the problem. While road racing gained early popularity in Europe, dirt oval tracks originally built for horse racing became popular in the United States for auto racing because they were numerous and the promoters could easily charge admission. But road courses were longer and had the potential to lure more spectators than any circle track. Between temporary grandstands, hillsides, and places to stand behind fences and hay bales, there was ample room to put eager, paying fans. The first road races in the United States were held in rural areas on open roads, however, making it impossible to charge admission for spectators that showed up elsewhere along the track's vast length.

In 1930 a new airport was built in Los Angeles and christened Mines Field. It was rudimentary, even for the time. The airfield had dirt runways and no buildings, but it was situated perfectly in the expanding metropolis. There were already two more popular airports in Los Angeles, Dominguez Field and Rogers Airport, but Mines Field had the backing of the city. The private investors who paid to have the airport built didn't put much money into it, though.

One man saw the potential of Mines Field beyond its intended purpose: publicist Will Pickens. After starting his career in 1900 with Henry Ford and his vaunted number 999 car, Pickens served as riding mechanic for Barney Oldfield when he won a match race at Agricultural Park in Los Angeles, and Pickens's career in all forms of motorized transportation blossomed. Pickens and partner George Bentel built Legion Ascot Speedway in Los Angeles in 1924 and brought in IMCA sanctioning, as Pickens was an IMCA founder. Pickens branched out to promote sports like track and field and tennis, but racing was what he knew best.

It took a significant amount of work, but Pickens convinced the city of Los Angeles to give him a chance to put on a race at Mines Field. Pickens's idea was to put on a AAA national championship race for big cars on a makeshift road course on the dirt runways at the airport. He secured a race for February 18, 1934. But in early January, AAA regional supervisor Art Pillsbury announced AAA big cars would not race and stock cars would take their place.

On a cloudy, crisp day, an astounding crowd of seventy-five thousand watched Al Gordon win the 250-mile race, dubbed the Gilmore Gold Cup.

Pickens wasn't around long enough to enjoy the fruits of his labor. While touring the airport during the race, he stepped on a rusty nail. Months later one of his legs was amputated. On July 20, 1934, he died due to blood poisoning.

After the success of the first Mines Field race, AAA agreed to try their two-seat, Indy-type cars at Mines Field and hoped the big names driving better race cars would draw a bigger crowd. They set the race for December 23, 1934, but on race day fog was so thick and the temperatures so frigid the race was nearly cancelled. Still, fifty thousand fans packed the airport to watch Kelly Petillo win the race—on the same day Rajo Jack won at Silvergate Speedway in Petillo's other race car.

The second Mines Field road race was miserable, and the city wanted to use its still-new airport for its intended purpose, so it was two years until another race was held at the location. It took a change in management at the airport to bring racing back to Mines Field in 1936. With AAA having essentially vacated California, there were few options for a racing series that could bring more than a handful of cars. Though Charlie Curryer was managing Oakland Speedway, he saw the potential in the earlier races at Mines Field.

Curryer set up a race he dubbed a stock car race, though it wasn't under his American Racing Association banner. It was a stock car race in theory, but they were the same type of *modified* stock cars—sedans with fenders removed and stock engines—that had raced in the 1934 race at Mines Field and were still racing at Oakland Speedway. Curryer declared no manufacturer would be allowed to have more than four cars in the race because he didn't want the Ford coupes to run away with the race and ruin the competition. And he rebranded the racetrack "Los Angeles Speedway," as it sounded better than Mines Field.

Once Curryer was involved, the first driver he booked was Rajo Jack.

Curryer's finishing touch was to dub the race the National Road Race Championship, implicitly promising nationwide prestige to glory-hungry racers. He was justified, mostly because there were few road races in the United States in 1936. The race was scheduled for October 18 and a few sections of grandstands were erected around the course, which by then had been shortened to one mile and had a distinct B shape.

On the day of the race, torrential rain soaked the dirt runways, to the point where there was no chance of anyone completing a lap. After all the buildup to the race, the airport's administrators took pity on Curryer's attempt and granted him a date for the following weekend. But races that initially rain out rarely drew much of a crowd, so there was reason for pessimism.

Though it was a long course of one mile in length, the field was capped at twenty-four cars for the race. Thirty-six entered. As the new October 25 race date loomed, the press named a few drivers as favorites. Bob McKenzie was feted as one of the finest road racers in America, though he was a relative unknown to the southern California crowd. Mel Keneally had given up his AAA standing and would race. Bud Rose had risen to the ranks of the best big car drivers on the coast. A promising upstart from the Bay Area, Fred Agabashian, signed up. And Duane Carter set fast time October 24 for the race.

Rajo Jack was not named as a favorite; like many other entrants, he had never raced on a road course. Even though he had become one of the hottest race car drivers on the West Coast, all Rajo knew was the consistent turns and terrain of dedicated racetracks, makeshift though they often were. The varied and winding route of a road course was completely new to him.

When the drivers first got on track at Mines Field under ominous skies at 10 AM on October 24, what they found was a track still spongy, as it never had time to dry out. Qualifying was a disaster. Many of the cars, with stock components such as control arms, broke under the strain of the quickly rutting track. But Curryer issued a last-minute warning to the drivers and pit crews about the necessity of stock parts and equipment.

The number 4 Ford Rajo Jack was driving was built with stock parts, or close enough, to not raise suspicion in tech inspection. Rajo's trick was he had extra stock parts in the car.

Between fifteen thousand and twenty-five thousand fans filled the airport to watch the race—plenty to turn a profit—but with a track that large it was impossible to know exactly how many fans were on hand, as many figured out ways to sneak in without paying.

As the twenty-four cars rumbled to the start, Pat Cunningham—a regular racer in a midget at Gilmore Stadium—took the initial lead, but Rajo Jack was the only driver who could keep him in sight. Rajo gave everything trying to stay up with Cunningham, but Cunningham managed to stay in front with a lead between 75 and 150 yards through the first fifty-five laps. Cunningham's car broke a spindle under the pounding on the fifty-sixth lap, handing Rajo Jack the lead.

The track was brutal and many of the twenty-four cars that started broke at an astonishing rate—eleven of the starters would finish. Six drivers and mechanics—Vernon Wade, H. A. Walker, Walt Harris, Dee Tolan, and Henry Becker among them—were injured in wrecks and required trips to nearby hospitals. To make it worse, fog rolled in late in the race and softened the dirt with more moisture, denying it the chance to dry and harden. So many cars dropped out that Curryer made the call during the race to cut it down to 200 laps from 250.

It all allowed Rajo to easily build a two-lap lead. Many of the other cars pitted to fix mechanical problems or add fuel; Rajo never stopped. What the tech inspectors failed to realize before the race was the stock parts in his car included *two* stock gas tanks—one in the regular position under the car and a second mounted in the trunk.

Three hours, forty-seven minutes, and four seconds after he started the race, Rajo won the biggest race of his life, two laps in front of everyone else. The $1,500 winner's check was the most money Rajo Jack had won in his thirty-one years.

What happened next was something Curryer—and Rajo—never expected. The big newspapers around Los Angeles, including the *Los Angeles Times*, had reporters at the competition who described it as the biggest race of the year in Los Angeles, which was true. Once the wire services noticed that a black driver won a national championship race against white drivers, the story spread throughout the country. It was the first time a black race car driver had won a major race. It made for a compelling story line.

Rajo Jack (with beer in hand) sits in his car after winning the 1936 two hundred-mile National Road Race Championship at Los Angeles Speedway on October 25, 1936, also known as the Mines Field airport. Charlie Curryer, in the white hat on the left, hands him a cigar. *Ted Wilson photo, Bruce R. Craig Photograph Collection, Revs Institute*

The story of Rajo Jack's win made its way into nearly every newspaper in California, and into mainstream newspapers in Phoenix, St. Louis, Nevada, Pennsylvania, Milwaukee, and Indianapolis, as well as black newspapers in places like New York.

And every story noted Rajo Jack was black. The *Indianapolis Star* called him, "one of America's foremost Negro race drivers." The biggest compliment he got for his race was when he was described as "probably one of the outstanding Negro race drivers in the country and certainly tops in the west" in the *St. Louis Post-Dispatch*, the same newspaper that ignored him when he raced in St. Louis in 1932.

Rajo Jack was becoming one of the most well-known race car drivers in the United States.

Over the following weeks, Rajo received letters and phone calls from his large group of friends in the racing community. To the racing elite, Rajo's win was a joke; the competition was mediocre, and the cars were not real race cars. To those who read about the win from afar, he was a star.

And for the first time in his life, Rajo Jack was appreciated by the black community in Los Angeles. Entertainers who previously knew him in passing—like dancer Bill "Bojangles" Robinson and boxer "Baby" Joe Gans—sought him out and befriended him.

Without ever seeing him race, many in the black community of Los Angeles were convinced this black man was the greatest race car driver on the planet. Over the next few years, many in the entertainment community would tag along with him to races. Black actors who previously had no interest in racing were determined to see their new star in his sport. Never before had a black man made such a successful showing in auto racing, partly because people of his race were so discouraged from racing. In one race, Rajo proved a black man could accomplish what the white racing establishment had always fought to prevent.

Even the owners of White Sox Park wanted in. The baseball stadium had been converted back to its intended use. The owners wanted to honor Rajo for his win at a baseball game at the stadium between the black Royal Giants and the White Kings. They included him in a long list of black athletes they intended to fete at the game.

Rajo Jack had become such an instant celebrity that promoters were clamoring for him. He was supposedly entered in a big car race on November 1 at the reopening of the mile oval at Kenilworth Park in Petaluma, but Rajo was back in Los Angeles that day; Southern Speedway was holding a sixty-lap race for big cars, and Rajo chose to stay close to home. A big crowd turned out for the race, many drawn in by the pre-race publicity of Rajo racing. And he was fast. Running third with twenty laps to go, he tangled with second-place Hal Robson. The number C10, Alex Podurgiel–owned car Rajo was driving flipped, and he was thrown clear out of the car—Rajo considered seat belts dangerous, like most drivers of the day. He broke an ankle and got a few cuts and bruises but received a huge ovation from the appreciative crowd after crawling out from under the wreckage and onto the track.

Rajo Jack races Alex Podurgiel's C10 big car at Southern Ascot Speedway against a roadster. He signed the photo, "To my Pal & Friend Alex Rajo Jack." *Podurgiel Collection*

Rajo Jack on the ground after being thrown out a car he was racing at Southern Ascot Speedway. *Podurgiel Collection*

Rajo Jack signed this photo of the C10 big car owned by Alex Podurgiel at Southern Ascot Speedway. *Podurgiel Collection*

Rajo appreciated the attention, but he hoped it would all be enough to convince the AAA he was worthy of being blessed with their approval—not that there were AAA races in California. After all the years of rejection by Art Pillsbury, Rajo tried to remain realistic.

But Rajo Jack soon learned that race car drivers can go from a nothing to a hero—and back just as quickly.

Rajo showed up at the November 5 race at Southern Speedway but only for ceremonial purposes, as he was in no shape to race. Three days later, though, he hobbled around at Oakland Speedway. Charlie Curryer was eager to pony up to get the driver who had become his biggest star. Jack Taylor once again offered up his Frontenac engine speedster, and Rajo was willing to try. As he made laps in practice, though, any time he pressed down on the throttle pedal with his right foot, he wanted to collapse in agony. It was not going to be a good time for Rajo Jack.

And Curryer was putting on an odd show. On the mile track at Oakland, he set up a hundred-lap race between big cars and midgets. The Offenhauser-powered midget driven by Pat Cunningham would lose pace down the front and back straightaways, but eventually took the lead for good in the turns and went on to win. Rajo soldiered on to place sixth, many laps back. His was the final car running. He knew he shouldn't have been racing, but Rajo was striking while the iron was hot. This was his time to get paid.

He had three weeks to heal before his next race, another one at Mines Field, still being billed as the Los Angeles Speedway, on November 29. This race was for big cars, though some midgets joined to fill out the field. The big cars were built solely to turn left on oval tracks and had no transmissions, which made them unsuitable for road racing. This was a bigger challenge for Rajo than his broken foot.

A hefty field of twenty-four cars and drivers—many of the best outlaw drivers California had to offer—showed up for the seventy-five-mile road race, but a disappointing crowd of seven thousand fans came. Pole-sitter Bud Rose led the first fourteen laps before breaking a connecting rod and giving the lead to Jimmy Miller, who would win in just under an hour. Rajo's car broke a few laps before the finish. In a short amount of time, Rajo had gone from a hero to an also-ran.

The race would be the last at Mines Field. The City of Los Angeles would buy the airport in 1937 and pay to make major improvements. Eddie Rickenbacker was lobbying cities to improve existing airports or build new ones to serve the needs of the growing commercial airline industry. After four major airlines—American, Trans World, United, and Western—moved flights to the facility in 1949, the airport was renamed Los Angeles International Airport.

Rajo was entered for two races on December 20: a hundred-mile stock car race at the Imperial County and another midget vs. big car race at Oakland Speedway. Rajo opted to go north for the guaranteed appearance money. The weather turned wet after a few laps of qualifying, though, and the race was cancelled due to rain. The fans weren't happy;

Linn Mathewson, who was promoting the race, became the villain. Rajo and a few drivers tried to calm the crowd, but it didn't work. A few upset men nearly grew into a riot, and police had to come to the track to calm them and get them to leave.

Rajo Jack spent nearly every moment of spare time building his new race car over the next month. Rajo was determined he would no longer be at the whim of other car owners in 1937. He wanted to race for himself. And he was achingly close. The car was mostly together: he had the remaining necessary parts and the money to get it done. To Rajo Jack, the new car represented independence.

8

INDEPENDENCE AND REACHING A NEW HEIGHT

HARRY EISELE BECAME ENRAPTURED with the hot rod scene while attending Franklin High School in Los Angeles. Before graduation, Eisele built his first race car and declared to his mother he was going to race it. She refused to allow such foolishness.

Resigned, Eisele took his race car to Silvergate Speedway in San Diego in 1934 at the age of nineteen—by far the youngest car owner—and hired other drivers to pilot the car. Eisele always warmed up his race car, but inevitably turned the car over to whichever driver he employed that day. He desperately wanted to race but feared his family would disown him.

Rajo Jack and Harry Eisele lived not far apart in Los Angeles and became quick friends, often towing their race cars to San Diego together in case one of the tow cars broke down—an inevitable occurrence.

On one of their frequent trips south Rajo offered Eisele a solution: an assumed name.

Eisele's friends already called him "Butch," and he was dating a woman named Rose, so he and Rajo invented the persona of Buzz Rose. When Eisele told the announcer at Silvergate his name, the man misheard him and mispronounced his name "Bud Rose." It stuck. As soon as he started racing, Bud Rose excelled and was bringing home noticeably bigger amounts of money each week. His mother inquired about his new driver, and Harry informed her he'd found a hot shoe named Bud Rose. His mother insisted on going to a race at Silvergate to see this new driver perform. Harry Eisele put on his helmet to drive in the trophy dash and won the race. He was so excited as he pulled to the start-finish line to collect his trophy that he took off his helmet in full view of the crowd—including his shocked mother. Harry had hell to pay when he got home, but Bud Rose was doing so well as a race car driver, his mother eventually relented and allowed her son to race.

Bud Rose so resembled Clark Gable that when a photo of Bud Rose winning a race found its way into the hands of executives at Metro-Goldwyn-Mayer, who had Gable under contract, they were incensed and asked Gable, "When did you drive race cars?" Rose was such a ringer he would be Gable's stunt driver in the 1950 movie, *To Please A Lady*.

Rajo Jack and Bud Rose were friends off the track and developed a rivalry on it. They could race side by side for laps at a time without touching a wheel, putting on a show. As trips to race in northern California grew frequent in the mid-1930s, they stuck together. On one trip to Oakland, the caravan of racers—Rajo, Eisele, and many others—stopped at a restaurant along the way. The large group walked in and sat around a table at the restaurant.

The manager came to the table and announced, "We don't serve colored people," in the direction of Rajo.

"Serve us all or we leave," Bud Rose announced.

Before the manager could answer, the group of nearly a dozen people stood in unison to leave, but the manager—seeing his business about to plummet—apologized and agreed to serve them all. After years of discrimination, Rajo learned to shoulder quietly through such overt racism; Bud Rose wouldn't stand for it.

Rajo Jack's profile in the racing world had grown so large, he decided to take a stab at his dream. In 1937, Rajo mailed an entry form and required fee to the Indianapolis 500, but it was promptly returned. He did the same thing each year for the next decade, but his entry was always returned. He never received a reason why his entry was being turned down, but he knew it was because of the color of his skin.

The black community in Los Angeles finally saw Rajo as more than a mechanic after his 1936 win at Mines Field. The most famous among them invited Rajo and Ruth to society events. For a couple who previously scratched out a living with meager blue-collar work, it was unexpected. But Rajo fit in surprisingly well. He had a gift for talking and could regale any group for any length of time with stories about his racing and his life away from the speedways. Rajo never bragged, was self-effacing and humble. But even the highest rungs of black society held him up as their hero. Rajo would spin wild, made-up stories about how he was the renegade black son of a state senator. He was ashamed of his real identity, and none of the celebrities would ever learn who he really was.

After years of work and planning, Rajo Jack had nearly completed his new car in time for the 1937 season opener on January 31 at Southern Speedway. The night before the race, however, he broke the driveshaft and couldn't get one in time to race. Instead he went to the track for the fifty-lap big car race and talked his way into another ride. Rajo placed a distant fourth behind winning Jimmy Wilburn, but was desperate to finish building his car, which he was convinced was going to be a superior machine.

By the time Rajo's new car was complete, a huge segment of the racing community had heard so much about it they expected it to be a miraculous machine capable of winning any race, even the Indianapolis 500.

Finally, on February 21, Rajo Jack's race car made its first journey to a racetrack. It was a single-seat big car immaculately detailed and painted, with a fresh coat of white paint and the number 53 painted on the tail tank. On the flanks, he painted "Rajo Jack Special." Few race cars of the time were christened with the driver's name, but Rajo wanted to be different. A few racers weren't impressed because some of its components came off their old cars. Rajo did as much of the sheet metal and fabrication as possible, and his work showed. It was the most pristine object Rajo Jack had owned in his life.

The one advantage Rajo's car had over the other cars at Southern Speedway was the former Francis Quinn Miller engine. Most other cars had engines with stock blocks and aftermarket heads and produced far less power. The Miller, though it had been sitting for years, was Rajo's ace.

Ten percent of the cost of admission to the February 21, 1937, race was earmarked to aid those in the Midwest who had been affected by flooding. Ironically, the race was originally to be run on January 17 but was cancelled due to rain, then rescheduled for February 14 only to be rained out again. George Robson led wire-to-wire to win the forty-lap main event barely in front of Swede Lindskog and Spider Webb, but Rajo Jack placed a respectable fourth in the car's debut. They were the first laps on the engine in years, and Rajo needed to make Francis Quinn proud. Still, Rajo had many problems to work out of the car.

At Oakland Speedway, Charlie Curryer set up another hundred-lap race featuring big cars vs. midgets, as the format had shown promise. This time only a few midgets arrived, and the big cars were up to the task. Charlie Thom won in a big car and Bud Rose was second, also in a big car. Rajo broke a steering arm, but somehow managed to bring his car home seventh.

Rajo Jack's name made promoters all over the West Coast willing to pay him significant sums to race. The promoter of Gresham Speed Bowl, the same track at which Rajo had watched his first race, offered him one hundred dollars to race on April 11. He was quick to accept, as he had never raced on the track. The tow to Oregon took almost three days, but the weather did not cooperate. The rain did not let up in the Pacific Northwest and the race was postponed a week. Promoter Jimmy Ryan offered Rajo and the other Los Angeles drivers who came the same tow money to race the following week and went as far to offer to find housing for them in the interim. But Charlie Curryer had taken over promotion of Southern Speedway, renamed it Southgate Speedway, and had a race scheduled for the same date. Rajo's loyalty was to Curryer this time.

Rajo needed a good run in his new car. Curryer was a proponent of longer races, so he scheduled a hundred-lap big car race at Southgate on April 18 under the American Racing Association banner. Longer races were how he could differentiate his races from other outlaw races and make his races closer in prestige to AAA races. Curryer loved to try out new promotional gimmicks to make the show better, this time inverting the field from qualifying and starting the fast cars behind the slower ones in hopes of more passing. The benefit fell to Rajo, who often struggled in qualifying. A crowd of three thousand watched Bud Rose lead early until he collided with Wally Schock, flipped, and left the track in an ambulance. Tex Peterson took the lead but spun in the closing stages, handing the lead to Rajo. It was exactly what Rajo needed. When Rajo assumed the lead, no one else was close and he won his first race in the new car, with Hal Robson second. Rajo jumped to second in American Racing Association point standings.

As thrilling as the win was for Rajo, it was less so for others. Most races at Southgate Speedway were held in the heat of Sunday afternoons, and dust would inevitably rise from the dirt surface and leave a fine layer over the entire crowd. Curious fans who watched a race tended not to return. Curryer convinced Alex Podurgiel to pave the half-mile oval, and the job started the day after Rajo's win.

Rajo performed well at many racetracks and in many types of cars, but the one track that vexed him was Oakland Speedway. He became convinced he was jinxed at the track. Rajo carried a lucky rabbit's foot in the pocket of his driving suit. Any psychological effect it had failed to pay off.

"I've carried that piece of fur and bone in every race that I've ever driven in on the Oakland Oval and it hasn't worked like it does in Los Angeles. A Miller Special is replacing it Sunday," he wrote in a telegram to the *Oakland Tribune*.

And at the April 25 fifty-lapper on the half mile at Oakland, the water pump on the Miller engine broke in qualifying and he didn't make a lap in the race. Rajo fixed his car for the May 9 race at Southgate, where he placed a distant fifth behind winning Tex Peterson. And on May 16, he was entered in two races including a three-hundred-lap stock car race at Oakland Speedway. When Rajo and Joe Wilber filled their entries for the race, they entered their wives as riding mechanics. Track manager Linn Mathewson was perplexed.

"I never heard of such a thing," Mathewson said.

It was a publicity stunt. And the race rained out.

The other race the same day didn't rain out. The Clovis Horse Show and Festival Association scraped together $20,000 to turn their horse arena into a half-mile dirt track. They had brought in Pop Evans to work the track, which gave them the connection to Rajo Jack. The American Legion posts in Clovis and Fresno sponsored the race, and a capacity crowd of four thousand arrived. Rajo gave them the hero they desired. Driving for Russ Garnant, the man for whom Francis Quinn had once driven, Rajo first won the ten-lap race for a trophy named after Don F. Conway.

But Rajo and Garnant could tell the track was going to go dry-slick, and quickly. It would be a miserable dustbowl for the main event. So Rajo and Garnant jacked up the trailer, took off the wheels and tires, and mounted them on the back of the race car. And then Rajo easily schooled the field in the sixty-lap main event for big cars and won big.

The rained-out three-hundred-lap stock car race for the mile oval at Oakland Speedway was rescheduled for May 30, and Rajo had a better idea than putting his wife in his race car this time. Originally entered in a Dodge passenger car, Rajo managed to procure a Ford sedan delivery truck. The truck's engine didn't have the horsepower of the passenger cars entered, but it had another advantage. Where most passenger cars of the day had a hard time surviving rutted and difficult dirt tracks like Oakland, a truck was one of the few vehicles capable of withstanding the pounding. Rajo removed the fenders and windshield of the truck—modifications allowed in the rules and common for the stock car class. The truck was nearly unrecognizable by the time he was done stripping it of its extraneous parts. And he painted the number 33 on the side. It was the first time in his career he used the number—the traditional number of starters in the Indianapolis 500—and it would become his trademark.

Oakland Speedway had a set of bathrooms for men and women in the infield. Though there were no signs the bathrooms were specifically for white people, it was assumed. But there were also no specific bathrooms for black people. If Rajo or Herman Giles—who frequently traveled as Rajo's mechanic—wanted to use the bathroom, they had to wait until the race was underway so it would be empty, and no one would see them use it. If there was a line for the bathroom, they would have to wait.

The Oakland race was minor in the racing world, but it was being billed as a national championship as Curryer was apt to do, and ten thousand fans arrived to bear witness. Joe Wilber led the other twenty-six drivers briefly from the pole position, but Duane Carter quickly passed him. On the fiftieth lap, a horse in the infield threw his rider and wandered onto the track through a gate mistakenly left open on the backstretch. The horse galloped along with cars down the backstretch for two hundred yards before being corralled and exiting uninjured. On the fifty-second lap, Ernie Criss—driving a Ford truck like Rajo's—took over the lead, but Rajo passed him on the ninety-third lap. Criss went back into the lead laps later and stayed there, though Rajo was never far behind. Criss pitted for fuel on lap 246, surrendering the lead to Rajo. Criss caught up to Rajo's truck but blew a tire with twelve laps left, and Rajo's lead extended to two laps in front of Les Dreisbach. Rajo slowed his pace greatly in the final laps and won after four hours and sixteen minutes.

"It should be called the Altamont Pass Sweepstakes. The trucks wouldn't let the autos by," purported IRS examiner John V. Lewis said.

The win was popular with Rajo's fellow competitors, especially after his previous hard-luck results at the track. And he took over the ARA lead with 730 points, ten more than Bay Area upstart Duane Carter.

Rajo's win made headlines across the nation again, spreading throughout California and into places like Oregon, Montana, Nebraska, Hawaii, and Washington. Some in the press proclaimed it to be a victory for the working man over the idle rich. All Rajo cared about was that it put him closer to winning the ARA championship.

For most of his career, Rajo Jack towed his cars to races in trailers—best described as makeshift—behind his well-used Ford. To tracks like Oakland, it made for difficult and lengthy trips. Though Rajo's Ford, "Sally," was more powerful than most cars on the road, the engine and suspension strained every time he loaded it down with the race car on a trailer, spare wheels and tires, parts, tools, and whoever he was bringing to the race as a crew.

Rajo longed for the setup he had while working for M. B. Marcell: a flatbed truck on which he could haul his race car effortlessly. There was one in Los Angeles he had been eyeing for years owned by Kelly Petillo's family, used for hauling produce for their grocery store. The truck had seen years of use, but Rajo saw the potential. The family wanted a princely sum of $3,000. Working as a mechanic, even with

Rajo Jack raced a Ford truck in a stock car race at Oakland Speedway in 1937 with his trademark number 33. *Tom Motter Collection*

other odd jobs and his prize money from racing, it would have taken years for Rajo to save up the money. Until he won at Oakland.

Rajo used his considerable winnings from the race to purchase the truck of his dreams. It was a half-ton Ford with Crager heads on its V-8 engine. The yellow paint was peeling from years of sitting in the sun. The wooden boards making up the flatbed were sunbeaten and a couple desperately needed to be replaced. But it had room for three people on the front bench seat and, most importantly, plenty of room for a race car and every needed spare part. For the rest of his years as a race car driver, Rajo Jack hauled his race cars in style in the truck.

With the new truck, he also decided to start a new business. Cars frequently broke down and few tow trucks existed in 1937 Los Angeles. When most people's cars broke down, they would tow their inoperable cars behind another car with ropes to get to his shop. Many times, he had to drive to the stranded cars to perform mechanical work to get his customer's cars running. With this new truck, Rajo started hauling cars for motorists to his garage. The road, not a garage, was where Rajo Jack belonged anyway.

The paving job at Southgate Speedway was completed in time for the June 6 race. The entire half-mile oval had a fresh coat of asphalt and was one of the first oval tracks in the country which was paved. For a racetrack often looked down upon by the racing elite, Southgate was now a showcase southern California track.

But the first race on the asphalt was marred by tragedy. Fred Krusky, a little-known twenty-five-year-old, broke a steering knuckle after taking the checkered flag of the second heat race and his car veered into the infield fence, killing him instantly. Rajo and the rest of the drivers shrugged it off. Rajo placed fifth in the fifty-lap main event won by Tex Peterson.

And then Rajo made a triumphant return to Oakland Speedway. In a sprint car race on June 13, Rajo led all fifty laps around the half-mile dirt oval in the infield to win. It was his fourth win of the year and a shot of confidence.

But the next race at Oakland Speedway, on June 27, was baffling. The race was billed as a hundred-lapper for big cars and seventeen drivers were scheduled to appear. But on the day of the race there were seven cars, Rajo included. And fewer than four hundred fans arrived, despite ample pre-race publicity. Rajo easily won his five-lap heat race, but promoter Lynn Mathewson decided to cut the main event to twenty-five laps because of the short field. Rajo won the pole position but gave up the lead on the start before taking it back on the sixth lap. While Rajo was trying to lap Bob Frame and Charlie Thorn on the sixteenth lap, Bud Rose slipped past Rajo for the lead. Rajo tried desperately to take it back, but Rose won and Rajo settled for second. The race was such a disaster that the few spectators who stuck around were given rain checks.

Rajo Jack had little experience racing on asphalt, but few drivers he raced against had much either. Rajo made quick adjustments after the first race at Southgate and on July 11 won the three-lap helmet dash and took the lead of the first turn of the forty-lap main event and led the first twenty-six laps until the Miller engine started misfiring, letting Spider Webb take the lead as Rajo soldiered on to a fifth-place finish. But once more, he showed he had the speed to be the driver to beat on the track for years to come.

With the AAA gone from the racing landscape in California in 1937 and midget racing still in its infancy, the outlaw drivers finally got their due. Newspapers needed drivers to play up to the masses as heroes. There were four drivers the press dubbed the "Four Horsemen" for their prowess on the outlaw tracks: Rajo Jack, George Robson, Spider Webb, and Bud Rose. It was a welcome boost of confidence and attention for each of them. At the next race at Southgate on August 1, Rajo led all forty laps to win, barely challenged by Tex Peterson. He showed the other three Horsemen who was the best.

Rajo was running fourth at the August 15 race at Southgate when leading George Robson was forced to slow while lapping Herb Kelley, letting Spider Webb, Tex Peterson, and Rajo by to sweep the top three spots. After the race ended, Robson and his pit crew were furious, convinced the other drivers had somehow colluded to knock Robson out of first, and attempted to fight Webb and his crew. Rajo tried to intervene and get between the two groups, but it didn't work. It took the police showing up to finally calm the situation. The long grind of the season was taking its toll on everyone and nerves were frayed.

The promoters at Flagstaff insisted Rajo come back for their August 30 race. Rajo set a track record of twenty-seven seconds in qualifying and won the trophy dash. He was far ahead of the pack in the thirty-lap main event, but two connecting rods broke and blew a hole through the side of the block of his prized engine. Rajo jumped in another driver's car and won a consolation race after the main event, but he had a lot of work to do if he was going to chase his prized championship.

After Harry Miller sold his engine business to Fred Offenhauser, Offenhauser consolidated the business into a more streamlined operation. He was more interested in building new, more innovative versions of the racing engines—which were being sold under his name—rather than the multiple versions of engines on which Miller had built his business. One of the obsolete pieces Offenhauser decided to sell for pennies were the molds for the 183-cubic-inch Miller marine engine like the one in

Rajo's race car. Rajo had one of the few engines of the size still in service by 1937 and bought the mold for a few hundred dollars. He had a new block cast and a couple new connecting rods built by the Offenhauser shop and spent nearly every cent he had putting the engine back together.

Rajo had taken a job in an auto parts and machine shop. He could ill afford the parts he needed, so after everyone else had gone home, Rajo would take whatever parts he needed. He didn't last long in the job when they figured out what he was doing.

Rajo spent the week after Flagstaff working on his engine. And Ed Winfield did most of the machine work. Rajo desperately wanted his race car ready for the Labor Day weekend. He had another crazy plan to execute.

Rajo placed third behind Spider Webb and Tex Peterson in a three-lap match race at Southgate Speedway on September 5 in the big car and won the ten-lap consolation race. In the main event, Rajo was moving forward through the pack until an oil line came loose, spewing hot oil on his right foot. In Rajo's haste to put the engine back in his race car, he had failed to tighten the oil lines. He refused to pull off the track until his car caught fire. The track workers doused him and his car with fire extinguishers.

But the best of Rajo's plan remained. He spent the next few hours after the race fixing the oil leak and cleaning out the extinguisher chemicals from the car. It was dark by the time he finished. Most in his situation would have headed home, but Rajo loaded his car and headed north. There was a race in San Jose the following day, hundreds of miles away. After a brief nap in an orange grove on the side of the highway along the way, Rajo rolled into San Jose Speedway as the sun started to rise just after 6 AM. He was so exhausted he didn't bother to unload the car, instead taking the tool box out of the cab of the truck, sprawling out on the bench seat, and going to sleep. A few short hours later, other drivers started showing up for the race, which was being sanctioned by *Coast Auto Racing Magazine* and promoted by the northern-based California Auto Racing Association. Rajo gave up on the idea of sleeping and unloaded the race car.

Qualifying for the hundred-lap race had taken place the previous day, but Rajo was given the chance to qualify immediately before the race. He was fast enough to earn a spot in the three-lap trophy dash. And by beating out Ernie Criss to win the trophy dash, Rajo was given a free order for auto parts. This was one of the few times he won a trophy dash, and he desperately needed it for the parts.

For the main event, Rajo started second among thirteen cars and easily passed Criss for the lead on the third lap. Criss wouldn't give up, catching up through the turns, but Rajo powered away down the straightaways. The engine was running better than ever, and Rajo took a firm lead on the thirtieth lap when Criss's engine blew. Fred Agabashian assumed second place and slowly gained ground on Rajo over the next thirty laps, but Agabashian's engine broke a connecting rod and he dropped out. Rajo suddenly held a comfortable two-lap lead and easily won with Lloyd Logan a distant second. It took Rajo days to catch up on the missed sleep, but the money he won eased any discomfort.

After a couple of rained out races, Rajo returned to Southgate Speedway; word was out that the paving job had been a success. The fans came to the races in huge crowds of eight thousand for the next few races. Not that it did any good for Rajo. He struggled with the Miller engine. In his haste, he accidentally bent a valve and now dealt with constant oiling problems.

But Rajo had reason to step up his performance for the October 24 race: Rajo's hero, Barney Oldfield, was being brought in as the race referee. Oldfield had officially moved to California in 1931, married his third wife Hulda, and adopted a girl named Elizabeth. Oldfield had resigned his job at Plymouth earlier in 1937 to open the Barney Oldfield Country Club in Van Nuys, and it was a failure from the start. Now Oldfield, who had been coerced into condemning racing in the press a few years before, gladly took money to come back in ceremonial capacities to races like the one at Southgate Speedway. It was an easy source of income: show up to a race, smile for the crowd, sign some autographs, and walk away with a pocketful of cash. It was the only way Oldfield could earn a steady paycheck.

Rajo's problems with his car had grown so severe he took a ride in the unfamiliar R4 car for this race, but the Crager-headed engine in the car was underpowered and Rajo qualified fourteenth. In the main event Rajo raced as hard as he could, coming from the back of the pack to place third, albeit a distant third behind winning Hal Robson and Swede Lindskog. It was the first time Rajo raced in front of his idol, Oldfield. He was almost giddy to talk to Oldfield after the race.

Oldfield claimed to remember him from their previous encounters; Rajo was ecstatic to see his hero again.

Rajo had a disappointing run at the following week at Southgate but had an offer from San Jose Speedway to race November 7. The race was being promoted as the Pacific Coast Big Car Championship. Rajo caravanned to the race with Wally Schock, another of the southern California boys. Duane Carter won, with Schock in a distant second. Rajo had engine problems again and didn't finish. He was frustrated.

Word got out about the race in San Jose, and Rajo and Schock were slapped with fifty-dollar fines by Western Contest Board chairman George Wright for racing at a track other than Southgate. Many of the drivers raced at venues like Southgate to get away from the miserable tactics the AAA used to strongarm the racing world. Rajo declared he was done with racing at the track, despite holding the points lead. He had other places to race.

Southgate had arranged to have Kelly Petillo referee the November 14 race, and as soon as Petillo found out about Rajo's suspension, he made wild threats to the promoters. Rajo was his friend and Petillo was loyal to his cause. The track needed Petillo and his name to bring in fans. Rajo's fine was suspended due to "extenuating circumstances." Schock's was not.

A huge crowd of eight thousand showed up for the fifty-lap race dubbed the Indianapolis Cup. Petillo predicted three drivers at the Southgate race would go on to race in the 1938 Indianapolis 500. As with most things in his life, Petillo was wrong, but for once he wasn't far off. George Robson won the Indianapolis Cup race, Hal Robson was second, Bud Rose was third, and Spider Webb won the trophy dash. They all raced in—or attempted to qualify for—the Indy 500 within the following decade.

Once his hurt feelings were mended, Rajo concentrated on racing at Southgate the rest of the season. He was leading the points and so close to winning a championship he couldn't risk racing elsewhere. Rajo's finishes at Southgate weren't great—fifth and sixth in main events—but were enough to accomplish his goal.

Rajo Jack (third from left) accepts a trophy at Southern Ascot Speedway.
Voohees Photo Service, Podurgiel Collection

Rajo Jack won the championship at Southgate, and he quickly painted the coveted number 1—reserved for the reigning champion—on his car's tail tank. Winning the track championship didn't earn him the recognition and acceptance of the racing world he had hoped. When white drivers won championships of the type, they were feted widely and gained acceptance. Though Rajo gained national regard for winning big races, few knew Rajo Jack won the 1937 track championship at Southgate Speedway.

9

LUCKY CHARMS
FAIL TO DELIVER

RAJO JACK WAS ONCE A SHY KID who tried to avoid crowds. Attention was something he had to learn to like.

After races, Rajo would spend countless hours talking to every person who sought his time. He had a soft spot for children, but there was one breed of people he liked even more: reporters. There weren't many who hung around dusty speedways to report on races, but the few who did became instantly drawn to Rajo. He could spin a story like no one else.

When Rajo Jack first started traveling to Oakland Speedway to race, he met a semi-serious fellow with dark, slicked back hair and nice suits—too nice for someone coming to a humble dirt track—who introduced himself as Alan Ward. Ward started working for the *Oakland Tribune* in 1922 and earned a sports reporter position by the 1930s. Few sports reporters attended sporting events in those times and fewer got bylines, but Ward was prolific. Ward started on the lowest rung as a sports reporter at the *Tribune* by reporting on races, but quickly became one of most well-known and respected sports reporters in the nation.

Like many reporters, Ward primarily covered stick and ball sports like baseball, but enjoyed the sports where real danger was involved. He made his name as a boxing writer and covered some of the biggest fights of the time. When Oakland Speedway was built, Ward drew the assignment of covering races. And he flourished, becoming as popular as some of the racers at the track.

Ward knew who Rajo Jack was before he arrived at Oakland from reading stories of Rajo's exploits on the dirt tracks in southern California. Their first interactions were pleasant, but the more Ward heard Rajo's stories, the more he sought Rajo out. Rajo had many grandiose stories of his past, most fabricated. Ward recognized how the story of Rajo being the only accomplished black driver on the Pacific Coast would play to his mainstream audience, but also saw the personality of the man. Many drivers of the day were terrible interviews, so Rajo quickly became Ward's favorite driver. When Ward wrote about an upcoming race and needed a quote from a driver, he would call Rajo. Rajo always obliged. And they started a frequent correspondence, sending letters back and forth about all manner of subjects, boxing among them. When Ward saw stories on wire services of Rajo winning races at far away tracks, he inevitably published the story in the *Oakland Tribune*.

While some southern California drivers were leaving in search of racing fame in other parts of the United States, Rajo remained and his star rose. Spider Webb had been racing in the Central States Racing Association in the Midwest throughout the summers, and when he returned to the west early in 1938, he brought a Midwesterner with him. George "Joie" Chitwood was born in Texas and started racing in Kansas in 1934. Promoters took one look at his slightly dark shade of skin and immediately labelled him an "Indian." Chitwood was white.

Like Rajo, Chitwood was feted by promoters for being different. But Chitwood wasn't prohibited from racing with the AAA because of the perceived difference. Still, they had an immediate rapport after Spider Webb introduced them.

To start the 1938 season at Southgate—which had been renamed Southern Ascot Speedway in an attempt at catching some of the magic of Los Angeles tracks Ascot Speedway and Legion Ascot Speedway—Webb won the fifty-lap main event with Wally Schock second, Chitwood third, Don Farmer fourth, and Rajo fifth. Rajo didn't know it would be his best finish at Southern Ascot for a while.

Even when they were in a slump, a bright spot for all drivers at Southern Ascot was the presence of Arrigo Balboni. A former pilot who owned the world's only airplane wrecking yard not far from the track, Balboni liked to refer to himself as the "original flying junkman of the air." Balboni was a former airplane racer who made large amounts of money by renting wrecked planes to movie studios. What the drivers liked most about Balboni was he brewed his own liquor and distributed it for free to grateful, thirsty racers.

Rajo expected a lot out of himself as a driver, but he struggled early in the 1938 season and couldn't figure out why. He tried different cars and different tracks, but he couldn't win. A fifth-place finish May 8 in the hundred-lap big car race at Oakland Speedway was his best finish for a while, but no reason to celebrate.

As a 250-lap stock car race at Oakland Speedway on June 5 approached, Ward quoted Rajo as writing to him, "Polish the trophy and get ready to engrave my name in it." It made good copy, but on Rajo's drive from Los Angeles to Oakland, he was involved in a crash on the highway. He broke two ribs but refused to withdraw. Rajo qualified twenty-first and struggled to bring the car home in tenth. The scenario played out often: Ward would give Rajo a huge amount of publicity before a race and Rajo failed to live up to it.

Rajo's performance improved slightly in the summer of 1938, placing third at San Jose Speedway on June 12, fifth in a big car race on June 19 at Southern Ascot, third again on July 10 at San Jose, and fourth on July 18 at Southern Ascot.

His on-track fortunes leveled out and Charlie Curryer, usually his greatest proponent, declared he would no longer pay Rajo appearance money. Race car driver's careers rarely lasted long and Curryer gave up on his star when he was down. With other southern California racers like Bud Rose and Tex Peterson performing better than Rajo, they wanted the same appearance money Rajo was getting. Curryer had found a crop of drivers up north and didn't need the southern California boys as he once did to draw a crowd.

Rajo wasn't going to enter the August 7 race at Oakland Speedway, but at the last minute, Rajo and Curryer came to terms for him to compete in the two-hundred-lap big car race. Rajo wasn't himself, placing fifth, eleven laps behind winning Bud Rose. People speculated Rajo Jack had lost his magic as a race car driver.

Two days later, on August 9, Rajo Jack's mother, Frances Gatson, died in Tyler, Texas. While working as a housekeeper, Frances suffered a cerebral hemorrhage, but her cause of death was listed as hemiplegia. She was fifty. Rajo had a list of races lined up over the West Coast but returned to Texas for the funeral. For once, Rajo didn't hesitate to take time off. Noah Gatson had always been hard on his children, but Frances had been the calming influence on Rajo's life. Rajo often wrote his mother about his adventures. Dewey Gatson idealized Frances.

Rajo didn't return to a racetrack until September 18 at Oakland Speedway. Charlie Curryer had dreamed of putting on a West Coast version of the Indianapolis 500. The idea of a major race on the West Coast had been percolating through racing minds for decades, but there was no venue on the West Coast near the grandeur of the Indianapolis Motor Speedway. Curryer was promoting the largest oval on the coast in Oakland Speedway's mile track, so he seized the opportunity to set up a five-hundred-mile race. To do so, and to have a shot at having any cars finish, Curryer put out cones ten feet from the inside of the turns, effectively lengthening the distance around the track to one-and-an-eighth miles so the drivers would only have to drive 444 laps.

The program would be drawn out over two weekends with qualifying beginning September 18. Rajo showed up late for qualifying, a frequent occurrence. When he grabbed the steering wheel of his number 33 car to guide it off the trailer, the wheel broke in his hand. He tried, in vain, to find someone to weld the steering wheel back together, but it was a Sunday and there were no shops open. Rajo found Pop Evans working as track superintendent and borrowed a length of wire so he could make the steering wheel usable again. When he drove his number 33 big car on the track for qualifying, the officials realized he hadn't signed a driver's release in his rush to get his car fixed and onto the track. The officials waved him into the pits, quickly explained he needed to sign the release and handed him a pen. Rajo angrily squiggled his name, sped back on the track in anger and was on pace for a remarkable 115 miles per hour average. But his car ran out of fuel and coasted across the finish line. He still completed the lap in 38.86 seconds at an average speed of 105.11 miles per hour to earn the pole for the September 25 race.

Rajo's superstitions had grown more intense than those of other race car drivers, a superstitious bunch to begin with. He was afraid of black cats crossing his path and broken mirrors, wouldn't allow his picture to be taken before a race, wouldn't use a pit spot beyond the start-finish line, and deemed the number 1 unlucky after his struggles and insisted the number 3 be on his car. When Rajo saw a full moon, he would take what money he had in his pocket and hold it to the sky to show to the moon. He also carried a rabbit's foot. In Rajo's version of the story, the rabbit's foot was something magical. At a race at Southern Ascot, so he said, a rabbit ran onto the track against traffic. Somehow the rabbit wasn't hit by any of the oncoming cars but came to a stop on the infield of the track, had a heart attack, and died. He said someone picked up the rabbit's body, for which Rajo paid ten dollars. He had the foot cut off and kept it with him in every race in which he drove. After that, Rajo reasoned, his luck at Southern Ascot changed. But it wasn't helping in 1938.

It wasn't luck that was causing his lack of results. When he first finished his own big car in 1937, its Miller engine was often the class of the field, but more modern Offenhauser engines and some other aftermarket engines were showing up in race cars throughout the fields. Suddenly the deficiency in the handling of Rajo's car was apparent. He couldn't drive the car as sideways as he once could and still be fast. It took Rajo time to realize he had to improve his car to win races again.

When Rajo started on the pole position at Oakland Speedway among twenty-nine cars for the September 25 race, christened the Gold Trophy 500, in front of ten thousand fans, he had reason for optimism. But Bud Rose, driving Gil Pearson's number 18 Miller, sped past him and into the lead on the first lap. Rose led the first hundred miles, briefly surrendering it to Tex Peterson. On lap 180, Rajo spun, and his car was hit by Charlie Thom, who subsequently launched completely out of the track. Rajo fell back to fifth and lost laps to Rose, but Rajo continued while other drivers struggled and blew up engines. By the time the five hundred miles were completed, Rajo was eight laps behind winning Rose but finished second. It wasn't a win, but it was a step forward.

In his next race, the hundred-lap Gold Cup race, held October 9 at Southern Ascot Speedway, Rajo led the first nineteen laps. But he was forced to pit as his car repeatedly jumped out of gear. A mechanic handed him a piece of rope and he tied it around the shifter to lock it in place. When Rajo made it back on track he was eight laps behind leading Tex Peterson. Rajo drove better than he had the previous weeks, but still placed fourth.

No one needed to remind Rajo he hadn't won all year. For the rest of the season, Rajo focused his attention at Southern Ascot. He decided number 33 was luckier than number 3, so he repainted his big car again. It didn't help. Rajo put together a strong run of races to finish the season, placing third on November 13, second on November 20, third on November 27, and second on December 4—all races won by Hal Robson.

After Rajo's mother died, he found solace in her religious teachings. After one race at Southern Ascot, while other drivers were loading up their race cars or talking with fans, Rajo walked up to the empty grandstands, took out a Bible and began reading it. He rarely went to church, but decided he needed to relearn what his mother had impressed upon him.

When the 1938 season came to a merciful conclusion, it was his first winless year since 1933, but he was strangely optimistic.

And it helped that a new force was taking over promotion of Southern Ascot to start the 1939 season.

J. C. Agajanian was born in California in 1913, months after his father, James T. Agajanian, smuggled his family out of Armenia amidst a war. James T. Agajanian amassed a fortune by building businesses others

Drivers pose at Southern Ascot Speedway. From left: unknown driver, Herb Koenig, Hal Cole, Don Farmer, Slim Mathis, unknown man holding trophy, Tex Peterson, Rajo Jack, unknown woman, Bud Rose, Alex Podurgiel, unknown driver, J. C. Agajanian, two unknown drivers, Hal Robson, three unknown drivers, and Roscoe Turner. *Walt Woestman, Podurgiel Collection*

overlooked—garbage collection and pig farming. He made plenty of money and gave his growing family what he couldn't provide in Armenia.

J. C. Agajanian desperately wanted to be a race car driver. After building his first race car, he informed his father at the family dinner table he was going to race. James unceremoniously informed J. C. he would be kicked out of the house if he did.

Much like Bud Rose, Agajanian became a car owner on the outlaw tracks around southern California at a young age, then gained his first promotional experience putting on races in Arizona. When the chance to take over promoting a track on a full-time basis was presented in the Southern Ascot Speedway, Agajanian snapped it up. Agajanian felt his flair for promotion could be a boon. While Curryer tried to squeeze every dime out of his promotions, Agajanian went big and spent lavishly to make his promotions bigger than other outlaw races. He always had a handful of tickets in his pocket and was quick to hand them out with unheard-of generosity to potential spectators.

Rajo helped Agajanian take his speedway promotion business to a new level.

Rajo Jack's disappointing conclusion to 1938 continued when he led the first twenty-five of fifty main event laps of the January 1, 1939, race at Southern Ascot only to place a distant second to Tex Peterson. Rajo did, however, win a twenty-five-lap semi main and a three-lap dash and was getting closer. He was frustrated by his big car and decided to make major modifications. After many crashes, the chassis was bent and in need of upgrades. With a flair, he sent word to the press that he had a new car. Though outsiders doubted Rajo Jack after his poor year in 1938, he didn't doubt himself.

"The rabbit foot didn't have a chance to get warmed up," Rajo said, "but this year it will be different. I gotta hunch I'm gonna have a GREAT season."

Rajo had never liked racing midgets, partly because he rarely had success in them—and, because of his size, he nearly felt claustrophobic every time he climbed into one.   But when Southern Ascot Speedway owner Alex Podurgiel offered a steady ride in a midget, Rajo reluctantly agreed. Many of the other top big car drivers at the track like Spider Webb and George Robson already had steady rides in midgets. Dominic Distarce promoted a fifty-lap midget race on January 8 at Southern Ascot under the banner of the American Midget Association. Rajo placed a distant seventh in the main event—barely able to hold on to the squirrely speed bug in the surprisingly slick conditions—while Perry Grimm swept the program.

After a forgettable big car race on January 15, Rajo looked forward to a midget race for the first time in his life. He was confident he could be competitive in the hundred-lap midget race at Southern Ascot set for January 29. Podurgiel's car was fast and Rajo figured if he got more experience in the midget he could win.

Midget racing was splintered in southern California in 1939. From the time it came into vogue in the mid-1930s, groups popped up to promote their races, with the American Midget Association becoming the top sanctioning body under Distarce's guidance. But for the class to gain acceptance at a wide level, it needed a premiere sanctioning body.

A group of forty midget owners and racers of the AMA held a meeting in Hollywood on January 23rd and agreed to dissolve their sanctioning and hand over control to the AAA Contest Board.

AAA Zone Supervisor Art Pillsbury had been essentially powerless since the 1936 demise of Legion Ascot. Pillsbury was working in his first profession as a civil engineer and worked a lot in Beverly Hills, which was planned to be an all-white community near Los Angeles. Only white people were allowed to own or rent property in the town; selling or renting property to Jewish people was prohibited. It was Pillsbury's kind of town.

Many among the AAA Contest Board considered midgets beneath them, but the AAA needed racing in southern California to regain relevance, so Pillsbury became a proponent of bringing midgets into the AAA. With the AMA's next race scheduled for January 29 at Southern Ascot, the AAA effectively allowed the race to happen but took no part in it. The drivers and car owners who signed up would be allowed to race as outlaws until the February 19 race at Gilmore Stadium, but then would be welcomed into the AAA fold.

The hundred-lap midget race, dubbed the Gold Cup Race, was hard on equipment. Tex Peterson and Hal Robson led most of the race, but both broke late and allowed Shorty Ellyson to win. Rajo, Spider Webb, and Hal Cole all experienced engine failures and pulled off before the finish.

Agajanian had ideas about how to turn races into events. For the sixty-lap February 12 big car race dubbed the Lincoln's Birthday Sweepstakes, Agajanian made a radical plan to invert the entire field from their qualifying times, starting the slower qualifiers in front of the faster contenders. Tex Peterson led early but broke a valve on the fifth lap and pulled off, surrendering the lead to Bud Rose. Three laps later, Rose spun and Rajo took the lead. Rajo had been on such a cold streak he was determined to finish this race off, unlike the season premiere. Rajo led the remaining fifty-two laps to win. In the span of twenty-seven minutes and fifty seconds, Rajo won his first race since September 6, 1937, well over a year earlier. To Rajo Jack, his drought had seemed like an eternity, but its conclusion was satisfying.

Agajanian decided naming his races would make fans think every race was special: he called the February 26 race the Midwinter Handicap. Rajo took the lead when Hal Robson spun out of first place after an altercation with Johnny Holmes on the sixth lap. But on the twenty-fourth lap, the front axle on Rajo's car broke, handing the lead and eventual win to Bud Rose.

A new manufacturer emerged onto the stock car racing scene from an unexpected pace. The Challenger Motor Car Company began importing the Citroen brand to Los Angeles from its factory in France starting in 1938. It was an oddity in the American car market, surprisingly nimble with its light curb weight and front-wheel drive, something unheard of in a passenger car at the time. Challenger had proven that the Citroen got thirty-six miles per gallon on an economy run between Los Angeles and El Centro, but few cared. The thought of buying a French car was repulsive to the public. What Challenger needed to earn trust in their Citroens was to prove the cars in races.

J. C. Agajanian devised a four-hundred-lap stock car race at Southern Ascot he dubbed the National Championship Stock Car Race, the longest stock car race ever on an oval track. Agajanian saw the potential a new manufacturer could have on his stock car races and convinced the unconventional Challenger company to field a Citroen for Bud Rose. Rajo was intrigued by the Citroens, but the best ride he could find was a reliable and unremarkable Ford sedan. The Ford trucks like the one he raced—and won in—at Oakland in 1937 were outlawed starting with this race, as they always made for terrible shows.

Rose took the lead on the 101st lap in front of a record crowd of twelve thousand and won by eight laps in front of second-place Rajo. But Agajanian pulled a move that baffled everyone: he declared he would hold off paying the top two drivers and they would race for the full winner's share in a twenty-five-lap match race on March 12.

Bud Rose was incensed. He demanded his winnings be paid immediately in cash. Agajanian didn't have the money to pay him. Rajo loved the idea as it gave him another shot at the money and a match race, two of his favorite things. For once the white man, Bud Rose, was getting the bad deal.

Agajanian brought in three-time Pikes Peak Hill Climb champion Louis Unser to be the official for the March 12 stock car race and Rose easily won the twenty-five-lap match race against Rajo by carving the turns faster and remaining smooth while Rajo's ill-handling Ford lost ground every lap. And in the 101-lap race that day, Rajo again placed second, this time behind Hal Robson.

As Gilmore Stadium was out of service for midget races early in 1939—it was being used as a temporary home for the minor league baseball Hollywood Stars—only Atlantic Speedway and Southern Ascot were suitable to hold midget races in Los Angeles. Since its inception, track owner Alex Podurgiel struggled to keep Southern Ascot open. He loved racing, but business wasn't his strong suit. When the AAA approached him about taking over midget racing at Southern Ascot, Podurgiel had no choice but to accept it. It was the only way he could keep the track going.

The move allowed the midget car owners and racers to race under the AAA umbrella. Except one. Art Pillsbury was adamant Rajo Jack would not be allowed to compete in the AAA midget races at the track. Even when the rest of the drivers at the track vouched for him and threatened to not race, Pillsbury wouldn't give an inch. And even though his steady midget ride was for the track owner, Rajo Jack wouldn't race a midget at Southern Ascot again.

In the rain-postponed April 2 big car race at Oakland Speedway, Rajo and Tex Peterson swapped the lead multiple times in the early laps. When Peterson's Duesenberg passed Rajo in the middle of the race, its tire kicked up a rock which shot into the left lens of Rajo's goggles. Rajo was dazed and attempted to soldier on with one good eye, but two laps later he blew a tire. He managed to muscle the car back into the pits. The tire was changed by pit men in quick order. Despite barely being able to see, Rajo returned to the race and soldiered on to place sixth, well behind winning Peterson.

The next day Rajo returned home to Los Angeles and went to an ocular specialist. A dozen slivers of glass were removed from his eyeball and lid, but the doctor managed to save his eye. The doctor told Rajo not to race for two months for fear he would further hurt the eye.

He didn't listen.

Rajo placed fifth, far behind winning Bud Rose, at the Easter Sweepstakes for big cars on April 19 at Southern Ascot. But the Miller engine in his number 33 was struggling and needed help.

The following week he pulled the engine apart and took pieces in need of machining to Ed Winfield. Winfield had paying jobs for other customers which required attention. But Winfield had held a soft spot for Rajo ever since they met in 1924, so he managed to fit in Rajo's machine work at night. Rajo picked up the parts two days before the April 30 race at Oakland Speedway. It was so late even an advanced engine builder with no other work would have a hard time putting the engine back together.

Rajo stood in his garage and stared at the car on April 29. The engine block was in his number 33 big car, but the parts which belonged in it were scattered around the floor of his garage. Fellow southern California drivers who were on their way to the race at Oakland stopped by, as they often did, to see if Rajo was ready to caravan north. One by one they saw his predicament, deemed it hopeless, wished him luck, and headed north.

The sun was setting, but Rajo Jack was too foolish to give up. He called Ruth into the garage. She saw the carnage and thought there was no way Rajo would be racing the next day. Rajo told her to get ready to go. She asked him if he intended on going to watch the race at Oakland.

"You drive. I'm going to put this thing together on the road," he told Ruth.

Rajo backed his Ford truck up to the garage and had Ruth help him push the race car onto the truck and strap it down. He took the engine components and needed tools and laid them on the bed. He told Ruth to drive slowly. Ruth cautiously managed to get the truck moving on the highway, trying not to hit anything which would cause her husband to slide off the truck. Rajo precisely put the engine together in the dark with the aid of a rudimentary flashlight. By the time they reached Oakland, the engine was ready, and they rolled the completed car off the trailer.

The other southern California boys were blown away the number 33 car was in one piece and apparently ready to race. Rajo qualified a surprising third for the hundred-mile race, something that stunned them after the carnage in Rajo's Los Angeles garage less than twenty-four hours earlier.

Wally Schock took off with the lead of the hundred-lapper at Oakland Speedway from the start, but Rajo quickly moved up to second place. Schock would win with Rajo nearly a lap behind, but that he managed to race at all made Rajo a legend among his fellow drivers. Only they could understand what he had pulled off.

Rajo placed second May 7 at Southern Ascot in a seventy-five-lap big car race, then went on to have a mediocre run driving an Alfa Romeo in a stock car race at Oakland Speedway. He sufficiently healed from his previous ocular injury, but July 4 was a catastrophe.

Agajanian had an appreciation for motorcycles and wanted to promote races for them. Many motorcycle racers made quick transitions to driving race cars on four wheels. As a preliminary for the July 4 hundred-lap big car event at Southern Ascot, Agajanian arranged to have a motorcycle race between his best-known big car drivers. Rajo Jack had ridden a motorcycle a few times in his life but had never raced one. None of the other big car drivers had either. As they were the only name racers competing at the track, Agajanian offered his big car drivers enough money to give the motorcycle race a try. Rajo hoped it would be an easy transition.

Going into the third turn of the first lap, another rider got inside Rajo and they touched wheels. Rajo laid the bike down on the pavement and came to an abrupt stop. He was taken from the track in an ambulance. The motorcycle race, which was a bad idea to begin with, was called off. Rajo had a fractured jaw and couldn't see out of his left eye. At the hospital, the doctor told him his left eye could possibly be saved, but he wouldn't be able to race again. Rajo was dazed and could barely speak, but he asked the doctor if he could race again if the eye was removed. The doctor said it was his best chance. Rajo told the doctor to remove his eye and replace it with a glass eye. It was a drastic move for someone in the prime of his life at the age of thirty-three, but Rajo

Rajo Jack poses in his number 33 big car in Victoria, British Columbia in 1939. *Pike Green Collection*

refused to give up the one activity that defined him and refused to give up his grand dream of the Indianapolis 500.

Curryer had been working on another lucrative northern tour for Rajo, and Rajo wasn't willing to give it up either. To drive a race car with two eyes was difficult enough, but he now had a significant change in depth perception with only one eye.

Rajo placed second in a B-Main event in a midget at Portland's Jantzen Beach Speedway July 14—which had been the site of a garbage dump when Rajo lived there—and fifth in a 250-lap stock car race July 16 at Portland Speedway. But Rajo had a more important race.

The promoters at Langford Speedway in British Columbia had been trying to get Rajo Jack to race in Canada for years. The trip was a risk on Rajo's part, and he put it off for years, but in 1939 the Canadian promoters offered enough money to make it worthwhile. For the promoters, it was a coup. For Rajo it was the closest he and Ruth would have to a vacation in a decade. And the promoters procured Rajo a sponsorship for the race by a local business, Brit's Diner, giving him more financial incentive.

The trek was rougher on Rajo than he anticipated. Rajo left his truck in Washington, unloaded the race car and pushed it onto the ferry that was to take him and Ruth from Seattle to Victoria, British Columbia. When Rajo and Ruth came on board, they were rudely informed by the staff they couldn't ride on the deck, as it was reserved for white passengers. They would have to ride below deck with the cars.

Below deck, fellow racer Jack Taylor had an empty casket he was shipping to Canada. He was sympathetic to their plight and offered Rajo and Ruth the casket to sleep in during the boat ride. The casket was lined with silk and was a workable accommodation. It wasn't the first time Rajo Jack felt the sting of racism. But it was disturbing, as Rajo was being hailed a champion race car driver by those who had been trying to bring him into Canada all those years.

Rajo's problems didn't end with the ride. When Rajo arrived at the Langford Speedway and got the car push started for hot laps, the rear axle in the car immediately broke. The problem was terminal. The hero who had been feted in the press as the star attraction was done before he completed a lap.

"I'll be back again soon and I'm quite sure I can get that track record down around the 15 second mark. I've got the car that can do it," Rajo said.

Rajo scrambled to put the rear end back together the following day. It wasn't a permanent fix, but it was enough to get him back to the ferry. And to get it back to the ferry, he got a push start and drove the race car on public streets to the landing. It made for a long and frustrating trip home, especially as he and Ruth had to ride the ferry back to Washington below deck again, this time without the relative comfort of a coffin.

By the time Rajo and Ruth returned to Los Angeles, the tale of how Rajo had performed in Canada grew, and Rajo was solely responsible for it. He told people how he won the Canadian national championship race in Ontario. But during his time in Canada, Rajo had been closer to Ontario, California, than Ontario, Canada.

Rajo Jack in his big car before the 1939 race at Langford Speedway (photo reversed). The year written on the photo is misidentified as 1937. *Pike Green Collection*

And when Rajo got his car fixed and was back racing in the United States, he was an also-ran again. He tried to race July 30 at Southern Ascot and won the Italian helmet dash but finished well back in the main event. He pulled out of the August 20 race at Flagstaff and started running well again in August at Southern Ascot. He led for a large part of the main event August 23 but broke a driveshaft. He placed fifth September 3 at Southern Ascot in the race billed as the Pacific Southwest Championship, which drew a huge crowd of ten thousand fans.

Rajo hadn't won a race since February, and word spread about his new glass eye. He was thirty-four years old, older than most of his competitors. And more southern California drivers against whom he had raced were moving on to race in the Midwest and the East Coast.

What few realized was Rajo Jack had plenty left.

10

THE SUPER-SUB
WINS THE OTHER 500

THERE IS ONE THING ALL PEOPLE involved in racing share: they're dreamers. Drivers dream of piloting better cars, winning races and glory, and getting rich; car owners dream of finding a driver who will pilot their cars to victory and earn them a fortune in prize money; and promoters dream of raking in cash by putting on races that spectators will never forget.

By 1939, Rajo Jack had become a recognizable force as a race car driver, both because he was usually the only black driver racing against white drivers in the United States and because he won huge races and earned headlines from coast to coast. Rajo had a better car than most of those against whom he was racing and was winning money—but he dreamt of making more. After losing his left eye in a racing accident earlier in the year and losing momentum, his results were improving, and he was showing flashes of becoming the great Rajo Jack again.

Charlie Curryer dreamt of making a fortune promoting races, but most of the time had to settle for getting by. His dream of a West Coast race which would rival the Indianapolis 500 started years earlier, but after the disaster of the inaugural 1938 Gold Trophy 500 at Oakland Speedway, few believed it would ever happen. Part of why Indy had grown so much in less than thirty years of existence was the gargantuan purse it paid: Wilbur Shaw earned over $27,000 for winning the 1939

Rajo Jack prepares for the start of the 1938 Gold Trophy 500 at Oakland Speedway. *Tom Motter Collection*

Indy 500. Curryer couldn't draw enough fans to a race at a dusty dirt track in California to raise the money to justify a purse near that. But after a relatively large field for the 1938 race, Curryer was encouraged that he was onto something. He knew if he drew enough cars, he could bolster the purse to levels never before seen for a West Coast race.

As promoter of Oakland Speedway, a one-mile dirt track in the San Francisco Bay area, Curryer had the power to make radical changes to the track. The downfall of the 1938 race had been the dirt surface deteriorating under the constant pounding of the heavy big cars in the heat of the day. The constant dust made watching the race unpleasant for the large crowd, and Curryer learned his lesson: to have a 500-mile race for big cars, he needed a paved track.

In 1939, Curryer scraped together every dollar he could, borrowed at every chance, and managed to put together enough money to pay for a layer of asphalt over the mile oval. But he didn't put together enough money to do the job right. No rock was put down over the dirt to form a stable base for the asphalt, and Pop Evans's smoothing of the oval with a road grader was questionable at best. It took two months in the hot sun to complete the paving, which meant two months with no income from the speedway, and that hindered Curryer's business.

Immediately after the 1938 Gold Trophy 500, Curryer had put the word out that the 1939 edition would be bigger and better. Whispers circulated that he would pay $10,000 to the winner in 1939, but it was only a rumor.

Curryer wanted a thirty-three-car field to mimic the Indianapolis 500. It seemed outlandish to gather that many big cars for a race on the West Coast, but it was necessary for the prestige. In the inaugural race in 1938, twenty-eight cars had started and only ten finished—an inevitability when cars built to race fifty laps at a time and drivers conditioned for no more than a hundred laps were forced to turn a sprint into an endurance race. Having thirty-three cars on a mile oval was a challenge for everybody, officials included. It would be close quarters, especially early in the race. And finding thirty-three big cars on the West Coast seemed impossible.

But if any promoter could draw that many big cars, it was Curryer. Curryer had grown the American Racing Association in the five years since starting it as a lower-level Class B group in 1934, extending his reach by promoting races up and down the West Coast. Since the American Automobile Association's Contest Board had no influence on big car racing on the West Coast after 1936, every big car on the West Coast was technically available. There were many fast cars—and hungry drivers—willing and ready to race for Curryer.

Word spread to every outlaw driver on the West Coast about how grand the September 24, 1939 Gold Trophy 500 at Oakland Speedway would be. Curryer managed to attract Art "Shorty" Scovell from Oregon, and the entire contingent of Los Angeles drivers like Tex Peterson, Bud Rose, Kenny Palmer, Shorty Ellyson (in a car fielded by J. C. Agajanian), Wally Schock, and—of course—Rajo Jack committed to race. Most of the drivers figured a win would be a positive on their résumé toward one day racing in the Indy 500.

Rajo Jack hadn't driven on Oakland Speedway's mile oval since it was paved, but he had edged out a second-place finish in the 1938

Gold Trophy, eight laps behind his best friend, Bud Rose, and Rajo was confident he could be faster this time. He was eternally optimistic.

In the first round of qualifying, September 17, Fred Agabashian won the pole position with an average speed of 103.10 miles per hour. Thirty cars qualified the first day, but Curryer wisely opened qualifying to the Friday and Saturday before the race as well so he could get a full field. Not every driver could justify spending a whole week at the race track.

Rajo decided he would be best served to stay home the first weekend of qualifying and save his equipment. He trekked to Oakland the Friday before the race to qualify; it saved money and time. The rare two-week break also gave him time to get his car ready. In theory, he was going to spend every waking hour working on it. The reality was he was behind on bills and was broke yet again. He needed any prize money he could win to keep his head above water. The Gold Trophy 500 promised significant pay, but even if he won, he couldn't pay all his bills.

In what little time Rajo spent on his race car leading up to the race—mostly late at night when the rest of Los Angeles' Watts neighborhood was asleep—he pulled the workhorse Miller engine out of "The Rajo Jack Special." Rajo tore it down to the bare block and inspected everything. Parts of the Miller were already eight years old and had been through many races, but Rajo found nothing concerning. He sought a hotter set of spark plugs to try to clean out the carbon that would inevitably build up over a long distance like the planned 500 miles. He found the plugs in the possession of fellow racer and engine designer Joe "Jiggler" Gemsa, who was building heads for Fords similar to the Rajo heads from which Rajo Jack got his name. From then onward, Gemsa always kept a set of the hottest spark plugs he could find in his tool box for Rajo Jack.

Showing up two days before the race and with no practice, Rajo qualified at an average speed of 106.5 miles per hour—the fastest of all starters—to earn a spot on the front row. Few were surprised; Rajo had always been fast at Oakland. Based on qualifying, he picked up sponsorship from Barnsdoll Oil for the race. It meant he could buy new tires, a rare luxury.

Officially, forty-two cars entered the race, including nine branded as Indianapolis cars. In theory, the cars with Indianapolis pedigrees would have an advantage. They had bigger engines, longer wheelbases, and—most importantly—larger fuel tanks. Some had the capacity for sixty gallons of fuel, compared to the thirty-gallon tank in Rajo's number 33 car. The Indianapolis-type cars also had drawbacks—with a shorter wheelbase, the smaller cars were lighter and nimbler. But an Indianapolis car could run the entire race with one—or possibly no—pit stop. Curryer leveled the playing field by mandating every car pit twice.

One of the cars with a purported Indianapolis 500 pedigree was a Duesenberg that had reportedly raced in the 1939 Indy 500. It was entered in the race by a mysterious woman who called herself "The Duchess." Oakland Tribune reporter Alan Ward couldn't figure out who she was and loved the mystery. She entered not only the Duesenberg with Jimmy Miller as driver, but also a second car, a Douglas to be driven by Gene Figone. No one bothered to check that no Duesenberg had raced at Indy that year.

With so many cars entered, Curryer could have expanded the field from the thirty-three he advertised to include all forty-two entrants. He struggled to draw cars for most races and had never turned cars away before. But on Oakland's mile, thirty-three cars were already too many.

When dawn broke on the Sunday race morning, clouds hung ominously over Oakland. They provided a needed respite for the drivers during introductions as they underwent pomp and circumstance unlike any they had previously been subjected to. As the cars gridded in their perfect eleven rows, one driver at a time rode forth in his car, pushed by crew members. A rundown of each racer's accomplishments was recited over the public address system in agonizing detail. By the time the final contestants in the race were announced, even the best-conditioned drivers were weary.

The race was scheduled to begin at 11 AM, which would have given ample time to finish the five hundred laps before sundown. But by the time all thirty-three cars were fired off, it was almost 1 PM. By that point, there were over ten thousand spectators at the track, and there was still a line at the ticket booth one hundred laps into the race. In all, thirteen thousand spectators would pay their way into the track—and more snuck

Rajo Jack didn't like having his photo taken early in his driving career. *Walt Woestman, Podurgiel Collection*

in. Every seat in the grandstand was full, and fans were standing around the outside fence to watch what had become the most prestigious West Coast race in 1939. The Gold Trophy 500 had already earned its status.

For one of the few times in his career, Rajo crafted a strategy. Even in the four-hundred-lap stock car races he won, Rajo typically concentrated on survival and let the results happen as they may. But in the 1938 Gold Trophy race, Rajo had tangled with Charlie Thom early and fell so far behind he was fortunate to finish second. Rajo decided this time he would take it easy at the start, cruise around the outside, bide his time until the end, and then make his move.

Flagman Bill Dreisbach attempted to arrange the thirty-three starters in a neat grid of eleven rows, three wide, for the rolling start. It didn't work. The track was barely wide enough for the cars to park three wide across the front straight. Racing three-wide was impossible.

Jimmy Miller started on the pole with Fred Agabashian in the middle of the front row and Rajo outside. With thirty-three cars accelerating at the same time, the track fell into chaos. It took four false starts to get the race under way.

When the racers finally put a clean start together, Agabashian took the initial lead as the engine in Miller's car struggled to get up to speed. Rajo tried to settle into third place, but in the close quarters of heavy traffic, his car was clipped from behind while entering the east turn on the fourth lap and went spinning into the inside of the track. His number 33 tore away twenty-five feet of wood fence, and he finally came to a stop with a sickening thud. It would be the only crash of the race.

But when Rajo Jack crashed, people noticed, and Rajo's initial plan was ruined. With the help of a few onlookers, he managed to get his car free and back into the pits, where he found a broken section of the frame. He made hasty repairs and lost six laps but managed to get under way again. He injured his left hand in the crash, though, and was having a hard time holding onto the steering wheel.

When Rajo pulled back onto the track, he could tell immediately his car wasn't right, and it soon became obvious to everyone else. But in a 500-mile race, he had time to make up for it. He managed to limp the ailing car along, but it drove so badly he could barely hang on.

Shortly after Rajo entered the pits, Miller's car coasted in with its engine dead and was the first car officially out. The Duchess's other car, driven by Figone, lost power just before the 200th lap. If either had an actual Indianapolis 500 pedigree, it was of no help at Oakland.

Agabashian set a blistering pace in Jack Stevens's car early and led the first 125 miles, but Tex Peterson, in Gil Pearson's number 18 car that had won the 1938 Gold Trophy, ran a consistent pace behind him in second. On the 125th lap, Agabashian could do no more and pulled into the pits—surrendering the lead to Peterson—and gave up his car to relief driver Dave Oliver.

The indomitable Wally Schock had the fastest car early, working his way from the back of the pack to ninth by the hundredth lap and then third 175 miles in. But while running second behind Peterson on the 221st lap, his engine blew up in a cloud of smoke. Schock waved in the car driven by George Fitzer, which he owned, and took over driving. Schock would make up five laps before the finish. The Jack Stevens car, now piloted by Oliver, broke a motor mount after 238 miles to end the day for Agabashian's car. By the halfway point at lap 250, attrition was taking a heavy toll on cars and racers alike.

Rajo was barely hanging on. His race car was handling worse than his big Ford truck on the highway and getting worse every lap. At lap 260 he was fortunate to be only ten laps behind leading Tex Peterson. Then the Miller engine in his car seized as he let off the throttle entering turn four. The rear wheels locked, and he skidded through the outside crash wall. Rajo was finally put out of his misery. He was exhausted from hanging onto the ill-handling car as long as he had. He managed to run back across the track to the pits as cars roared past. His perseverance paid off, as he was later credited with fourteenth place.

As soon as he reached the pits, though, Rajo recognized drivers were pulling in and giving their cars over to relief drivers at a staggering rate. The heat and humidity increased as the afternoon wore on, and the pilots were struggling. Rajo went to car owners and volunteered as a relief driver. At first, none were interested. They all knew Rajo Jack—most liked him, as he had driven for many of them at one point or another—but they also knew he was rough on equipment.

Still, Rajo kept looking for a chance to get back on the track. He couldn't leave if he wanted to—he needed to collect his prize money to be able to afford to make it home to Los Angeles—but he also wanted another shot in this race.

Cars continued dropping out at a prodigious pace and Tex Peterson found himself leading by ten laps with 200 laps to go. But then, with no warning, he brought the number 18 car into the pits. Peterson shouted at Gil Pearson and the rest of the crew that something was wrong with the rear axle.

Rajo was not far away in the pits when he noticed their dilemma. He joined in with the rest of the crew as they quickly jacked the car up, slid the rear end out, and put in another one from a broken race car. They performed the swap so fast with Rajo's help that Peterson lost only a few laps and was still leading the race. It was a miraculous mechanical feat.

Seeing Rajo's dedication to the cause, Pearson told him to stick around because he might be needed as a relief driver after all.

The intense heat of the day and the pounding of the cars took their toll on the asphalt. The thin pavement broke up in places and the rough surface wore on the remaining cars. The most alert drivers avoided the forming potholes, but the track was deteriorating fast. Bud Rose hit a hole, breaking a shackle on the front leaf spring. He soldiered on a few laps before mercifully calling it a race.

Tex Peterson continued a steady pace and built his lead a lap at a time. By the 440th lap, Peterson was twelve laps ahead of second-place Wally Schock. But Peterson got sideways a couple times—with no other cars around—and at one point appeared ready to drive the car through the outside crash wall. Pearson decided Peterson had had enough.

"Get that guy out of there," Pearson yelled as Peterson wove through traffic. Still, it took Pearson six laps of frantically waving his driver into the pits before Peterson finally complied.

Spent from exhaustion and five consecutive hours of choking on exhaust, Peterson had to be dragged out of the cockpit by a half-dozen crew members.

Rajo was well rested and ready to go. He leapt into the still-running machine and got ready to get back into the race. He knew this was a winning car, and it was still eight laps ahead when Rajo took it back on the track.

"Keep 'er on the track and win," Pearson shouted at Rajo as he sped away. Rajo couldn't hear him.

Just keeping the Pearson car going was a more difficult proposition than anyone realized. Part of the reason Peterson had struggled the prior fifty laps was that the hand-operated fuel pump was failing. Normally it took one or two pumps per lap to maintain enough fuel pressure to keep the engine running smoothly. This fuel pump was failing spectacularly. To get the engine to run consistently, Rajo had to pump it constantly with his injured left hand and hang on to the steering wheel with his right. The crowd wondered if Rajo was capable of finishing, and Pearson, not realizing the immensity of the task Rajo was performing, searched desperately for a third driver to put in the car to finish the race.

No matter how out of control Rajo appeared to be, he was doing what he needed to finish.

There was another challenge, though. It was already 6:30 PM when Rajo got in the number 18, and the sun was setting rapidly. There were no lights at the track.

Curryer had to act fast. He and his officials started up their street cars parked in the infield, drove to different locations around the track, and turned their headlights on. They rounded up everyone who had a car at the track to do the same. They even got cars passing by on the street to stop and shine their headlights on the track from the outside, even though the beams barely filtered through the wood fencing around the track. It gave the drivers enough light to finish. And none of the thirteen thousand in attendance would leave before they'd seen the race's conclusion, even when the sun set completely just past 7 PM.

They finally got their wish when Rajo took the checkered flag at 7:20 PM, six hours and twenty minutes after the race started. He was elated and exhausted. He barely got the winning car back to the pits after his victory lap.

Officially, Schock—in the car Fitzer started—placed second, eight laps behind the Tex Peterson–Rajo Jack combination. Bill Johnson placed third and was the top finishing driver who drove the same car the entire distance. Of the thirty-three cars that started the race, ten finished. Most of those cars—and their drivers—spent incredible amounts of time in the pits for repairs. Gil Pearson's Miller had been the class of the field.

The Pearson car had been such an exhausting beast Peterson and Rajo could barely stand after the race. Rajo gladly would have stood in victory lane, though. But when Charlie Curryer presented the trophy, he shooed Rajo away. Though normally Rajo Jack's greatest proponent, Curryer decided that, because Peterson started the race in Pearson's car, he was the rightful winner.

Some in the press agreed with Curryer and declared Peterson the rightful winner of the race, some said Rajo won because he was the driver who took the checkered flag, but most argued they should be cowinners. But no matter who the official winner was, word reached far and wide that the combination of Tex Peterson and Rajo Jack had won the 1939 Gold Trophy 500.

Gil Pearson earned $3,000 for the win and split the money between Peterson and Rajo.

Dozens of newspapers printed the story of Tex Peterson and Rajo Jack teaming to win the biggest race of the year on the West Coast. But there was something more notable about this win for Rajo: for the first time in his life—unlike after the stock car race he won at Mines Field in 1936, the stock car race he won at Oakland Speedway in 1937, or the dozens of other wins—none of the papers noted he was black. In every media account, however, he was noted as a race car driver. It was how he always wanted it.

For the previous sixteen years, every time Rajo Jack was better than an also-ran, every mention labeled him as black or some other race he pretended to be. The other racers had accepted him as a race car driver, but he was finally accepted by the press as a race car driver.

And for once his luck held more than one week.

On October 1, Rajo Jack got his chance to race one of the strange and wonderful Citroens in a three-hundred-lap stock car race at Los Angeles' Southern Ascot Speedway in a race promoter J.C. Agajanian billed as the National Championship Stock Car Classic. Rajo found out why Bud Rose had beaten him in their last stock car race—the Citroen Rose had piloted was a superior-handling machine and its mileage surpassed any Ford stock car he had raced.

Rajo took the lead early among the forty-car field, but shortly into the race, the Citroen engine developed a problem and the French car struggled. Rajo had to pit many times to get it fixed. In one stop, Rajo fell back to seventh place, but he drove with determination back up to second in a matter of laps and easily passed Hal Cole's Ford with a few laps left to win in two hours and thirty-five minutes. He was on a roll.

The next month, Rajo decided to try his luck driving a midget at Oakland Speedway for Fred Frame. Rajo first met Frame at a race in Culver City in 1924, and they had remained friendly but had never been close. For a time—after winning the Indianapolis 500 in 1932—Frame was one of the biggest names in auto racing, but he desperately wanted to quit driving. He had few other skills, though; racing was what he knew. So, like many other significant Indianapolis 500 drivers, Frame made money on the side by owning midgets and hiring drivers to race them. Rajo Jack never liked racing the tiny cars, but when Frame offered him the chance to race on the half-mile inside Oakland Speedway November 11 and 12, Rajo couldn't pass it up. The *Oakland Tribune* proclaimed the race as Rajo's first in a midget. It wasn't true, but when he got on the track, it looked as if he had never seen a midget, let alone raced one. The car he was driving broke early in the 150-lap main event and he watched Gene Figone win.

Despite an injury-plagued summer of races, Rajo finished the season at Southern Ascot Speedway third in points. In a poll of drivers, car owners, and promoters, Wally Schock was voted the number one racer on the West Coast in the 1939 season. Rajo was lauded for the most impressive comeback and was reported to have finished no lower than sixth in any race. Rajo wasn't going to correct them.

After months of rained-out races in southern California, Rajo Jack wondered if the 1940 season was doomed. The American Racing Association and Charlie Curryer had returned to promoting big car races at Southern Ascot Speedway, but the fields grew thin as most of the top drivers joined in the exodus to greener pastures in the Midwest.

The March 3 race at Southern Ascot should have been easy for Rajo. But in the third heat race in front of six thousand fans, he was involved in a six-car crash that included Jimmy Robson (the older two Robson brothers had left California and were racing in Midwest AAA circuits). Rajo's car was the most damaged of the bunch, and he could only manage a distant fourth place behind winning Bud Rose in the forty-lap main event.

The promise of a big race the following week encouraged Rajo to fix his car quickly. Though Agajanian had given up promoting Southern Ascot, he was far from done promoting. He scheduled a race for March 10 at a new track far north in Madera under the sanction of Southern California Car Owners and Drivers Association, a new association Agajanian had started. The race had been scheduled for February, and fifteen drivers had shown up the first time, but when the race rained out, most didn't return. Only seven cars came back, and Rajo was the class of the thin field. He placed second to Bud Rose in the trophy dash, won his four-lap heat race, and dominated the twenty-five-lap main event. The show overall was a flop for the four thousand spectators, but Rajo Jack had earned new fans.

For many years, Rajo had the distinction of being the only black driver racing in California—not counting the ill-fated White Sox Speedway stunt—and he was the only competing driver who wasn't white once Sey Sugi gave up after years of struggling. But in 1937, one of the black drivers against whom Rajo had raced at White Sox Speedway, Mel Leighton, bought his first big car with a Riley four-port head. It wasn't a great car, but Leighton drove it at every race he could. Many of his first races were outlaw races a step below the races in which Rajo was driving, and it was two years until Leighton would do anything worth noticing on a race track. But Rajo and black mechanic Herman Giles didn't get along with Leighton. Unlike Rajo and Giles, Leighton tried to assimilate into black society, including going to a black church—but he also lived in a nice neighborhood in Santa Barbara and had a good job with the city of Los Angeles.

Rajo would place third behind Bud Rose and Bud Sennet in the March 17 race at Southern Ascot—a race named the Irish Derby. But Leighton left the track in far worse shape: he crashed through the outside wall, flipped twice, and landed upside down. He was taken to nearby Maywood Hospital and released shortly after. It was not an unusual finish for Leighton.

Big car fields were waning all over California. Rajo placed third again in the March 24 Easter Sweepstakes at Southern Ascot. He drove Vince Podurgiel's midget to a seventh-place finish at San Diego Stadium

Rajo Jack poses in a car before one of his few midget races with car owner Vince Podurgiel standing in the center behind the car. *Douthell Photos, Podurgiel Collection*

and a fifteen dollar paycheck. And then Rajo broke through again and won the first of two twenty-five-lap big car main events on April 14 at Southern Ascot Speedway. He followed that by placing third on April 21 at Southern Ascot.

The promoters of Los Angeles' Atlantic Speedway, a track built primarily for midgets, had made significant efforts over the years to get Rajo to race a midget at their track, no matter how many times he said no. They desperately wanted the biggest name remaining in Southern California big car racing. Midgets had outstripped big cars in popularity and were drawing tens of thousands of fans to each race. Vince Podurgiel wanted Rajo back in his midget.

When the AAA took over sanctioning midget racing at Southern Ascot Speedway in 1939, it also took over the sanctioning of midgets at Atlantic Speedway. But with vaunted Gilmore Stadium back in full operation in 1940 and hosting a full slate of midget races, AAA Western Zone Supervisor Art Pillsbury proclaimed that Southern Ascot and Atlantic Speedway were no longer tracks of the AAA's caliber, and the AAA abandoned both tracks. The newly-formed United Midget Association took over and brought in its cars. The UMA's cars were deemed second-class, as they were not powered by Offenhauser engines, and the AAA didn't want them anyway. The AAA only wanted the best.

Rajo drove in a series of races in April 1940 at Atlantic Speedway, but each time the engine in whatever midget he procured expired.

Rajo also brought his big car to the tight one-fifth-mile paved oval. He wasn't there just to race—he was there to put on a show. At each race, he would issue an open challenge to the thousands of spectators on hand. He would wager $100 dollars against all comers in various challenges. In one instance, he challenged someone in the crowd to race him in reverse. An old man came down and gave it a try; Rajo easily won. On another occasion, he challenged the spectators to race him while he wore a blindfold; Rajo again won. It was easy money. And he made far more from the gimmick races than he ever did racing a midget at Atlantic or any other track.

Around this time, Rajo found he had earned a new nickname among the legion of mechanics around the speedways: "Abracadabra." It was appropriate. Rajo could do things with a race car that seemed like magic. But Rajo hated the nickname.

———

Since the first, hasty paving job at Oakland Speedway, Curryer had faced constant problems. When the weather finally dried out enough in 1940, Curryer borrowed more money to have the track repaved. He scheduled a hundred-lap race for May 5, but the track wasn't ready in time. The new surface was finally done for a May 12 race, but it still wasn't great.

An astounding field of thirty-one cars showed up to race on the Oakland mile, which was amazing considering it was a humble ARA race and not the Gold Trophy 500. Curryer capped the field at twenty cars. After the chaos of having thirty-three cars on the track in the 1939

Gold Trophy race, Curryer decided twenty cars for a hundred-lap race was crowded enough.

Wally Schock took the lead early, and Bud Rose challenged him several times before falling off the pace. Rajo came on late in the hundred-lap race to place second behind Schock. Schock claimed he had lapped Rajo, but it didn't make a difference in the final results, so the officials didn't follow up on his protest.

Once again, Mel Leighton ended a race with a trip to the hospital. On the ninety-first lap he drove through the fence lining the outside of the far turn, plunging over an eighteen-foot embankment. Leighton had taken to carrying a rabbit's foot like Rajo, but it didn't seem to work for him either.

Over the years, Rajo Jack and Bud Rose battled on race tracks throughout the West Coast and put on many entertaining races. The May 19 Stars and Stripes fifty-lap big car race at Southern Ascot was no exception. There, the pair lined up for a ten-lap match race. Rose easily won the match race and the main event, with Rajo second in both. Rajo always loved match races, but he never was good at them.

As the 1940 season wore on, the big car fields continued to thin. For years, Fred Frame's desire to quit driving race cars had been no match for Charlie Curryer's ability to convince him to keep racing. But in qualifying for the June 2 Pacific Coast Stock Car Championship race at Oakland Speedway, Frame crashed and was critically injured. Frame had been trying to end his race car driving career for a long time; the crash did it for him.

A bomb was detonated to start the race at Oakland. Rajo had to come from the eighth starting spot in a Citroen, and the car's advantage was negated on the mile oval, as each car was required to make three pit stops. Early in the race, a rock came flying up from a car passing Rajo and smashed his windshield, forcing him to pit. The crew members worked to remove the damaged glass, but after a few frustrating minutes, Rajo accomplished it by kicking the windshield out from inside. Rajo whizzed back into the race with determination. He had fallen back to ninth place by lap seventy-five in his freshly air-conditioned car, but he gradually made his way forward to fourth by lap 150 of 250. He picked up second place when Walt Davis blew a tire with five laps to go. Frank Phillips, a car dealer from Chowchilla in a Ford, won, but Rajo placed a respectable second, nine laps off the pace at the finish.

"Boy, oh boy, what a lucky break for me," Rajo said. "I never won a race on Thursday in my life. I have more luck on Sundays."

Two weeks later, in the same car—with a new windshield—Rajo took the early lead five laps into a 250-lap race at Southern Ascot, but Wally Schock went past just as fast. Rajo surged back into the lead on lap 185 and led the rest of the way to win. The Citroen got great mileage and could turn well on shorter speedways like the half-mile Southern Ascot, but Rajo still missed his old Ford Sedan Delivery.

Stock car racing existed in small segments of the United States. The AAA Contest Board abandoned it after a few early tries, and few other groups thought stock cars were exciting to watch and would be able to handle the rigors of racing. But stock car races frequently drew large fields, much larger than the more prestigious big cars. And they drew far more fans, even for races which often became mediocre. Rajo excelled when he got behind the wheel of a stock car. If anyone could nurse a lesser car through a long race, it was Rajo.

Rajo Jack was a firm believer in luck because occasionally his luck was good. When the four leaders—Tex Saunders, Ed Barnett, Ernie Miller, and Bud Rose—crashed on the thirty-first lap to wipe each other out of the June 21 Night Sweepstakes big car race at Southern Ascot, Rajo capitalized and won. Then Rajo made it three straight wins on June 23 in a miserable thirty-lap big car race at Valley Speedway in Goshen. He placed second in a two-hundred-lap race on July 4 at Oakland Speedway and third in a hundred-lap jalopy race at Southern Ascot three days later.

Rajo was building momentum, and track promoters capitalized; his name was used heavily in the promotion of a hundred-lap stock car race at the half-mile dirt track in Riverside. But he never showed up. Many in the crowd were upset.

"Where was Rajo Jack?" asked a fan who paid to witness the race.

Rajo Jack was getting ready for what he hoped would be his greatest adventure yet.

11

THE BIG CRASH AND
ROAD TO OBSCURITY

THE BRIGHT CENTER OF THE RACING UNIVERSE is the Indianapolis Motor Speedway. The grand stadium was originally conceived as a test track for the burgeoning automotive industry in Indianapolis but soon became the racing mecca due to its marquee race, the Indianapolis 500. The allure and prestige after its first running in 1911 grew at a quicker pace than any other race in the world. Talented, capable race car drivers often congregated in other areas of the country, but it didn't matter until they proved themselves to the men who owned the Indianapolis cars. To make it to Indy, the drivers had to race in front of the men who owned the cars.

California had been an epicenter of the racing world in the early 1930s—with plenty of money and prestige at stake—thanks largely to the reputation of Legion Ascot Speedway. But with the AAA giving up on big car racing on the West Coast and a perception that midget racing wasn't going to be a path to greater things, the boys believed they could never reach the Indianapolis 500 if they stayed in California.

By 1940, most of the top young drivers against whom Rajo had previously competed were racing elsewhere in the country. Drivers like Duane Carter, Fred Agabashian, George Robson, Hal Robson, Hal Cole, Duke Dinsmore, Spider Webb, and Bayless Levrett had left for the big time of racing elsewhere in the United States. Most of the California boys found immediate success on new circuits. The irony is that many would land Indy 500 rides through car owners they met around Los Angeles.

Bayless Levrett was one of the first of the southern California group of outlaw drivers to leave in 1934 when a lucrative offer came along to race with the International Motor Contest Association. After founder J. Alex Sloan died in 1937, his son John A. Sloan took over as head of the sanctioning body and ran the organization. The difference between J. Alex Sloan and John A. Sloan was the son immediately recognized the need for new blood.

Throughout the 1930s, the IMCA was dominated by Gus Schrader and Emory Collins. They could draw a crowd anywhere they went and consistently be counted on to put on a great show at every race. At some smaller races, the competition was so poor outside Schrader and Collins that the rest of the racers were instructed to let them win and put on a good race amongst themselves for third. It wouldn't have mattered as Schrader and Collins were normally the fastest drivers. These races were dubbed "hippodromes" as they were, for all intents and purposes, fixed. J. Alex Sloan had loved to play up the rivalry between his two star drivers. The rest of the drivers barely mattered.

John A. Sloan wanted to bring in new drivers to challenge Collins and Schrader, specifically the southern California contingent.

While some of the California boys went off to race in promotions in the Midwest like the Central States Racing Association or raced in one of the AAA's regional tours, in 1937 Levrett accepted an offer to race with the IMCA. His agreement with Sloan was that he would be paid $200 per week, plus whatever purse money he won. That guaranteed money never happened with the AAA, which considered itself above that kind of tactic. And the IMCA had so many races, sometimes Levrett raced five days a week and made more money than his guarantee in winnings. The masses ate up John A. Sloan's angle of the California invaders coming to take the money from the hometown boys.

Levrett made several trips to the Midwest to race in the IMCA in the summers and at every opportunity told John A. Sloan how he needed to bring Rajo Jack to race with the IMCA. Levrett kept in contact with Rajo as his career blossomed back in California. John

A. Sloan knew who Rajo Jack was and was immediately interested. And his great champion Gus Schrader vouched for Rajo too. Schrader had known Rajo for over a decade and knew what he had to offer as a driver. Schrader's voice carried more weight than any other when it came to the IMCA. Sloan called Rajo in an attempt to convince him to come to the Midwest and race with the IMCA. Rajo was wisely holding out for more money. The rumor was, according to Levrett, that Schrader, and Collins were making $1,000 per week beyond their purses. Schrader had raced in the Indy 500 in 1932 but found he could make far more money with the IMCA.

After years of negotiations, Rajo and Sloan finally reached an agreement in 1940: Rajo would be paid $500 each week plus whatever purse money he won. Rajo Jack was worth the money. The IMCA was the highest level of racing for outlaw drivers like Rajo and a way to prove himself to the Indy 500 elite.

When Charlie Curryer found out about Rajo's deal with the IMCA, he was upset. Curryer had lost most of his top drivers to similar organizations. Rajo, he figured, would be the last of his boys to leave. It was widely known the AAA would never allow a black driver to race in the Indianapolis 500, and Curryer thought it foolish of Rajo to venture so far from home. There were several big American Racing Association races coming up, including the 1940 Gold Trophy 500, and Curryer wanted Rajo's name to bring in fans. Curryer offered to raise Rajo's guarantee from his standard $100 per race, but he could come nowhere near the $500 a week the IMCA offered.

As soon as Rajo agreed to the IMCA offer, John A. Sloan set up an aggressive schedule for him. Beginning in early August, Rajo would race in the Warren County Fair in Des Moines, Iowa, the Steele County Fair in Minnesota, the Minnesota State Fair, the Missouri State Fair, the Sioux Empire Fair Raceway in South Dakota, the Kossuth County Fair in Iowa and the South Dakota State Fair, along with smaller IMCA races on other nights. The IMCA schedule was so aggressive that its drivers were so busy they didn't have time to race elsewhere, though they were allowed. Some IMCA races were at huge fairs that would pack in thirty thousand fans a night to watch a race on a first-class track. Other IMCA races were at tiny fairs that would draw two thousand fans at worse tracks than any on which Rajo had raced coming up.

The schedule Sloan put together for Rajo required him to crisscross the Midwest, sometimes driving hundreds of miles a night to the next race. The prospect of spending that much time on the road driving from race to race thrilled Rajo Jack. Not that he would tell Sloan. But Ruth told Rajo if he was going to go on such a tour, she wouldn't be coming along. And with the Midwest being unfamiliar territory, Rajo was going to have to stick with Levrett every mile of every highway as segregation was more overt in that part of the country—especially compared with California—and Rajo could run into problems at any time.

But there was another lurking problem. The IMCA was accepting drivers of any race or creed. If the driver could get a car and pay the entry fee, the IMCA welcomed them. John A. Sloan was excited about a black man racing in the series, especially one who could be competitive. The reason Sloan wanted Rajo Jack was the widespread publicity about how he was the greatest black race car driver in the country. But Sloan knew the Midwest wasn't ready for a black race car driver.

He and Rajo crafted a new yet old identity. Rajo would become Rajah del Ramascus again, one of the identities he had first tried while working for M. B. Marcell in the 1920s.

Rajo had to update the story of Rajah del Ramsacus. In this version, Ramascus was a road-racing star born and raised in Oporto, Portugal. He had been a volunteer aviator during the Spanish Civil War in the 1930s but fled to California during the war. Rajo even commissioned a photographer to take a set of photos in which he wore a turban adorned with a feather and a cape in his race car. Fortunately for him, no one from California ever saw the photos; Rajo was sitting in his well-known number 33 big car. The picture of him in a cape was all the authenticity most small-town newspapers near IMCA races needed. Sports editors, understandably, ate the story up. But they also had problems with the name. They alternatively called him Raj del Ramascus, Raja del Ramascus, Rajah del Ramascus, Rajah Ramascus, and Roger Ramascus.

Many of the IMCA racers read about this new mystery man and the rumors spread quickly among them. Most were shocked—except

Gus Schrader and Bayless Levrett—when the mysterious stranger who showed up was Rajo Jack, the Negro ace driver from California.

Rajo followed Route 66 through Oklahoma then up into the Midwest, a dangerous trek for black men like him. Many of the cities were sundown towns, banning all black people from entering town after dark. There were printed guides for black people traveling the Mother Road called "Green Books" listing businesses that would serve black people. Rajo didn't know they existed.

Rajo's haul to Iowa from California was unlike any he had previously undertaken. Compared to a Ford sedan, his truck with a race car on the flatbed made him incredibly conspicuous.

It was a route of sixteen hundred miles from Los Angeles to the first race in Des Moines, and it took Rajo five days driving alone along roads through backwater towns. Though he was being hailed as a conquering champion coming to race in the Midwest, he wasn't ready for the ways of the society in the middle of the country. But his race car always drew a crowd of curious folks who had never seen one. While locals went home and slept in their beds, Rajo slept in the truck. He couldn't risk renting a hotel room and letting his car and truck out of his sight, even for a minute. Not that he had the money for hotel rooms. The race car was Rajo's identity. Without it, he feared he would go back to being Dewey Gatson.

Bayless Levrett had been racing primarily in Indiana with the Central States Racing Association in 1940, so when Rajo showed up for the first race of their tour at the Warren County Fair in Des Moines on August 8, it was a warm reunion. The years of separation disappeared quickly as they traded stories of their successes.

The half-mile dirt oval at the Des Moines Fairgrounds wasn't much different than most of the dirt ovals Rajo had raced through the years, except for its massive grandstand with room for thirty thousand spectators. Rajo was confident he could keep up with the best drivers in the IMCA, despite having an engine half the size of Schrader's Offenhauser. In races at Oakland Speedway and with the American Racing Association, Rajo had been fine because many of the cars against which he had been racing were inferior; with the IMCA he was going to have to work to be competitive.

Rajo was confident, though he was starting well back in the field for the main event. But on the first lap, Glen Coffman slid sideways directly in front of Rajo, and Rajo had no choice but to hit him head on. The impact spun Rajo into the air. Bayless Levrett also had nowhere to go and crashed into both. Gus Schrader barely avoided the pileup and would go on to win the race, not that Coffman, Rajo, or Levrett would see it.

Levrett was unconscious when the track workers reached him. The first ambulance that arrived took Levrett to a nearby hospital. Beyond a head injury, Levrett was badly bruised. Coffman had a broken arm and the next ambulance took him to the same hospital. Rajo had a broken left arm, a fractured skull, and a bad concussion. A third ambulance arrived at the track. Track workers attempted to carry Rajo on a stretcher to the ambulance, but when the ambulance driver saw Rajo, he said he wouldn't take the black man anywhere. Track workers explained this was Rajah Ramascus, a Portuguese man. The driver said he wasn't taking him anywhere and left behind a badly injured man. This type of treatment was not surprising to Rajo, even if he was barely conscious.

Fellow car owners saw how badly Rajo was injured and one offered a ride in the bed of his truck—not in the front seat—and Rajo accepted. He would take medical attention by any means.

Rajo was taken to the same hospital already occupied by Levrett and Coffman—a hospital reserved only for white people—and given a room next to Levrett's. The car owner told the attendants he was Rajah Ramsacus, the great Portuguese racer, and the hospital workers believed him. Levrett regained consciousness a few hours later. Days later, Rajo's head cleared. Over the next few days Rajo and Levrett were constantly found in each other's room regaling each other with stories and playing cards. The nurses frequently found them together in Levrett's room and quickly shooed them apart. They eventually tried to strap them to their beds to keep them separate. Neither Rajo nor Levrett had memory of the crash, but they vividly recalled their time as young, hungry racers in California.

The doctors put Rajo's left arm in a cast. Gus Schrader came by to check on Rajo and Levrett only to find them rioting with laughter over a story of Rajo spinning into the infield mud at Silvergate Speedway. John A. Sloan also came to check on them. His motive was to find out if his California boys would be in any shape to race. They confirmed what Sloan could tell with one look: the lucrative racing tours were over for Rajo and Levrett.

It was almost a week until they were discharged. Both of their race cars were significantly damaged. A group of racers at the track saw Rajo's predicament after the crash, loaded his car on his truck and brought it to the hospital. Rajo's truck sat outside for days with his mangled car on its flatbed, ready to head back to Los Angeles. Rajo cut off the cast as soon as he got out of the hospital. It was a long drive home for Rajo.

What hurt Rajo worse than driving home with a broken race car is he was going home without any of the $500 per week guaranteed money.

Rajo wasn't going to be earning any money as a mechanic—or any of his other brief professions—for the next few months, but at least he could make money as a race car owner. He fixed his car with the goal of having it ready for the 1940 Gold Trophy 500 at Oakland Speedway. Rajo previously had procured a ride in Russ Garnant's car for the race but was in no condition to drive his own Ford sedan on the streets, let alone a race car. Rajo barely got his number 33 car back together in time—with lots of help from Herman Giles and others—to let Van Edwards drive it to ninth on September 2, many laps behind winning Hal Cole, who was piloting the same Gil Pearson car in which Rajo had won the race in 1939. But Rajo made money, something he desperately needed. He left unpaid hospital bills in Iowa, and with no other income and no savings he needed every cent.

Charlie Curryer wanted Rajo back racing. He understood how serious Rajo's injuries were but needed his name recognition to draw fans.

Rajo tried. On October 20, he came to the ARA race at Clovis Speedway. He took his car out on the track but within a few laps pulled off, complaining of back pain. He put another driver in his car for the rest of the race.

Rajo tried to race again in the IMCA races at the Arizona State Fairgrounds on November 11 and 19—which weren't part of his initial deal with Sloan—but the best he could do was win a five-lap heat race. He spun on the first turn of the first lap of the main event and came to a stop. Rajo was done for the year. He should have been finished after the crash in Iowa in August, but he was too stubborn.

Rajo finally healed enough to race January 12, 1941, in the two-hundred-lap Gold Cup race at Southern Ascot. Rajo led the first 110 laps in a Citroen, but the car suffered head gasket problems and was overheating. He spent the remaining laps in and out of the pits—eight times in all—to have the radiator refilled with water, but he placed fifth, far behind winning Wally Pankratz.

Adding to Rajo's problem, he could no longer straighten his left arm. He never gave it a chance to properly heal after the wreck in Iowa. He couldn't physically work as a mechanic and took a job operating a steam cleaning rack. That business soon failed.

Rajo repainted his big car white and blue with number 3 on the tail before his next race, April 20 at Oakland Speedway. He placed a distant seventh behind winning Hal Cole. Rajo Jack still wasn't the driver he once had been. Friends implored him to retire. With his physical impediments, he looked nothing like the driver he was in 1939.

But Rajo Jack made his career out of proving others wrong. He again tried to put together an Indy 500 effort, going as far as trying to enlist car owners he knew, but none were willing to take a chance on him. Even if he could get in the gates of Indianapolis Motor Speedway, his physical ailments would prevent him from passing the required physical. But he had enough friends racing at Indy that year, including Ted Horn, Joie Chitwood, George Robson, and Kelly Petillo, he made the drive to Indiana to watch the race again. Only this time he didn't try to go in the pits until after the race. He was already used to the "coloreds only" grandstand.

Shortly after Rajo returned to California, he placed second to Tex Peterson at a hundred-lap big car race June 8 at Southern Ascot Speedway and won the Floyd Clymer Trophy, named for the noted racing author, by beating Kenny Palmer in a two-lap trophy dash. It was a positive sign.

He showed up almost a week early for the July 4, two-hundred-lap big car race at Oakland Speedway. Most, including reporter Alan

Rajo Jack, in car, with a trophy after a big car race at Southern Ascot Speedway. *Podurgiel Collection*

Ward, surmised Rajo was anxious to race. But his relationship with Ruth was deteriorating, and he needed to get away. On the track his marital problems didn't matter. Hal Cole took off with the lead from the start, but Rajo ran steadily and finished a strong third, three laps behind the winning Cole in Gil Pearson's number 18.

Somehow that finish gave Rajo the lead in the American Racing Association championship chase with 473 points, three more than Tex Sanders. In the fifty-lap big car race at Southern Ascot on August 3, Rajo spun and watched Bill Sheffler win the fourteen-car main event. Then Rajo won twice at Southern Ascot Speedway on August 24. Sheffler led the first fifty-four laps of the hundred-lap race before Rajo passed him and won. Tex Peterson protested the win, claiming Rajo was a lap down. Peterson's appeal was disallowed by referee Dave Dillon. It was Rajo's first win in over a year, and his first since the crash.

Racing in the United States was about to be halted, and Rajo was one of the few racers who saw it coming. War engulfed large parts of Europe and spread, though the United States was not yet involved. The threat of rationing materials needed for race cars like gasoline and tires cast a pall over the racing community. Many younger drivers wondered if they would be called upon to serve in the military; Rajo knew the military would never take a disabled thirty-six-year-old black man, but he still registered for the draft.

"I don't believe there will be any racing next year," Rajo told Alan Ward. "Too many pilots are going into high pay defense jobs as expert mechanics, and too much of our equipment is being snatched by the government. Well, it has been fun while it lasted."

Rajo wondered if racing would ever return if it was halted in the United States. Many viewed the sport as a barbaric pursuit of men who wished for death.

Going into the final points race of the American Racing Association's 1941 season, the Gold Trophy 500 on September 1 at Oakland Speedway, Rajo led the ARA points by a huge amount. He figured if he placed sixth or better in the race, he would win the championship. Hal Cole and Wally Schock took turns leading the race by huge margins, but each broke. Rajo ran a conservative race and finished sixth, well behind winning Ed Barnett in front of fifteen thousand fans.

Rajo's math was wrong. Tex Saunders won the ARA championship and Barnett placed second. Rajo's long-desired championship slipped through his fingers. And he placed third again.

Rajo returned to Southern Ascot Speedway for the October 12 race to place eighth while Bill Sheffler won. J. C. Agajanian—taking a page out of Rajo's book and billing himself as a Syrian pilot—was promoting a race at the Arizona State Fair. Rajo entered. He passed Dave Champeau in a thrilling finish to win the fifteen-lap Australian pursuit race, then in the fifteen-lap main event spun out into the infield fence on the tenth lap and dropped out of the race. In the Arizona heat, Agajanian bought a white cowboy hat in the fair's midway to protect himself from the harsh sun. For the remainder of his life, Agajanian was rarely seen without one.

Rajo would go on to place third in the fifty-lap big car race on November 23 at Southern Ascot Speedway.

———————————

On December 7, 1941, Japanese pilots bombed the US naval base at Pearl Harbor. The following day, the United States entered the war. On December 21, AAA Contest Board president and Indianapolis Motor Speedway owner Eddie Rickenbacker announced all AAA racing would be cancelled through the duration of the war. The outlaw circuits could still race as much as they wanted. And they had a monopoly on racing in the United States. Some of the biggest name drivers volunteered to join the military, as the draft was imminent, and sought to enlist to get safer assignments; many drivers so desired the lucrative wartime jobs.

Southern Ascot held its first race of the 1942 season on January 4, and Rajo placed fourth after initially challenging eventual winner Bill Sheffler. Rajo placed seventh in the February 15 twenty-five-lap big car race behind Sheffler, who passed newcomer Johnnie Parsons for the lead. Promoters shortened races in hopes the government would allow them to continue to hold races if they consumed fewer resources. Rajo raced April 25 at Southern Ascot, but few fans were coming to races anymore. Gasoline was rationed, and it was hard for most people to use the precious fuel for their street cars to travel to watch races. Many California promoters stopped scheduling races. Then the US government banned all automobile racing on July 15, 1942.

———————————

World War II was hard on Rajo Jack. He tried to get jobs with defense contractors during the war, but none were willing to hire him. Rajo then tried to get a job at numerous machine shops around Los Angeles. Many engine builders around southern California took on work building other parts for military contractors, including the Offenhauser shop. Most who owned machine shops were already at full staff by the time Rajo approached them.

As much as he dreaded it, Rajo went back to working as a mechanic. There were no cars being produced by the manufacturers in the United States, and Rajo found steady work as those who had cars needed to keep them running. For once he was getting equal work from black and white customers.

Many of Rajo's friends were sent overseas in the military or worse. Sey Sugi—though born in California—was sent to an internment camp in Wyoming based solely on his Japanese heritage.

Rajo registered for the draft in 1940 under the name Rajo Jack DeSoto, but at the age of thirty-five with one eye and a left arm that wouldn't straighten, he was never called for service. Two of Rajo's brothers, Gerald and Warren Gatson, enlisted and served in World War II. Warren was stationed in the Pacific Theater when a bomb struck the ground near him and riddled his body with shrapnel. He survived and was honorably discharged and moved to Berkeley, California. And his father Noah Gatson died in 1943. Rajo couldn't go home for the funeral due to the gasoline rationing. Not that he wanted to.

While Rajo had always been religious, he became more so during World War II. Before he crossed streets, he would stop and say a prayer. He picked up rocks, believing each to be a prayer, and put them in his pockets. He would deposit each rock in the front yard of his house until it resembled a quarry. Friends worried Rajo Jack had gone crazy.

Though racing was banned in the United States, a few outlaw promoters put on races just across the border, in Mexico. In 1944 and 1945, a few outlaw drivers raced hastily assembled dirt tracks in towns like Juarez and Tijuana. Rajo was thrilled at the prospect, but the reality of wartime rationing set in. Gasoline rations made long trips almost impossible. Even if he had been able to save up enough gas rations to haul his race car, there were no sources for high-octane gasoline for his race car. And tires for race cars hadn't been produced since 1941. The closest Rajo got to the races was hearing about them second-hand.

The longer the war dragged on, the worse Rajo's demeanor became. Already distant from Ruth, he grew despondent, as his identity had been taken. In the worst times of their marriage before the war, Rajo would get in his car and drive a long distance. It wouldn't be unusual for him to drive to Nevada on a whim. During the war, the farthest he could go was the other side of Los Angeles, and even that was a sacrifice. During the war, many of the racetracks on which he became a star were sold off and developed into housing for men who were returning from war with cash in their pockets.

With the one thing that made him Rajo Jack—racing—taken away, he was lost.

12

RACING AROUND
THE FRINGES

WHEN RAJO JACK MARRIED RUTH, she immediately declared she wanted children. Rajo Jack did not, and though he would not explain why, he was adamant. None of the Gatson siblings wanted children or would have them.

However, Ruth's younger brother Eugene Ball—who she previously barely knew—moved in with Rajo and Ruth in Watts for a time and was essentially raised by them

Before Rajo and Ruth were married in 1933, Rajo had promised to put her name on the deed of his house in Watts. It was less than a decade old and already in desperate need of repairs. Any money Rajo made beyond paying bills, however, went to racing. When a floorboard on the back porch broke, Rajo took the sheet metal off an old tail tank of a race car and used it as a patch. He was proud of his handiwork and showed it off to friends who came over. When Ruth first saw his patch job, she was devastated. When she agreed to move to California, Ruth imagined she would be leaving behind living in squalid conditions.

Ruth maintained steady employment as a domestic worker, cooking and cleaning for white families. While Rajo became famous, she was scrubbing floors. She never earned much, but anything she could spare was put into renovating the house. She paid for venetian blinds, linoleum, a bathtub, and new stucco. She spent countless hours and about $1,000 she couldn't afford for repairs.

No matter how much work Ruth invested, the home inevitably would fall back into disrepair. From a young age, Rajo and his family always kept animals. Even when his house was nice, the front and back yards would decay. The interior could be teeming with cats, dogs, birds, or any number of other animals. At one time, Rajo started a hog farm in the backyard. It didn't go over well with Ruth or the neighbors. And somehow, he lost money.

The one thing Rajo maintained through the years was a coop of chickens. When his financial circumstances prevented him from being able to pay bills—which happened frequently—Rajo would gather eggs from the coop and deliver a dozen a week to those whom he owed money. For years Rajo would deliver a dozen eggs each week to Ed Winfield for machine work long-since performed.

From 1942 to 1945, Rajo Jack was often found in his garage, working diligently on his race car with nowhere to take it. There wasn't anything broken, but even on cold nights, he was in the garage, drinking a beer, smoking a cigarette, and dreaming about racing. He was afraid that day would never come again.

Rajo Jack's funk ended on September 2, 1945, when World War II officially concluded.

There were hundreds of race car owners with cars that had been sitting for years, and when the US government lifted its ban on auto racing, promoters were anxious to put on races. But rations on gasoline had not been lifted, and tire manufacturers were not producing tires for passenger cars, let alone race cars. Many racers who served in the military were slowly making their way home with money and nowhere to spend it. The drivers who stuck around California and worked for defense contractors during World War II also had large amounts of money. Rajo didn't.

They all had one thing in common: they wanted to race again. The AAA was in no hurry to get going, but promoter J. C. Agajanian was. Most of the tracks he previously promoted had closed during World War II—Southern Ascot had become housing—and Agajanian had to search out a new location. He found a potential venue at the Imperial County Fairgrounds in El Centro. At one point, the AAA had held races there, but after years of neglect, the track needed a lot of work to be a suitable venue for racing again. Grass grew through the dirt on the oval and the wood grandstands looked about to collapse. The best thing about the track was it was available and cheap. The El Centro fairgrounds races previously had been held on dirt tracks of one-and-one-eighth miles and a quarter mile, but those wouldn't do. The big track was too big, and the smaller track too small. Agajanian cut out a half-mile oval. And he did it fast.

Most of the former southern California drivers returned immediately after the war. Agajanian's job was to gather them. He set a date of October 21—the race was rained out and postponed until October 28—for a big car race at El Centro and had an outstanding field of drivers. George Robson, Bayless Levrett, Tex Petersen, Mel Hansen, and Bud Rose signed up for the race, but not before Rajo. Rajo installed young Art George to drive his beloved Model T "Sally" against the big cars while he raced his trusty number 33. Most of the drivers who came had raced as outlaws early in their career and transitioned to racing with the AAA, but with the AAA not sanctioning races, big-time drivers figured they would be fine racing in an outlaw race to knock off the rust. Agajanian limited the laps of races and most races were uncompetitive, as tires were unavailable. Still, a decent crowd of five thousand witnessed Bill Sheffler set fast time and Rajo win his heat race. Rose won the twenty-lap main event. The racing was a needed respite for everybody.

———————

Eddie Rickenbacker still owned the Indianapolis Motor Speedway and was technically the president of the AAA Contest Board in 1945. But during World War II, the track was neglected. Rickenbacker focused his time prior to the war on his duties as president of Eastern Air Lines. During the war, he supported the war effort as a civilian. While touring air bases in the Pacific, a plane on which he was flying crashed into the ocean, and Rickenbacker was stranded at sea for twenty-four days. When the war ended, he was disinterested in racing. Rickenbacker considered selling the track to developers who wanted to turn the land into housing.

But retired driver Wilbur Shaw convinced Terra Haute businessman Tony Hulman to purchase the track for the same $750,000 Rickenbacker paid in 1927. Hulman named Shaw president and general manager, and Shaw began renovating the track to get it ready for the 1946 Memorial Day race.

After reinstating racing for 1946, the AAA Contest Board decided rules for the 1946 Indianapolis 500 would remain unchanged from 1941. And the AAA declared an amnesty for all drivers who had been running as outlaws prior to the 1946 Indy 500. Drivers from around the world sent entry blanks and their $125 entry fees as early as January 1946.

Rajo Jack saw this as his final chance at Indy. He was forty-one years old and limited physically. He took his long-expired AAA mechanic's license, filled out an entry blank, scraped together $125, and mailed it to Indianapolis. Rajo didn't have a car to race in the Indy 500, but he figured he could pick up a ride by cashing in on his name, if only the AAA would give him an overdue shot. His backup plan was to stretch the wheelbase on his big car and procure a more competitive engine for the race. It was a long shot.

Of the seventy entries filed for the 1946 Indianapolis 500, sixty-one were accepted. Rajo Jack's entry was returned. The AAA said in its rejection he was physically incapable of racing at Indy with the missing eye and left arm that wouldn't straighten. The AAA's doctors never performed a physical examination on him. Rajo was devastated but not surprised. There were some new faces among the AAA authority, but the racism remained.

"In case they got their back up against the wall, they would manufacture a way so you didn't make it," said Herb Spivey, a mechanic at the Indianapolis 500 in the 1940s and 1950s.

The AAA Contest Board accepted the entries of a ridiculous number of Rajo's compatriots, however. Hal Cole, Ted Horn, Rex Mays, Duke Dinsmore, Joie Chitwood, George Robson, Jimmy Wilburn, Hal Robson, Bill Sheffler, Mel Hansen, and Bud Rose all had entries accepted. Each had raced against Rajo, and he frequently beat them. Kelly Petillo

From left, unknown driver, Rajo Jack, George Robson, Van Edwards, and unknown driver. *Bill Bagnall photographer, Podurgiel Collection*

also filed an entry, but he was denied too. He sued the speedway for $50,000 and lost.

Rajo decided this wasn't a time to be timid. He drove to Indianapolis and, during the month of May, constantly pestered the officials to let him in the pits. He figured if he could make his way into Gasoline Alley and the dozens of race cars, one of his many associates would rally to his cause. The old guard of officials who wouldn't let him in years prior held fast—neither Rajo nor any black man would be allowed in Gasoline Alley. Rajo snuck past them occasionally, but he was caught and thrown out. And he didn't have as close a friend like Francis Quinn or Petillo who would let him use the janitor excuse for being in Gasoline Alley.

Rajo stayed at the track as much as he could and was a constant presence through the month of May. Rajo again watched an Indy 500 from the familiar vantage of the "coloreds only" grandstand. Rajo recognized his final chance to race at Indy ended with the rejection. He was proud of his old friends but couldn't resist being jealous.

When George Robson took the lead of the Indianapolis 500 in the Thorne Special, Rajo Jack applauded. Even back in their Southern Ascot days, George Robson was never the hard-edge driver Rajo was. George Robson came from the fifteenth starting spot through conservative driving and high attrition to win the Indy 500 by a margin of forty-four seconds.

Chickie Hirashima, Robson's engine builder, made a brief appearance in victory lane, but was quickly ushered away by officials who didn't want a Japanese man in their hallowed ground. Like Sey Sugi, Hirashima spent time in an internment camp during World War II.

It took Rajo the better part of the evening to reach the elder of the Robson brothers to congratulate him. On his drive back to Los Angeles, Rajo grew more determined to keep racing. He would show everyone he was still one of the greatest drivers in the world.

Oakland Speedway had closed and was demolished during World War II. The Coelho family who owned the track wanted to subdivide the land and sell it for homes, but the idea ended during the war.

In 1946, the Coelho family hired Charlie Curryer and his business associate, William Linn, to build a new racetrack, one like no other. Because of the shape of the land, Curryer designed a five-eighths-mile paved oval to be built essentially on top of the existing mile oval, cutting across the older track at several points. Because of the site limitations, one set of turns would be tighter than the other. Turns one and two were built with thirty degrees of banking, more than any other asphalt speedway in America. The tighter turns three and four were built with a heart-stopping sixty-two degrees of banking on the outside groove, roughly wide enough for one car. Curryer envisioned the banking to be used as a safety wall and assumed the racing would take place on the wide, flat apron. But as soon as Lenny Low drove up the banking and found it was the fastest way, everyone went high. The stadium's monster banking allowed drivers to go faster than ever. But to be fast, the driver had to hold the car wide open right up to the outside rail, often bouncing the car against it as he flew around at breakneck speed.

And, per the terms of the deal with the Coelho family, Curryer would promote the races.

Curryer was no longer willing to pay Rajo's appearance fee of $100 for the grand opening of Oakland Stadium, so Rajo stayed home for the first race on June 30. But, at the last minute, he decided to go to the second race on July 14. Early in the afternoon, with the race at Oakland Stadium hours away, Curryer and driver Art George sat in the track's office.

"Rajo ought to be calling now," Curryer pronounced.

Curryer explained Rajo should be arriving in San Luis Obispo on his way to Oakland, and just then the phone rang. It was Rajo. He explained that his truck broke down on his way to Oakland, and he needed the promise of appearance money so he could make a deal with the owner of the auto parts store for needed parts. Rajo's truck was fine, and if it hadn't been, he could have fixed it. Curryer agreed to pay him twenty-five dollars in appearance money.

"This is standard," Curryer explained to George. "I already know how much I have to pay Rajo, but he strings it out so he feels like he's hustling me all of the time."

When Rajo finally saw the new track, he didn't like it. Even if Rajo Jack had been the young and brave thirty-one-year-old he was in 1936, instead of the forty-one-year-old he was now, he still would have been hesitant.

While qualifying for the July 14 race at Oakland Stadium, Rajo hit a slick spot in the high-banked turn. His number 33 car got loose and made a hard right-hand turn into the wall in front of the grandstands. He hit the wall so hard, his car ripped out a huge chunk of concrete. It didn't help he was racing on a set of decade-old tires that had seen their best days when he raced on them at Southern Ascot in 1941. The front of the frame of the number 33 car was bent over six inches in the wreck. Rajo's brother Warren, who lived nearby in Berkley and was acting as his pit crew, stood defeated at the sight of the wrecked race car. It would take a month to get it back together.

Rajo returned to the Oakland Stadium on September 1 for another big car race, but in the semi-main event, while riding high in the north

Rajo Jack takes a checkered flag at the Sacramento Fairgrounds in his iconic number 33 big car in 1946. *Bruce R. Craig Photograph Collection, Revs Institute*

turn, his car clipped the wall. He went into a spin and nearly flipped the car, but mercifully came down on all four tires. The car again needed major repairs. Rajo Jack declared he was done with Oakland Stadium.

What made things worse was Rajo found out George Robson had been killed the following day at a race at Lakewood Speedway in Atlanta, Georgia. Many of Rajo's friends died racing, but this was different: Robson had gone from their shared circumstances to win the Indianapolis 500. Still, it didn't stop Rajo from getting back in a race car.

Rajo's car was repaired in time for the J. C. Agajanian–promoted September 22 race at Gardena, California, billed as the first big car race in southern California since 1941. It sounded plausible, as many of Agajanian's promotions did. Rajo won his heat race but was mediocre in the main event won by Orville Brummer. Rajo didn't race again until another Agajanian-promoted race, this time at the five-eighths-mile dirt oval at the Arizona State Fairgrounds in Phoenix. Rajo managing only a third-place finish in the semi-main event.

––––––––––

After Kelly Petillo gave up driving in 1941, his life went downhill. He purchased a bar in Hollywood, Marco's Café. For someone who drank heavily and had a quick temper, it was a terrible combination.

In the years that followed, he allegedly drove in front of a moving train, assaulted a couple with a wood bat at his bar, fired a rifle at customers, punched a police officer, attacked another police officer, attempted to bribe a police officer, assaulted and attempted to rape a girl, and was arrested for speeding. Somehow, the only punishment that stuck was a twenty-five-dollar fine for drunkenness and disorderly conduct in 1944. But when his wife, Val, filed for a divorce, the judge granted it at lightning speed.

Despite all the horrible things Petillo did, he and Rajo remained friends. Petillo owned a five-unit apartment complex in Huntington Park, and Rajo was the only of Petillo's old racing friends to come over to visit him. No one else from that world wanted anything to do with him.

Racing never left Petillo's blood, and he had a plan to return. With all the racing in southern California, there had never been a showcase racetrack like the Indianapolis Motor Speedway. Petillo had been brewing a plan to build a string of super speedways and a racing empire for years.

The first plot of land he sought was in Orange County, but its cost was prohibitive. He ended up with an option on a piece of land in Kearny Mesa in north San Diego and christened it the new home of the San Diego Motor Speedway. He envisioned the track to be a one-and-a-half-mile asphalt oval, shaped as a near-perfect circle. Even with every dollar he had, Petillo wasn't close to having enough money to build the place as he envisioned it. He reached out to a large group of friends and family members—including Rajo Jack—to invest in it. Petillo managed to convince twenty-one members of his family and friends to invest between $500 and $3,000 each in his new track.

Rajo needed a boost in his career, and Kelly Petillo offered one.

Though he didn't have money to invest, Rajo offered something of more value: he committed to race at Petillo's track. With only Rajo signed up for his race, Petillo started his own outlaw sanctioning body, the Independent Racing Association.

He told the press he would start putting on races at his new track as early as November 15, 1946, and the track would be a grand shrine to racing.   But as much as he tried, the track wasn't coming together in time. He wasn't paying his construction crews, and workers often walked off the job. Petillo planned to have a five-hundred-mile race around January 1, 1947.

On December 10, 1946, just days before his new track was supposed to open, Petillo was driving through Santa Barbara when he made an illegal U-turn at Fifth Street and Mt. Vernon Avenue at 10:30 PM. He sped north and ran a stop sign. He was charged with drunk driving, speeding, illegal turning, and running a stop sign. In the car with him was his secretary and girlfriend, twenty-five-year-old Naomi Roberts, who was also arrested on a charge of intoxication.

When taken to the police station, Petillo was abusive and refused four times to let the officers see his driver's license. Petillo punched officer C. C. Vineyard in the face and broke his nose.

He and Roberts were released the next day on twenty-five-dollar bail apiece, but Petillo was rearraigned later in the day on the battery charge. He pleaded not guilty to that charge and was again released on $500 bail.

The San Diego Motor Speedway was finally ready for testing on January 1, 1947, far behind schedule. The track wasn't paved—Petillo couldn't raise enough money—but there was a heavy mix of oil and crushed rock placed on top of the dirt surface. Still, it was far better than most of the dirt tracks around southern California. Most tracks of the time used concrete walls and fences to surround their tracks, but Petillo could only afford an antiquated wood guardrail—much like many fairgrounds tracks which started as horse racing tracks—in places around the oval. One driver showed up for the first practice, Rajo Jack. Petillo's loyalty to Rajo years earlier was being repaid.

Rajo started his first laps on the track cautiously. He had driven thousands of laps on racetracks of all varieties and never showed fear, but he had reason to be cautious at this track. In his first laps the surface deteriorated. He gradually built up speed, but with the track being a near perfect circle, he was in a constant, broad slide and had no time to rest.

As Rajo drove into what was labelled as turn one, a pothole suddenly appeared. Rajo didn't see it in time to avoid it. He hooked his right front tire in the hole at nearly ninety-five miles per hour. The car turned right and launched through the wooden guardrail. His car flew through the air and Rajo, not wearing a seatbelt, was ejected. He landed with a thud, bruised all over and with a cut on his leg. The car, which had been through so much in its decade, appeared demolished. Rajo was taken to Mercy Hospital and was fortunate to be released the same day.

Even if Rajo were in any shape to race January 5, he no longer had a car capable of racing. When race day came, a surprising six thousand fans filled the hastily assembled wood grandstand for what was supposed to be a fifty-lap race for a field of twenty cars. Only five big cars showed up, and they were some of the most archaic big cars since Silvergate Speedway shut down in 1936; a couple actually were old Silvergate cars that had been sitting for decades. The main event was cut to fifteen laps and later to thirteen, as only the car of Joe Rand was running after the twelfth lap. Had it not been for a small group of roadster drivers who were recruited at the last minute for their own ten-lap race, the event would have been even worse. Petillo advertised he would pay a $5,000 purse, but Joe Rand was fortunate to walk away with fifty dollars.

The fans were angry, and Petillo tried to smooth things over by offering free admission to the next race at the track. There wasn't one. A San Diego attorney organized the stockholders who invested in the track and sued Petillo. A judge ruled Petillo would have to pay back twenty-one creditors a total of $52,482. Petillo was broke. The track would be his financial ruin.

For Rajo, though, the crash and failure to make as much as a lap at the San Diego track was enough to convince him he was through. After twenty-four years of racing all over the country, winning some of the biggest races, seeing his name in lights and becoming a star, Rajo Jack finally determined his career as a race car driver was over. The people who told Rajo he should give it up finally got their wish.

But Rajo was not done with racing. When he started in 1923, there was little guidance and seemingly no avenues for black race car drivers. In 1947 he took on the altruistic goal of ushering a new generation of black drivers into the sport. No one else was giving black people opportunities in racing in the 1940s. Rajo had problems finding black drivers with even rudimentary skills which would translate to driving a race car. Much like he had done while helping recruit drivers for races at White Sox Speedway in 1936, Rajo began to scour garages, delivery companies, and taxi services for potential racers. It took time, but he eventually found a protégé. It still took months for him to put his number 33 big car back together.

Charlie Curryer had always been a good mark for Rajo for appearance money. But when Rajo contacted Curryer about paying tow money for him to bring his car with a new driver to race at Oakland Stadium, Curryer balked. Rajo called on his greatest proponent, Alan Ward, who had become the *Oakland Tribune's* sports editor. Rajo wrote a letter detailing how he had found a young black driver who he viewed as the next golden boy. Rajo tried to convince Ward to contact Curryer and David Bolton, president of the track, to convince them his new driver was worth the extra money. But Rajo failed to write the name of his protégé. Ward wrote a column detailing the letter in the *Oakland Tribune,* but it made no difference. Rajo Jack was the one who drew fans to the races, not some unnamed kid he was tutoring.

Rajo eventually found a pair of black brothers, John and Charlie Dawson, who were interested in racing and entered them in big car races at Carrell Speedway in Gardena, the track promoted by J. C. Agajanian. The track was named for Judge Frank Carrell, the former land owner who sentenced Kelly Petillo to prison. The Dawson brothers joined fellow black drivers Mel Leighton and Leroy Nooks racing at the track in the 1948 season. Though none produced significant results, to have that many black drivers racing at one track in that time was astounding.

Rajo also worked as a crew member on a few occasions in 1949 for car owner Emil Diedt and sponsor Bob Jaffe, a Long Beach car dealer; their vehicle was a former big car converted to race on dry lakes like El Mirage. Rajo knew how to make cars go fast. But the work he did on the dry-lake car, alongside chief mechanic and old friend Reg Swimmer, was mostly in an advisory capacity. It was ultimately an unrewarding experience.

Rajo's work as a car owner was also unrewarding. His impact was minimal, as most young drivers he tried to field were incapable of winning. And worse, they were costing him money.

Early in Rajo's career, he could pass for white or younger than he was; now he looked older than his forty-four years. He put on weight, his hair was slowly graying, and he wore glasses—though people still recognized him at first sight.

But Rajo Jack could only be Rajo Jack when he was driving a race car.

13

RISING FROM THE ASHES

WHEN LOUIS VERMEIL BOUGHT HIS HOUSE IN CALISTOGA, California, he saw the structure for what it could be. The house in northern Napa Valley had once been owned by Robert Louis Stevenson, author of *Treasure Island* and *Strange Case of Dr Jekyll and Mr Hyde*, and had plenty of room for Vermeil's growing family. But Vermeil also figured he could build a shop out back from which he could operate his business as a mechanic.

The shop would become known as the "Owl Garage," because Vermeil was often found late at night working on race cars in it. In the house, the dinner table was the focal point. Family dinners were an event and a place for Vermeil to hold court. It was where he educated his young sons about the legend of Rajo Jack.

Vermeil was a mechanic by trade, but his passion was racing. While living in San Francisco as a teenager, Vermeil witnessed a board track race at the San Francisco Speedway in San Carlos and was hooked. For years, Vermeil hitchhiked to races around the San Francisco Bay Area. Vermeil settled in Calistoga and bought his first big car in 1936, the same time he was starting a family. He hired Jimmy Joy as his first driver and entered a few races at the Oakland Speedway as well as the Calistoga Speedway when it opened at the Napa County Fairgrounds in 1938.

There was one story he told his sons repeatedly. While traveling through San Mateo to attend a race, Vermeil noticed a billboard advertising a race at San Jose Speedway. What struck him was the billboard advertised in huge letters that two drivers would be racing at San Jose, and Rajo Jack received top billing. For a black race car driver to receive such status made Vermeil pay attention. He had yet to see Rajo Jack race, but he quickly learned of Rajo's reputation by fielding cars against him.

After World War II, decent venues for big cars were hard to find. Many privately owned tracks had been sold to property developers. Most that survived were fairground ovals, ones built for horse racing and largely ignored during the war.

Vermeil was instrumental in returning racing to the half-mile dirt oval at Calistoga Speedway in 1948. When Charlie Curryer took over promoting the track, he brought with him his American Racing Association, and the track soon became a needed mecca for big car racing.

When Rajo Jack showed up to race at Calistoga Speedway for the first time in 1949, Vermeil's young sons, Dick and Stan, were awestruck by how someone they considered a legend carried himself. When they asked him to autograph a program after a race, Rajo was gracious and spent as much time as possible with the adoring boys.

"He was very sort of warm and joyful with us kids," Dick Vermeil said.

———————

Off the track, Rajo Jack was the same person he had always been. But recapturing his on-track glory was difficult, as a comeback is never as easy as it sounds.

To make a comeback, you need to have reached such a level of competition—and sustained that level—to become familiar to an average fan. Then you must give up the activity for a period long enough for the fans to miss you. When you do decide to come back, you must rekindle the drive you once held to participate—and that drive must grow. And if you don't produce results at the same level or higher, fans will think you should have stayed retired.

Rajo Jack held a lingering, romantic notion about the American Racing Association. In Rajo's formative years as a racer, during the

ARA's halcyon days, the group provided such competition it became a springboard to the highest level of racing. Many drivers Rajo raced against in the ARA and associated racing series like Johnnie Parsons, Joie Chitwood, Duane Carter, Duke Dinsmore, Bill Sheffler, Hal Cole, Bayless Levrett, Fred Agabashian, and Spider Webb—as well as eighteen-year-old Troy Ruttman—raced in the 1949 Indy 500. Indy was out of the picture for Rajo, but he figured he could be competitive in the ARA.

Rajo had a couple false starts in his attempts at a comeback. He entered a stock car race at Carrell Speedway in 1948, but the race car he lined up for the race didn't show. He entered a couple ARA races early in the 1949 season in California but couldn't get his battered race car ready in time.

The American Racing Association bred a couple young, hot-shoe drivers to be the series' stars. Mike Reilly and Jack Pachateau were the most successful drivers but had far less name recognition than Rajo. Reilly and Pachateau were both in their early twenties and capable drivers, but they were drastically different people.

Reilly came out of nowhere to become a champion racing driver. When World War II ended, Curryer recognized the need for cars to keep his series afloat. Most new car owners were building midgets, as the class thrived. To make big car racing viable again, Curryer placed a huge order with Grant Douglas for twelve cars. Douglas needed help in the shop to fill the order and hired Reilly, a star athlete fresh out of high school in San Francisco. Reilly quickly became a partner in Douglas's business. Douglas installed the neophyte Reilly as the driver of his house car in 1948. Reilly acclimated quickly and became a winner, eventually running away with the ARA championship in 1949. The dapper Reilly was quickly accepted by the racing community in northern California and proposed marriage to Laura Vermeil, Louis's daughter, while she was still in high school. The engagement didn't last.

Pachateau came from the opposite world. His hard-working mother owned a major hot springs resort near Calistoga and accumulated wealth, lavishing significant amounts on her son. Pachateau started a business hauling gravel but was so enamored with racing he only worked a couple days a week. In 1947, he bought an old big car powered by a Model A engine and, with a great deal of help from Louis Vermeil, turned it into a competitive car. He used the money he won from driving the big car to purchase an engine for a midget he would race four or five days a week. Working hard was not in his DNA, but racing was. Most of his fellow racers considered Pachateau a spoiled brat.

Both Reilly and Pachateau won races and were championship-caliber drivers, but they were nobodies compared with Rajo Jack.

For the first race of his comeback in September 1949, Rajo Jack opted to race in a familiar place, but one where few knew him. Portland Meadows was a new, one-mile dirt oval for horse racing in Oregon that shared a border with Portland Speedway, a track on which Rajo raced thirteen years earlier on its opening night. Portland Meadows promoters struggled with horse racing at the start of their new venture and decided to put on an auto race. It meant importing cars and drivers. Rajo Jack and Mike Reilly were the two California hotshots brought in for the first race at the track.

When Rajo arrived in Portland, the town was going through myriad changes. It was a different place than it had been when lived there over thirty years prior. Industries like ship building had come to town, and with them housing, which now rose where groves of trees once stood. The city was transforming into a modern metropolis. And the black population had grown significantly since the repeal of Oregon's Negro Exclusion Laws in 1926.

But Rajo was focused on the racing. He had driven race cars only in practice over the prior two years. He didn't realize how difficult it would be to learn to really race again.

The mile at Portland Meadows wasn't what he had hoped for, either. The dirt was soft and rutted, but Rajo had seen worse. A year before, the track had been under many feet of water after a massive flood wiped out the city of Vanport across the street.

When Rajo pulled his car onto the grid for the Northwest 100-Mile Dirt Track Big Car Championship, he was surprisingly nervous, more nervous than he had been in years. The number 33 car was ready, but he wasn't. Early in the race he was running wheel-to-wheel with unknown Conrad Christensen well back in the pack when Christensen's car collided with Rajo's left rear wheel. They both went into a devastating spin. Christensen's car hit the inside guard rail while Rajo's car came to an abrupt stop with a broken axle. What hurt Rajo was the newspapers called him "Roger Jack"—the writers had no idea he had been racing in the area for twenty-six years. Reilly, the young upstart, won the race.

While some would have been devastated by a poor result in their comeback race, Rajo grew more determined. On September 30, he was back in a different big car, the McDowell Special, for a race at the quarter-mile dirt track in San Mateo named Belmont Speedway. Al Benoit won, but Rajo placed a strong fourth. He needed more time behind the wheel to win races again.

In what was scheduled to be the final race of the 1949 ARA season at Calistoga, on November 13, Rajo drove to a tenth-place finish. But at the last minute, the ARA added a race at the Stockton Fairgrounds' one-and-one-quarter-mile dirt oval and dubbed it the National Invitational 100-Mile Racing Championship. While Mike Reilly and Jack Flaherty were racing for the ARA championship, Rajo Jack was racing for relevance.

A robust field of fifty cars attempted to qualify as an electric clock—an oddity and recent revolutionary advance in technology—marked their time. About half the drivers went home without racing a lap, as Curryer capped the field at twenty-four cars. While Reilly was busy driving away with the lead to win the race and the ARA championship, Rajo steadily passed car after car to place second.

Rajo spent most of his racing career driving at tracks around his home in Los Angeles, but those options were now closed to him.

In the early years of J. C. Agajanian's career as a promoter—he preferred the label "race organizer"—Rajo and his compatriots had been vital to Agajanian's promotional efforts. Outlaw racers like Rajo made up the fields for Agajanian's races for the Western Racing Association. In turn, Agajanian had been vital to building the legend of Rajo Jack.

But Agajanian's desire to be part of the Indianapolis 500 meant making a choice.

In 1948 Agajanian purchased a Kurtis chassis championship car and filed an entry for the Indy 500 with Johnny Mantz as driver. His entry was immediately rejected, but it had nothing to do with his Armenian heritage. The AAA stated Agajanian's entry was rejected because he was promoting the outlaw Western Racing Association. To get around the outlaw label—for the moment—Agajanian had two of his mechanics, Clay Smith and Danny Jones, enter the car under the team name of Smith and Jones Company. Mantz placed thirteenth. After the Indy 500, Agajanian was told he had to make a choice: compete at Indy or continue to promote the WRA.

In April 1948, Agajanian resigned from his position as president of the WRA, and the association disbanded soon after. In November of that year, Agajanian received sanctioning from the AAA for Carrell Speedway. And Agajanian also appropriated the name Pacific Southwest circuit from the AAA for his new racing series, harkening back to the series that Francis Quinn won in 1930. Many who raced for Agajanian previously became the star attractions at his AAA races.

But while large segments of the fields of the WRA races at Carrell in 1947 had been black drivers, after the track went over to AAA promotion, none of the black drivers raced there again—though Mel Leighton often fielded his big car for white drivers. In 1949, 1950, and 1951, Agajanian allowed the California Sports Car Club to hold foreign car races at Carrell Speedway, during which Fay Taylour, an Irish woman and former flat-track motorcycle star rider, competed in a series of match races. After promising results in different cars, including a midget, she was barred from competing when the AAA entry form was changed to state, "No Women Drivers." The AAA also did what it could to keep women out of racing.

By 1950, Rajo had accepted he would never race in the Indianapolis 500, but he could still accomplish one thing he had been chasing his entire career: winning the American Racing Association championship.

Rajo Jack had to repair his race car numerous times, mostly because of wrecks, and occasionally he put in the effort to repaint it. At times, he would paint on a sponsor's name or change his number. On occasion, he would paint his car because he believed in something. For the opening race of the 1950 season for the ARA at Calistoga, Rajo painted his car bright red with the words "Roy Land Governor" on the sides. He wore a light-blue leisure suit and distributed campaign literature to the crowd between races. The platform of the Los Angeles gubernatorial candidate, whom Rajo met on another of his adventures, was that all California residents would be given $125 each month when they reached the age of sixty. Rajo was claiming he was fifty-seven years old when he was forty-five. Roy Land was easily defeated in the governor's race.

Rajo Jack arrived fashionably late to the April 24 race at Calistoga. The trophy dash was lined up on the front stretch and ready to be pushed off when Rajo pulled into the pits in his truck with the race car on the back. The announcer alerted the audience that Rajo Jack had arrived, and the crowd broke into applause. Then Rajo came from the back of the field in the twenty-five-lap main event to place third behind Al Benoit and Jack Pachateau.

Rajo was one of the first black people to come to Calistoga. When he showed up for his first race at Calistoga, he had slick tires—leftovers from his car being raced on the asphalt at Carrell Speedway—and Stan Vermeil asked Rajo why he was running those on a dirt track.

"These are the only tires I have," Rajo replied.

Rajo's number 33 car was antiquated. It was essentially the same car he debuted in 1937, with some updates, mostly dictated by needed repairs after crashes. But with the ARA, he could still be competitive. Rajo had the same 183-cubic-inch Miller engine under the hood. The engine was an antique and had more laps than entire fields of drivers, but it was superior to the stock-block Studebaker and Plymouth engines in many cars on the circuit. The engine was solid, but other pieces of Rajo's car broke often, and he failed to finish many races. At the Stockton Fairgrounds for the May 7 100-mile race at the big oval, Rajo finished sixth after completing 116 of 125 laps, far behind the winning Joe Baker and second-place Reilly.

Rajo always had a way of surprising people. There was another new track Curryer lined up for a race. It was a three-eighths-mile dirt oval named Shasta Speedway, far north in Anderson at the Shasta County

Rajo Jack counts his winnings after a race. *Action Photos, Podurgiel Collection*

Fairgrounds. The field for the May 12 race was thin but included many ARA regulars. Rajo was the class of the field and won his first main event in nine years.

Rajo Jack was back.

Rajo returned to Calistoga for the May 30 race with a different outlook. The race was scheduled to be the thirty-five-lap Memorial Day Sweepstakes but was cut to twenty-five laps when few cars showed. The race concluded earlier at fifteen laps when fourth-place-running Dave Lee drove over the bank and tore out a huge section of fence. When he did, Rajo Jack was leading and awarded the win. Going from nine years between wins to two weeks was a record pace, even for Rajo.

By that time, Rajo was telling people the reason he never raced in the Indy 500 was he didn't want to be the first black man to race at Indy. Jackie Robinson broke the major league baseball color barrier in 1947 and faced much resistance. The tales of how the white establishment resisted black baseball players were widely reported, and Rajo related to the toll of institutional racism. The fiction about his aspirations of racing in the big time were easier than the truth.

To follow up his win at Calistoga, Rajo placed second behind Mike Reilly June 5 at Orland Raceway, a new half-mile dirt oval at the Glenn County Fairgrounds in Orland. More importantly, Rajo took the American Racing Association points lead from defending champion Reilly. Rajo thought he was finally on his way to the ARA championship.

Rajo and Reilly, along with occasional ARA competitor Dave Carter of Stockton, were engaged to race June 11 at Portland Meadows. Rajo's first trip to the track a year earlier didn't go well, but Rajo never let the past get in his way. It took the California boys two days to tow to Portland, and they brought with them a straggler. Reilly brought along Dick Vermeil, the thirteen-year-old son of Calistoga promoter Louis Vermeil, to crew on his car.

When the California contingent arrived up at Portland Meadows, there was a solid field of seventeen cars, even with another big car race scheduled at the same time on the same day at Portland Speedway, spitting distance from Portland Meadows. Dave Carter beat Howard Osborn to win the twenty-lap race at Portland Meadows while Rajo placed sixth, one of his best performances at a race in Portland. Rajo loved Portland, but he rarely did well there.

Rajo had work to do back in California. He raced at the resurrected fairgrounds track at Dixon on June 17, placed third on July 3 in Calistoga, then followed it with a fifth-place finish the next day at the same track in a race for the Napa County Fair.

After the races ended the first night at Calistoga—as with all the races at the track—Louis Vermeil invited the racers back to his house.

Vermeil let racers work on their cars in his shop and sleep on the property. The drivers were often in need of equipment to fix their cars, and for a two-day show, they needed to keep as many cars running as possible. Most important to the racers was that Alice Vermeil, Louis's wife, fed them all. She would stay up the night before the races to cook huge spreads—a couple turkeys and hams, cold-sliced tongue, and huge dishes of pasta, among other items—to feed the inevitably huge crowd of famished racers. The drivers would eat like kings.

When Rajo showed up at the Vermeil house after the race the night of July 3, his truck was directed to the parking spot of honor by Stan Vermeil: under the big tree out front. When Alice Vermeil had the post-race meal prepared, Louis called all the racers into the house for dinner. Rajo slowly approached the house and stood in the doorway. While the rest of the drivers found places at the table and passed huge plates of food among them, Louis Vermeil noticed Rajo wasn't coming in. Rajo was hesitant entering a stranger's house, especially when the stranger was white.

"This is my house, you're going to come in and eat," Louis told Rajo, making sure he was loud enough for everyone to hear. "If anyone doesn't like it, they can get up and leave." Rajo found a seat at the table next to Stan Vermeil, his biggest fan at the time, and ate the best meal he had in a while.

Rajo slept in the front seat of his truck that night, which wasn't unusual. But he also needed to do some laundry. Alice had a wash tray on the back porch, and Rajo asked her permission to use it. Alice was impressed that he asked and gladly gave permission.

After the first day's race, Louis Vermeil wondered if Rajo's Miller engine was low on compression. Rajo had been using increasingly hot spark plugs in the engine to keep it running. The engine occasionally blew out a puff of blue smoke, and it wasn't unusual for the headers to glow red when he came off the track. Louis had a compression gauge and offered to let Rajo use it. Rajo first declined, embarrassed his machine might be lacking.

"Rajo, let's test the compression," eleven-year-old Stan Vermeil said, and Rajo relented.

Rajo took Vermeil's compression gauge and screwed it into a spark plug hole in his engine. A group of men got behind the car and pushed it to build compression. It produced 220 pounds of compression in all four cylinders, far more than any other car in the place. Many of the other racers were shocked. Many parts in the engine were from the one Francis Quinn purchased decades before, but it was still capable.

———

Promoters around California—and in the rest of the West Coast—took note of Rajo's resurgence. They approached him about racing at their tracks, and some offered to pay him large guarantees to race. The younger version of Rajo Jack would have taken the money and gone on the adventures. The older, more realistic Rajo Jack recognized that if he was going to finally win a championship on the ARA tour, he had to focus on it and skip any races outside the series. But in August, Rajo was falling back in the championship chase. Mike Reilly had earned 1,077 points with Rajo in a distant third with 781. Despite his determination, Rajo's chances were slipping away.

Rajo won the fifteen-lap main event at the Plumas County Fair on August 13 in front of a slim field, placed third in the August 26 race at Salinas, then struggled the next week at Calistoga Speedway. Two days later at Stockton 99 Stadium, Rajo broke early after completing thirty-six laps and struggled to a tenth-place finish. He was falling further behind Reilly with each race.

The long season was taking its toll on Rajo. At the age of forty-five, he was struggling physically. Between his limited left arm and one eye, he was already behind, but drivers in their twenties like Reilly and Pachateau were resilient and in better equipment. There were several races where Rajo would run well for a short period and then his car would break.

But Rajo, along with Reilly, still made the tow back up to Portland Meadows to compete in a hundred-lap championship race in September. The Portland Meadows promoters desperately needed the California drivers and were happy to shell out a couple hundred dollars of guaranteed money to each of the California boys to race. This time the race would be on a newly carved, half-mile track inside the mile oval on which the horses competed. It didn't go well for Rajo or Reilly. New drivers from the northwest like Len Sutton and the Claude Walling were transitioning up to big cars from roadsters and midgets, and the California drivers couldn't keep up.

And the inevitable happened: Rajo's Miller engine threw a rod through the side of the block. Rajo still had the original Miller pattern to make a new block but was low on money after scraping to get by to make it from race to race. He didn't have the money to get the engine back together before the season ended. Rajo had fallen so far back in the ARA points chase, and Mike Reilly had driven so well that Rajo could see the championship was out of reach. It was a defeating finish to the 1950 season. Reilly clinched his second straight ARA championship on November 5 at Calistoga Speedway, one race before the season ended. Rajo didn't come to the race. His season was already over.

For Rajo to race in 1951, his old number 33 car wasn't going to cut it. Rajo learned of a used big car for sale with a provenance that sounded good. The car was said to have once been owned and raced by Gus Schrader. The many-time IMCA champion had died in a race on October 22, 1941, at the Louisiana State Fairgrounds. The first time Rajo showed up to a race in the Schrader car, few believed its legendary origins. Schrader was known for his impeccable cars with miles of chrome. This car, which bore number 99, looked like it had been through a demolition derby. The car was outdated and had clearly suffered a hard existence. But it had a 270-cubic-inch Offenhauser engine that could keep up with any other engine in the field, unlike Rajo's antiquated Miller.

Charlie Curryer assumed Rajo would want to race his new car with the ARA in 1951, but Rajo's time with the ARA was over. Curryer had taken back promotion of the Oakland Stadium and offered Rajo appearance money. Rajo had no desire to ever see the track again after his hard wrecks there in 1946. Curryer optimistically promoted that Rajo would drive in the ARA races early in the 1951 season, but after Rajo repeatedly didn't show, Curryer gave up on his biggest star.

Rajo had unfinished business with the IMCA after his disastrous stint with the tour in 1941 ended in the hospital. The closest IMCA races were thousands of miles away, but Rajo looked forward to the travel.

His marriage to Ruth had collapsed and the only times they spoke were to fight. Being separated for weeks at a time while Rajo was traveling was the happiest they had been in a while.

In Rajo's years of racing, one area he had long wanted to race was his home state of Texas. But it was with mixed emotions Rajo returned to his home state. Most of his family had moved away or died. Rajo still had two siblings living in Texas. Brother Gerald Gatson was twenty-four years old and living in Fort Worth after serving in the army. Gerald, like the other Gatson men, was working as a menial laborer, drinking heavily and frequently getting into fights. His sister Jennie—by then going by Geneva—was thirty-five years old, living outside of Dallas, unmarried, and one of the least likable characters in the family.

Rajo recruited Gerald to serve as his pit crew for the June 24 IMCA race in Texas.

Arlington Downs was a former horse track outside of Dallas and just over a mile in length. The year before, it—along with Carrell Speedway and Indianapolis Motor Speedway—had been used as a location for filming the Clark Gable/Bud Rose movie *To Please a Lady*. The track previously hosted AAA races, but its condition deteriorated and the IMCA scooped it up. The IMCA always welcomed Rajo. The difference this time, as opposed to 1941, was that he was now billed as Rajo Jack.

Though the segregated grandstands in California had long since been integrated, at Arlington Downs, there were separate grandstands for white people and black people. Rajo could race in front of white people but not sit with them.

And Rajo struggled badly in his new race car. The best he could do was place fourth in the six-lap consolation dash. Rajo Jack finally raced in Texas, but he left his home state for the final time, defeated.

Rajo wasn't used to being outclassed in a race. His new race car was partially to blame—he didn't realize how bad it was when he bought it—but Rajo's physical ailments were catching up with him. Finishing heat races, let alone main events, had become a challenge.

In late August, Rajo traveled to Des Moines, Iowa, to compete in the IMCA races held in conjunction with the Iowa State Fair. He showed up late for the August 26 race, as was his custom, in front of twenty-three thousand spectators—one of the largest crowds to ever watch him race. He placed third in the ten-lap heat race for drivers who didn't make time trials, then made a respectable fourteenth in the twenty-lap main event behind winning Bobby Grim, Frank Luptow, and third-place Bill Holland, the 1949 Indy 500 winner.

The Iowa State Fair races were split over two weekends, so Rajo spent the next week living on the fairgrounds and sleeping in the cab of his truck. Some drivers ventured out to race at other tracks in the interim, but Rajo spent his days at the fair. He played carnival games and enjoyed himself. He still had the spirit of a carnival worker, even years after his work with M. B. Marcell.

Then a familiar face arrived. Joie Chitwood's Auto Daredevils performed at the fair on August 30. Since Rajo met Chitwood in 1938, Chitwood had raced at the Indianapolis 500 seven times—despite his purported Cherokee lineage—and finished fifth on three occasions. Chitwood had built his thrill show to a premier attraction at fairs and stand-alone performances throughout the United States. Chitwood tried numerous times in 1951 to quit driving race cars so he could focus on his more profitable auto thrill show on a full-time basis.

The Joie Chitwood Thrill Show garnered headlines across the nation for daring stunts, and Rajo was finally able to see why Chitwood got so much attention. Stunts like driving up ramps and onto two wheels and jumping cars impressed even the most skeptical fans. Rajo figured there was no way Chitwood would remember him, so he didn't try to talk to him after the show.

For the September 1 race at the fair, Rajo qualified a surprising sixth with a time of 28.10 seconds on the half-mile oval. But the rear end in his car broke during his heat race. By the time Frank Luptow won the main event, Rajo had loaded his race car and was headed back to California.

Rajo recognized he wasn't the same driver he had once been. His glory days were over.

14

THE INDY
500 DREAM

THE WORLD OF BLACK ENTERTAINERS in Los Angeles was not large in the 1930s. The major players—be they actors, comedians or singers—were centered in Los Angeles. And their world often overlapped with the world of sports. Boxers, actors, and baseball players could often be found at the same parties. The athletes would show up at shows, and entertainers would show up at sporting events.

When Rajo Jack rose to fame in 1936, many of the top black entertainers sought to include him in their society. He regaled them with his tales of racing—and other adventures—and made his desire to compete in the Indianapolis 500 known. The entertainment industry was integrating faster than sports, and some of Rajo's new friends in entertainment believed they could help end the segregation in racing too. Though entertainers like actor and dancer Bill "Bojangles" Robinson became friends with Rajo, most didn't understand racing.

But Rajo planted a seed in another man. Eddie Anderson was born in Oakland in 1905 and started as a vaudeville performer as a teenager while he developed many talents, including dancing, singing, and later comedy. While on a tour of the East Coast he met Jack Benny, the most famous radio host in the United States. In 1937 Anderson made his first appearance on the *Jack Benny Program*. After a couple of early appearances, Benny cast Anderson on the show full time in the role of his valet, Rochester van Jones. With Anderson's distinct gravelly voice, he became instantly recognizable. Rochester became one of the most beloved characters in entertainment, and Anderson would play the role on radio and television until 1965.

In real life, Anderson owned a limousine—among his fleet of high-end cars—and had his own valet. Rajo and Anderson had become friends in the 1930s, and when one of Anderson's many cars needed work, he often engaged Rajo for jobs.

"You babies come down to Los Angeles," Rajo Jack told Louis Vermeil's children. "I'm friends with Rochester. We'll go for a ride in his limousine."

Anderson had many hobbies and interests outside of show business. He owned a company that made parachutes for the military during World War II. He managed boxer Bill Metcalfe. He built model airplanes and advocated for black people becoming pilots of real airplanes. He was the skipper of his own boat. He owned race horses, which usually ended up costing him money rather than making any.

Rajo convinced Anderson to give driving race cars a try, not that he needed much persuasion. In 1941, Anderson entered an American Racing Association race at Oakland Speedway in Rajo's old Model T, "Sally." Anderson entered under his real name—not Rochester—and most at the track thought the biggest star in the field was either Rajo Jack or IMCA champion Gus Schrader.

In the late 1940s, Anderson attended a few sports car races with the group that would become the Sports Car Club of America and decided to try road racing. The problem was that Anderson loved Cadillacs. He wanted to race one, but they were the most ill-suited car to race. The heavy, boxy cars with atrociously small brakes were terrible for road racing, especially compared with the lighter, exotic European sedans that filled the fields. But Anderson had money—he reportedly earned an unheard-of $150,000 in 1946—and wasn't shy about spending it.

Nearly every race car builder worth knowing located their businesses in southern California, as did most who built components for race cars. Rajo knew them all. When Anderson decided he wanted a car in which

Radio and television actor Eddie "Rochester" Anderson, a friend and associate of Rajo Jack, in a Kurtis Kraft midget at Carrell Speedway. *Podurgiel Collection*

he could be competitive in sports car races, Rajo introduced him to car builder Emil Diedt. Diedt built his reputation by building cars for the Indianapolis 500, like the vaunted Novi. Much like the car with a Cadillac engine Anderson desired, the Novi cars were nose-heavy with a powerful anchor for an engine. After many discussions, Anderson engaged Diedt to build a one-off race car for road racing. It would be a departure for Diedt, but Anderson was willing to pay the steep price of $20,000 for the proposed project. It would have been cheaper and easier for Anderson to go with any other number of engines available, but Anderson would only have a Cadillac engine in his race car.

In 1948 Diedt started to build a car unlike anything else on any race-track. The creation was a tube-frame chassis—based largely on the Indy cars Diedt was constructing—with a swoopy, aluminum body designed by Roger Evans Bacon, similar to the lines of cars that European

manufacturers were producing. A 331-cubic-inch Cadillac V-8 was sent
to an engine builder for improvements and was mated to a Lincoln
transmission, a quick-change rear end, and Alfa Romeo drum brakes.
It was a radical creation built solely to win road races. And it took two
years to complete. When Diedt finished it in 1950, Anderson drove it
a lot. He took to the car, driving it on the street and racetracks. He
didn't win races, but he grew a greater appreciation for racers and more
respect for the sport.

And he developed an interest in the Indianapolis 500.

Mel Leighton gave up his career as a race car driver after he lost a finger in
one of his many crashes. He had received his AAA car owner's license in
1948 with the help of AAA champion Rex Mays, fielding cars on lower-tier
AAA tours. In 1948 Leighton became the first official black mechanic for
a car in the Indianapolis 500 when he crewed for Jack McGrath. He tried
to enter the Indianapolis 500 in 1949 as a car owner but was turned down.

"The only thing that might stop me is the unwritten lily white clause
of the American Automobile Association," Leighton said.

The AAA's official position, however, was "New drivers must pass
a driver's test before a license will be issued to them. If and when
Mr. Leighton files an application, he will receive the same consideration
as any other applicant."

Rajo still didn't like Leighton—Leighton claimed he first became
interested in racing after seeing Barney Oldfield race when he was eight
years old, copying Rajo's story. But Leighton did much for the career
of another burgeoning black driver.

A twenty-four-year-old black man from Kentucky named Joie Ray
bought his first big car after winning a lottery and started racing in 1947
at outlaw tracks in Kansas, Kentucky, and the Midwest. It was there that
Ray became acquainted with Leighton.

On October 9, 1949, Ray became the first black driver to officially
break the AAA's color barrier when he raced at Salem Speedway in
Indiana in a car owned by Leighton. Rajo had broken the barrier years

before, but it was in secret while this was public. One of the drivers who vouched for Ray and helped him get his AAA license was Spider Webb, Rajo's friend for years.

Word of what Ray was doing in the Midwest filtered back to Rajo. It seemed a miracle a black man had done the impossible and received a AAA driver's license. But in Rajo's mind an idea brewed.

Rajo's driving career was supposed to be over in 1952, but he was talked into driving in one of the worst races in California history. He was recruited to race the half-mile dirt oval at De Anza Park at the Riverside County Fairgrounds on May 19, 1952. It was the same track at which Rajo was supposed to join a stock car race in 1940 that he never attended. Many of the cars brought for the race were reportedly last run at Carrell Speedway in 1947, but most looked like they had been sitting in barns since Legion Ascot closed in 1936. The race was nicknamed the "bolt, bailing wire, and petrol series."

Rajo placed fourth in the semi-main event behind nobodies in "Sally." Leroy Nooks, one of the black drivers who raced at Carrell Speedway, made his first start in years, but it became his last start as his car caught fire in the twelfth lap of the main event and almost burned to the ground.

If Rajo wasn't going to be the first black driver to race in the Indy 500, at least he could help someone else accomplish it. He hatched a plan to create the first team of black men to race in the Indy 500. He had the black driver in Joie Ray, or so he thought, but he needed money.

Rajo broached the subject of owning a race car for the Indianapolis 500 with Anderson. Rajo explained how expensive it would be to put a competitive effort forth for the Indy 500, but Anderson loved the prospect of being involved in a groundbreaking effort to break the color barrier. Anderson, who flirted with owning a midget in 1948, had plenty of money and this seemed important. But in public, Anderson said "he refuse[d] to propagandize," as his credibility with the large *Jack Benny Show* crowd was at stake.

The catch was this group needed a car owner with a AAA license that the officials of the Indianapolis Motor Speedway wouldn't reject out of hand, as they had with Leighton. Rajo knew a willing participant:

Andy Granatelli. Granatelli, with his brothers Vince and Joe, entered the 1946 Indianapolis 500 as the Grancor Racing Team and in a few years had become one of the top car owners in racing.

Eddie Anderson, Andy Granatelli, and Joie Ray met at the Palmer House in Chicago on November 3, 1952. Rajo did his best to keep his name away from the deal for fear his involvement would cause AAA officials to reject the deal. At the meeting, a handshake deal was struck: Granatelli would field the car for the 1953 Indianapolis 500, Anderson would fund the operation (which would cost over $50,000), and Ray would drive the car. Part of the deal, however, was Ray would have to step up his performance as a driver.

"So I felt like if Andy was going to build the car and Rochester was going to spend the money that I had a real chance to make the race," Ray said.

Rajo had tried on many occasions over the years to gain reinstatement by the AAA. The AAA mechanic's license he first received in 1929 was long expired, but he rarely let the piece of cardboard out of his possession. His previous attempts at reinstatement were never through proper channels and always denied. In 1952, Rajo Jack officially applied for reinstatement to the AAA and hoped for the best.

He wasn't alone. Many drivers and mechanics had their AAA licenses revoked over the 1952 season for many reasons. When most drivers had their licenses revoked, they were assessed fines between $5 and $500. Paying that sum of money was all the contrition necessary to put them back in the AAA's graces.

Rajo figured if he could get his mechanic's license for the Indy 500, he would be able to drive the car in practice. Rajo secretly hoped if Ray couldn't get the car up to speed to qualify, he could. Rajo Jack always was a dreamer, and involvement in the Indianapolis 500—preferably as a driver—was his life's goal.

In December 1952, the AAA had its annual meeting at the Palmer House, and, after the meeting, the AAA's Contest Board reinstated most who applied for reinstatement. Nineteen drivers were reinstated, including Jim Rathmann, Jud Larsen, Eli Vukovich, Bob Gregg, and Allen Heath. Frank Luptow was reinstated after getting his license revoked for driving in the IMCA—including races against Rajo in the Iowa State Fair. Fay Taylour, the Irish motorcycle queen who raced a midget at Carrell Speedway, was rejected for a license to compete in Pike's Peak Hill Climb. The AAA explained it did not license women drivers.

Rajo Jack was denied reinstatement by the AAA. No reason was given.

The deal Rajo orchestrated to bring the first black racing effort to Indy fell apart shortly after. Anderson's wife, Mamie, was diagnosed with cancer at age forty-one that year. And Anderson's adopted son, Billy Anderson, who had a brief career as a fullback for the Chicago Bears, was arrested in 1952 for transporting marijuana and faced serious charges.

Joie Ray didn't develop to be the driver everyone had hoped. The most notable thing he did in a car was when he was nearly arrested driving home after a race in 1952. The police mistook the black Joie Ray for a white man named Joie Ray. The other Joie Ray, from Portland, Oregon, had raced in the NASCAR beach race at Daytona in 1952 and had a lengthy rap sheet.

And there weren't many other prospective black drivers on the horizon. As perfect as the operation once seemed, it fell apart quickly.

15

HAWAIIAN INTERLUDE

RAJO JACK ALWAYS HAD A SCHEME. His plots were either about how he was going to get rich with a new business or how he was going to get a ride in a great race car and once again become Rajo Jack, the greatest black race car driver ever.

By the mid-1950s, he was done driving race cars but still entertained friends from the racing community and the entertainment community at his house in Watts. No one was surprised at the condition of his house, which seemed to decline with each visit. Rajo insisted on playing them his favorite record, "I'm Going to Move to the Outskirts of Town." He regaled friends with stories about how he used chewing tobacco to cauterize wounds received while racing.

By 1954 he was hauling oranges for a living. It was less glamorous than some of his previous pursuits. Rajo had not driven a race car in two years and was beyond rusty. Even worse, his personal life was a disaster.

Rajo Jack entered a March 15, 1953, race at Corona Speedway in California in a Miller engine big car. Three days before the race, March 12, Rajo filed for divorce from Ruth. They had been married for twenty years, but over the previous decade had become confrontational. At times Rajo would move out of their Watts house and in with friends, in Long Beach or other neighborhoods of Los Angeles, for weeks at a time. There were times he would tell Ruth he was going out for groceries and instead drive to New Jersey. He wanted out of his marriage.

Ruth filed a countercomplaint to Rajo's divorce filing, alleging extreme cruelty. Rajo didn't race at Corona.

At the end of the 1947 season, Bill France and a group of men met in a hotel boardroom in Florida, and from the meeting came the sanctioning body called the National Association for Stock Car Auto Racing (NASCAR). In the 1930s, France had been an outlaw big car driver around Washington, DC, though not a successful one, and had served on a crew at the Indianapolis 500 before World War II. But after starting NASCAR he borrowed a garage pass at the Indy 500 to gain entry into Gasoline Alley. AAA chief steward Harry McQuinn heard France was in the garage area and corralled a couple police officers. When McQuinn found France, he ordered the cops to escort France out. France once hoped to gain the backing of the AAA for his new sanctioning body, but out of spite decided he would be a success on his own. NASCAR started by staging races solely in the American South, and the national part of the name was an aspiration. In the early 1950s, NASCAR branched out across North America by sanctioning races and tracks in the northern United States and in Canada. The strangest place NASCAR sanctioning reached in its early days was Honolulu, Hawaii.

Honolulu Stadium, a baseball and football venue, opened in 1926. A grand, wooden stadium in a perfect tropical climate in which games could be played year-round, it had seating for twenty thousand and was the largest venue in Hawaii. Famous athletes like baseball players Babe Ruth and Joe DiMaggio and black track-and-field Olympic gold medalist Jesse Owens competed there.

Lou Abrams received NASCAR sanctioning for a dirt oval he built around the football field in 1952. The simple oval was a quarter mile in length, and as soon as Abrams started promoting races, stock cars flooded the track to compete. He promoted the races under the label Hawaiian Auto Racing Promoters Limited.

Abrams found his star driver from an unexpected place. Jerry Unser Jr. was an upstart, twenty-one-year-old, second-generation driver—his uncle, Louis Unser had won the Pikes Peak Hill Climb eight times—from Albuquerque, New Mexico, striving to make a name in the racing world. Unser had raced a few times growing up in Albuquerque, but after enlisting in the navy in 1952, he was stationed in Honolulu. While on active duty, he picked up rides in the NASCAR stock car races in 1953 at Honolulu Stadium and quickly became the best driver on the island—he won the championship in the Sportsman Class in 1953. The navy supported Unser's racing so much that, no matter how many hundreds of miles from Hawaii his boat was on patrol, the navy would send an airplane or helicopter to pick him up and deliver him to Honolulu. But the crowds for the races at Honolulu Stadium were nowhere near what they were for baseball or football.

In December 1953, the promoters and racers came into conflict over money. The drivers claimed the races in the season had brought in $235,000—not including expenses—and the drivers were paid about $53,000. The local drivers threatened to boycott the stadium. The promoters needed race cars and drivers.

Aspiring promoter Ed Johnson had an idea: Johnson approached Alan Ward about importing a field of big cars to Honolulu Stadium from California to race.

In his time at the *Oakland Tribune*, Ward's influence in the sports world had grown. And from his seat of power, Ward had been afforded opportunities. People would come to Ward with events and offer him a piece of the profits if he would provide publicity. Ward took on many of the lucrative opportunities.

The logistics of Johnson's plan seemed impossible. And there was the question of where Ward would find drivers and cars to fill the field for a race—a AAA race was out of the question. Even if the organization had agreed, the costs would have been astronomical.

Ward reached out to old friend Charlie Curryer. It would be a stretch, but the American Racing Association was the only group that could get enough cars and drivers together for a race like the one Johnson was proposing. They wouldn't be great cars or great drivers—the ARA had fallen on hard times—but it would be an actual field.

Ward struck a deal that required a huge outlay and commitment on Johnson's part. Ward would get together fifteen cars and drivers to come to Hawaii, and Johnson would pay for one driver and one mechanic for each car to come to the race. That was a skeleton crew, but it was workable with the right cars and drivers.

And Ward needed a name driver. Many of the ARA drivers who had made headlines after World War II had retired, such as Mike Reilly and Jack Pachateau. There were a few drivers around who were capable, like Bob Willis, Al Benoit, Claude Walling, and Jack Flaherty, but there wasn't an active ARA driver who was known outside of the San Francisco Bay Area.

Throughout his career as a sports writer, when Ward needed a driver he could play up as a star, he always relied on Rajo Jack.

Rajo, however, hadn't raced in over a year and was barely physically capable of driving his truck on the road, let alone a race car. And with the late notice—and little money—he had no chance of putting back together the number 33 car, which was still torn apart in his garage. Between paying for lawyers in the divorce fight and having another failing business—he was collecting scrap—Rajo had to sell much of his racing equipment to pay the bills.

When Ward called Rajo with the proposal, Rajo was enthusiastic. But Rajo warned Ward that car owners didn't want him anymore. Rajo had been hustling in attempts to get rides for races, but no car owner was willing to take a chance on a washed-up black man, even if he once was the great Rajo Jack. Ward set Rajo up in the best car he could find, a number 5x Offenhauser-powered car owned by Hank Henastead.

Ward and Johnson arranged a ship to pick up cars and spare parts in early January 1954, leaving from San Francisco. The drivers and mechanics would take a flight from Oakland Airport on January 20, 1954.

As soon as the cars were unloaded in Honolulu, there was a hold up on the docks, as the workers had never seen anything like them. Most of the big cars were nothing fancy. There were a couple with Offenhauser engines. But there were also cars powered by a Ford six-cylinder, a couple Mercurys, a couple overhead-valve-conversion Fords with Hal heads, a couple GMCs, and even a Studebaker. Some of the cars were built in the 1930s.

Johnson spent about $2,700 to ship the cars to Hawaii and estimated his outlay to put on the races at $15,000. He set the race dates for January 22 and 29 at Honolulu Stadium. To make the venture work financially, the races would need to draw at least ten thousand fans to Honolulu Stadium for each race.

Johnson also told people he had lined up a third race to be held on the island of Maui in the week between, but it would require a venue. The only suitable track in Maui was at the Kahulu Fairgrounds, but the mile dirt track shut down in 1953. The chances of it reopening for one race were slim, and the cost of ferrying the menagerie to Maui would have been prohibitive.

Alan Ward did everything he could to bring publicity to the races. Not only did the Honolulu newspapers and other publications around Hawaii carry stories about the races, Ward also succeeded in reaching the mainland.

One of the media outlets Ward reached was the new *Jet* magazine, considered a novelty publication intended for a black audience that was slowly catching on in the mainland. In Ward's prose, Rajo Jack was a legend in the racing world. Ward wrote Rajo had been one of the greatest drivers in the United States in the 1930s. He claimed Rajo had competed in several Midwestern races the year before—it had been three years earlier—but didn't note Rajo's performance. And Rajo's longevity was compared to that of baseball great Satchel Paige. He also called Rajo sixty years old, despite him being forty-eight.

Ward's advance publicity painted Rajo as one of the greatest drivers ever to get in a race car. But it didn't mention he hadn't been competitive in a race car in four years and had a hard time finishing races. The people of Hawaii didn't know any better.

The flight to Hawaii was the first time Rajo, and most of the drivers, had been on an airplane. That experience made the operation worthwhile for Rajo. The island of Oahu was a paradise like nothing he had ever experienced. Rajo had seen many sandy beaches in his time, but Hawaii was more than he had hoped.

A paying crowd of 7,476 piled into Honolulu Stadium, though more than nine thousand watched, as children under age six were allowed in for free. Waiting fans flocked to Rajo before the race. They only knew what they had read, but Rajo Jack was the most famous race car driver who had ever come to the island of Oahu, and he was a celebrity again.

But in qualifying, Rajo was far off the pace, placing thirteenth out of fifteen cars in 18.5 seconds around the quarter mile. He showed promise in the eight-lap heat race for the six slowest qualifiers, winning easily, but in his next heat, he placed fifth.

By the time the main event started, the track was in terrible condition. There had been significant rain the previous few days, and the dirt rutted horribly as the big cars drove on it. And the track was so narrow it was nearly impossible for big cars to race side by side. There were no crashes in the program because the track was too tacky, and the drivers drove cautiously, worried about tearing up their vehicles with another race on the horizon and few spare parts on hand.

Flaherty was the class of the field in the main event. Few cars finished the race, and Rajo's wasn't one of them.

For a man who spent most of his life running up front in every race, this was a new low. The fans lured to the race with expectations of Rajo being one of the greatest race car drivers on the planet were shocked at his mediocrity.

"We had a tough time getting used to this track," Rajo said. "The wet terrain was troublesome because of the rains, but I know we can put on a better performance once we get the feel of this track."

They didn't.

After the decent crowd in the first Honolulu Stadium race, the January 29 race needed a boost, and the promoters had an ace up their sleeve. Jerry Unser was flown from the deck of a navy ship to Honolulu in time to race.

The January 29 race was split into two twenty-lap main events. But Rajo wasn't any faster. He qualified fourteenth out of fourteen cars and his best result was third in the first heat race. Clyde Palmer won the first main event, but when the second main event—which was shortened to fifteen laps—started, there were only eight cars left running. And Rajo was the one driver among the eight starters who didn't finish.

Johnson lost money promoting the races and would never bring big cars back to Hawaii.

Rajo Jack would never race again. His career ended after thirty-one years with a whimper. This time he made no proclamations and wouldn't admit he was done.

After returning to the mainland, Alan Ward reported to *Jet* magazine that Rajo Jack won two races and placed second in another race. But Ward also reported in the *Oakland Tribune* the races were a financial disaster and the track was ill suited for sprint cars. Rajo loved the attention. Even though he knew the reports were false, it gave him a sense of hope he could once again recapture his past glory.

Hawaii had been a welcome respite from the rest of Rajo Jack's life. Not long after he returned to the mainland, on April 27, 1954, Rajo's divorce from Ruth was granted. She fought the divorce petition for a year, arguing that the house on 114th Street in Watts should be considered community property.

No matter how well Rajo's lawyers, Gladys Towles Root and Joseph M. Rosen, fought, they couldn't get the judge to look past Rajo writing a deed in November 1949 conveying the property to himself and Ruth. After sixteen months of official separation, the divorce was granted.

As was usual in Rajo Jack's life, the names in the case were made up. Rajo was listed as Rajo Jack DeSoto and Ruth was listed as Ruth King DeSoto. When they married in Kansas in 1933, Rajo was using his alias of Jack DeSoto.

Ruth had to finally admit she didn't know who he was when she married him.

16

A NEW DREAM

WITH RAJO JACK, a grand comeback as a race car driver was always imminent.

After World War II, classes like midgets, roadsters, and jalopies saw huge spikes in popularity, and other classes were virtually ignored. But by 1954, stock car racing was booming in popularity, and as Rajo had been one of the top stock car drivers before the war, he wanted another shot at it.

In its infancy, NASCAR promoted its modified class, cars that resembled the bootlegger cars around which the sanctioning body built its legacy. They were faster than the strictly stock cars Bill France wanted to promote. But France foresaw the largest area for growth was in a strictly stock class as it would better appeal to the average person. NASCAR started the Strictly Stock class in 1949 and soon changed the name of the class to Grand National.

Bob Barkheimer got out of driving midgets and became an aspiring promoter in California. In 1954, Barkheimer took over West Coast promotion of NASCAR races and made the Grand National series truly national. Barkheimer's previous experience in stock car racing came in handy.

Barkheimer had raced against Rajo Jack in an ARA stock car race at Oakland Speedway on June 2, 1940. Rajo placed second that day, while Barkheimer finished many laps down.

Rajo saw his opportunity with Barkheimer's promotion. He was missing one thing to make stock car racing work for him again: a race car. So, he hustled.

The problem was Rajo didn't know any owners of modern stock cars. These stock cars were unlike the Citroens and Ford trucks Rajo raced in the 1930s and 1940s. Those cars had been truly stock, except for a few items like fenders and headlights being removed. These stock cars were enhanced with the highest-powered engines available from the factory, roll cages, stronger wheels, and stiffer springs. But Rajo figured his best chance of finding a stock car to race was to be *seen*. Rajo's name still held weight in racing, especially in California.

NASCAR held a race for its Grand National Series on May 30, 1954, at Carrell Speedway in Gardena—the swan song for the track. The State of California was building a new freeway and decided it needed to go through the track's property. J. C. Agajanian returned to promote the race, as he had done from 1947 to 1950. Agajanian promoted the May 30 event as the "Poor Man's Indianapolis," making it a five-hundred-lap race on the half-mile dirt track, complete with thirty-three starters.

Rajo put on white pants and a white shirt, as was custom for pit men, and talked his way into a pit pass, claiming he knew the promoter, which was the truth; he had known Agajanian for decades. Many people at the track recognized him as he entered the pits.

"He was pretty iconic up and down California," said Ken Clapp, then a fifteen-year-old boy attending the race for his birthday present.

At the end of the marathon, four-and-a-half-hour race, which John Soares won, Rajo believed he had talked one of the lesser car owners into fielding a stock car for him. Rajo Jack thought he was going to get a chance.

The race Rajo had his eye on was a NASCAR Grand National race at the Bay Meadows Racetrack—which primarily was a track for horse racing—in San Mateo. Bob Barkheimer was promoting a 250-lap race on the mile dirt oval. Rajo filed an entry for the race with a 1953 Lincoln. Barkheimer played up Rajo's name as an entrant for the race. Rajo Jack still held more weight in California than top NASCAR drivers like Bill Amick, Dick Rathman, Lee Petty, Herb Thomas, Lloyd Dane, Marvin

Panch, and Buck Baker, all of whom would be racing at Bay Meadows. This wasn't some small race like at Carrell Speedway. It was important enough that Bill France decided he needed to be in San Mateo.

But the person who never arrived was Rajo Jack. It's possible that the car Rajo planned to race wasn't ready or wasn't as secure of a ride as he figured, but whatever kept him from the track that day prevented Rajo from being the first black man to race in a NASCAR race.

Rajo Jack was still so well known in 1954 that twenty-five-year-old Hershel McGriff, who led all 250 laps from the pole position to win his first NASCAR race, was disappointed Rajo never arrived.

On May 25, 1955, the Second District Court of California upheld the lower court's ruling that Rajo's house and property were joint tenancy and not community property. To keep his house, Rajo was ordered to pay Ruth a hundred dollars for her share, far less than she had spent. He was in such poor financial shape he had to borrow the money to pay her.

———————

Rajo relentlessly hustled in his attempt to restart his driving career.

He knew a person who had purchased a 1952 Ford and wanted to build it into a race car. Rajo optimistically entered a two-hundred-lap race for a new NASCAR series dubbed the Pacific Coast Late Model Series at Gardena Stadium, to be held May 29, 1955. In the press, Rajo was billed as fifty-seven years old—he was fifty at the time—and a headliner of western auto racing in days past. Rajo showed up for the race; the 1952 Ford never did.

Rajo was the first black driver to enter a NASCAR race, but the NASCAR color barrier wasn't broken until 1955 at Bay Meadows—another race promoted by Barkheimer—when Elias Bowie, who made his money operating taxi cabs and buses, placed twenty-third at the July 31 race in a 1953 Cadillac.

Shortly after World War II, Rajo had taken on an apprentice in Art George, the white driver and transplant from Washington against whom Rajo had raced a few times. The rest of the racing world gave

Rajo Jack stands over a race car with a Rajo head. *Kem Robertson Collection*

up on George after a 1949 crash at Portland Speedway that killed Indy 500 veteran Les Anderson and left George with serious shoulder injuries. George showed promise as a driver and Rajo let him drive his race cars on multiple occasions. George brought a sixteen-year-old kid, Herb Spivey, to Rajo's house to help on multiple projects. Spivey was awestruck as he had read about the legendary Rajo Jack most of his life, but Rajo treated the kid as a peer.

"I never heard him swear," Spivey said. "It was mostly 'Pick up that' or 'Do this or do something else.' I'm sure I gave him lots of opportunities."

After the death of his first wife, Mamie, Eddie "Rochester" Anderson put his personal life back together and by 1955 was dating a beautiful woman named Eva Simon.

Anderson's desire to be a pioneer in the Indianapolis 500 had not diminished. He and Rajo hatched a new plan to reach Indy: Anderson would put up money, George would drive, famed champ-car and

midget-car builder Frank Kurtis would make a new chassis, and Ed
Winfield would build a supercharged engine like the Novi V-8 he had
helped design. Rajo would be the chief mechanic. The brain trust of
some of the finest minds and craftsmen in auto racing were determined
to make a concerted effort at the 1957 Indy 500.

Rajo finally would have had a legitimate chance at getting into Indianapolis this time. The American Automobile Association pulled out of
racing at the end of the 1955 season after multiple tragedies, including
the death of Bill Vukovich (against whom Rajo had raced) and a crash
at the 24 Hours of Le Mans race that killed eighty-three spectators. A
new sanctioning body called the United States Auto Club, headed by
Indianapolis Motor Speedway owner Tony Hulman, had been formed to
take its place. Some former AAA officials worked for the new organization, but it was more progressive and the thought of a black car owner
at the Indy 500—or a black driver—wasn't out of the question.

Rajo was working on a ranch in Bakersfield, but he was also still working
as a junk dealer out of his house in Los Angeles. Rajo's brother Warren
was living in the Bay Area, and the two grew close—more so than Rajo
had been with any other member of his family. Rajo got Warren started
as a junk dealer, and they would make long trips in Rajo's truck to pick
up antiques from all over California and take them home to sell. Warren's
injuries from World War II limited his career options, and he took to
the profession.

Since his struggles in the Great Depression, Rajo constantly squir-
reled away anything that looked like he might eventually be able to use.
He was reluctant to get rid of anything; it was hard to tell which bits of
junk in his possession were new and what was his old stuff.

On February 27, 1956, Rajo and Warren were on a trip in Rajo's truck,
headed north from Los Angeles with a load of antiques. While passing
through Inyokern at about one o'clock in the afternoon, Rajo felt a stabbing
pain in his chest. He wrestled his truck to the side of the road. Recogniz-
ing something was seriously wrong, Warren moved his brother into the

passenger's seat and sped to nearby Ridgecrest Hospital. By the time they arrived, Rajo Jack was dead. He was fifty years old.

At the hospital, Warren signed the death certificate as the family member. It would have been confusing for Warren to sign the death certificate as Warren Gatson, so he signed "Warren Jack."

At the time, obituaries were reserved solely for famous people. Rajo Jack's obituary appeared in the *Los Angeles Times*; he was called "Roger Jack Desota," and it stated he first gained fame racing at Legion Ascot Speedway.

One thing was correct: "He drove in hundreds of sprint car and stock car races around the country. He never accomplished his one big ambition, to drive in an Indianapolis 500-mile classic."

Rajo Jack's funeral was held March 5 at South Los Angeles Mortuary and was packed. Rajo was buried at Lincoln Memorial Park in Carson, California. As was often the case in his life, his gravestone was a mix of fact and fiction, reading: "In memory of Noal Gatson Famous Race Driver 'Rajo' Jack DeSoto. 1898-1956."

Ed Winfield was named the executor of his estate. Most furniture in Rajo's house, such as couches and chairs purportedly from Italy, his trophies, and his collection of toy cars went with Warren and ended up at his house in Berkeley. Winfield kept some of Rajo's machine equipment. What was left of Rajo's two race cars—the number 33 car was in pieces, and the 183-inch Francis Quinn Miller engine was mostly intact—was given to Art George. Winfield had to sell or give away a vast number of parts Rajo had collected over the years. Rajo's final racing helmet ended up with Herb Spivey, who hung onto it for sixty years. Rajo's broken goggles, from when he lost his left eye in 1939, were given to Herman Giles.

There are few physical traces of Rajo Jack left.

Epilogue

RAJO JACK AS
A WORK OF ART

SALVATORE SCARPITTA ARRIVED AT THE DESK of his New York art studio one day in 1964 and found a picture of an old big car lying on it. Scarpitta was intrigued. He recognized the name on the car. As he closely studied the form of the car, an idea grew. Could he make a race car into art? He started with a huge block of wood and began to carve a full-size replica.

Scarpitta was born in New York in 1919, but his family moved to Los Angeles when he was an infant. As a teenager Scarpitta was transfixed watching races at Legion Ascot Speedway. He frequently pestered neighbor Wilbur Shaw, the three-time Indy 500 winner, and idolized that generation of racers. Scarpitta found work painting numbers on racing cars while still in high school. But six months after Legion Ascot closed in 1936, Scarpitta left for Italy to attend art college at the Royal Academy.

When Italy entered World War II on June 6, 1940, Scarpitta was stuck. He fled to Romania before returning to Rome, where he was arrested and sent to an internment camp. He escaped the camp into the Apennine Mountains and lived as a refugee for nearly a year. He escaped with a group of seventy-eight people and immediately enlisted in the US Navy. With his fluency in Italian, Scarpitta was given the job of interpreter. Scarpitta became attached to the Allied Monuments, Fine Arts, and Archives program, which was tasked with locating and preserving art stolen by Nazis.

After World War II, Scarpitta studied at the American Academy in Rome, working primarily on two-dimensional canvases and three-dimensional sculptures featuring found items. By the time Scarpitta returned to the United States, he had developed a unique style. But he never got racing out of his system.

Scarpitta went to every dirt track race he could. At Langhorne Speedway in Pennsylvania, Scarpitta witnessed the fatal crash of driver Bobby Marvin and after the race, gathered pieces of the destroyed car and made a painting from them.

When the photo of the big car landed on Scarpitta's desk, he studied it intently. It was Rajo Jack's big car from his disastrous 1938 season with number 1 on its tail tank and "The Rajo Jack Special" on its flanks. Scarpitta never learned who placed the photo on his desk, and it wasn't of great quality. The beat-up car in the photo made the sculpture more challenging, but Scarpitta was determined to make it realistic. Scarpitta used some real items, such as wheels, but also made do with found items like a motion picture reel, which he modified into a steering wheel. Scarpitta painted on the sculpture car's flank what would become the title for the piece, *The Rajo Jack Special*, just as he had painted the lettering onto race cars in his youth. The car became the first in a series of seven race car sculptures Scarpitta created.

The Rajo Jack Special was Scarpitta's prized piece. Scarpitta went on tours with it around the world. At a 1979 exhibition in Portland, sixty years after Rajo Jack first arrived in the city, Scarpitta—then an owner of sprint cars competing with the vaunted Pennsylvania Posse—said he wanted to recreate "the magic of the man" and described Rajo as the first professional, black racing driver ever to win a national championship.

"This man was so eloquent in his situation, considering the history of the United States," Scarpitta said.

The Rajo Jack Special was last sold for the equivalent of about $100,000, more money than Rajo Jack made in his entire racing career. It resided in storage in the Civic Gallery of Modern and Contemporary Art in Turin, Italy, as of 2019.

In the years after his death, the legend of Rajo Jack grew. He spun so many stories in his lifetime, people who thought they knew him well didn't realize until much later they barely scratched the surface.

People wondered if he really was Dewey Gatson. He had been known as Jack DeSoto, Roger Jack Desota, Roger Jack Desoto, Rajah Ramascus, John DeSoto, Jack Sota, Rajo Jacks, Rajo Jock, Rajo-Jack, Rago Jack, Rajo Jack Miller, Raja Jack, Dewey Gadson, Rajo Jackwn, Rajah Jack, Noal Gatson, Rogo Jack, Roger Jack, Rajah del Ramascus, Raj del Ramascus, Raja del Ramascus, and Roger Ramascus.

And the stories of his driving ability as a race car driver grew with each passing generation.

A group called the Black American Racers Association was formed in 1973 to promote black race car drivers. Among the founders was NASCAR driver Wendell Scott—the first black man to win a NASCAR race—and drag racer and car owner Leonard W. Miller. The organization built a program around driver Benny Scott, the son of Rajo's former White Sox Speedway recruit and competitor, "Bullet" Bill Scott. One of the sponsors of the team was oil company STP, whose CEO, Andy Granatelli, had tried to put together an Indy 500 effort with Rajo.

The BARA held a convention in 1976 to honor the accomplishments of black drivers. The organization gave an award to a black driver who had significant success in racing and named it the Rajo Jack DeSoto Memorial Award, sponsored by STP. When Miller approached STP executives to sponsor the award in Rajo Jack's name, they told him, "We know about Rajo Jack," and quickly gave money for it. The ceremony featured entertainers and athletes like comedian Bill Cosby, football player O. J. Simpson, and singer James Brown. The first—and last—Rajo Jack DeSoto Memorial Award was given to drag racer Malcolm Durham of Maryland.

It was a Californian who eventually broke the color barrier at the Indianapolis 500: Willy T. Ribbs, from San Jose. With an effort largely funded by Cosby—much in the same manner entertainer Eddie Anderson tried to fund Rajo's efforts—in 1991 Ribbs became the first black driver to qualify for the Indy 500. He placed thirty-second of thirty-three. Joie Ray was a constant presence at the Indianapolis Motor Speedway while Ribbs was making history.

In 2002 Leonard Miller's late model, driven by black driver Shanta Rhodes, had "Salute to Rajo Jack" on its hood at Concord Speedway in

North Carolina. The car was taken to NASCAR tracks like Charlotte Motor Speedway and Michigan Speedway and used as a show car.

The 2003 ESPN documentary *The Forgotten Race* highlighted the accomplishments of black race car drivers, but the shortest segment was about Rajo Jack. Few details of his life were reported, and most were incorrect. His first name was repeatedly mispronounced "Ray-Joe," like Joe Jagersberger's products.

In 2017, Freewheelers and Company of Japan produced a line of work shirts bearing "Rajo Jack California" and created some with a picture of his first race car from 1923. The shirts were priced at 40,000 and 8,000 yen (about $400 and $80 in US dollars), more than Rajo won for most races.

When the West Coast Stock Car Hall of Fame was formed in 2002, it included J. C. Agajanian, Charlie Curryer, Hershel McGriff, Troy Ruttman, Ken Clapp, and Bob Barkheimer in its inaugural class of inductees. In its second class of inductees was Rajo Jack.

There were no living members of the Gatson family on hand for the Hall of Fame ceremony. Gerald Gatson died in 1970 in Fort Worth, Texas, after being shot following an argument outside an acquaintance's house. Warren Gatson died in 1976 at the veteran's hospital in Martinez, California, from cirrhosis of the liver. Geneva Gatson died in Kern County, not far from where Rajo died, on June 15, 1995. None of the Gatson siblings had children.

The restored number 18 big car Rajo raced to the co-victory at Oakland Speedway in 1939 for Gil Pearson was put up for sale in 2019 for $550,000.

There was one place Rajo Jack belonged most: the National Sprint Car Hall of Fame. From the first class of inductees into the National Sprint Car Hall of Fame in 1990, many of Rajo's contemporaries and friends were inducted each year. And the men who kept Rajo Jack and all black men out of the Indianapolis 500, like Art Pillsbury and Eddie Rickenbacker, were inducted. But Rajo remained excluded—that is, until Rajo's former competitor Don Radbruch championed his cause.

Radbruch raced in the ARA in 1950 and 1951 and later became a notable historian and author on racing history. In Radbruch's 2004

Rajo Jack in his trademark Rajo Jack California driving uniform and Gilmore Lion helmet. *Podurgiel Collection*

book *Dirt Track Auto Racing 1919–1941: A Pictorial History*, he included a section about Rajo Jack. A voter for the National Sprint Car Hall of Fame, Radbruch took up the cause of Rajo's induction.

"Perhaps some prejudice still exists—for some reason, Rajo Jack is not in the National Sprint Car Hall of Fame where he belongs," Radbruch wrote.

In 2007 Rajo Jack was inducted into the eighteenth class of the National Sprint Car Hall of Fame.

RAJO JACK'S WINS

March 25, 1934, Silvergate Speedway (San Diego), 35 laps, big car
August 26, 1934, Silvergate Speedway, 50 laps, big car
September 23, 1934, Silvergate Speedway, 200 laps, stock car
December 23, 1934, Silvergate Speedway, 19 laps, big car
March 17, 1935, San Jose Speedway, 100 laps, big car
June 23, 1935, Valley Speedway (Goshen, CA), 30 laps, big car
July 29, 1935, Flagstaff Fairgrounds (Flagstaff, AZ), big car
February 9, 1936, White Sox Speedway (Los Angeles), 10 laps, midget
March 29, 1936, Silvergate Speedway, 25 laps, big car
August 2, 1936, Flagstaff Fairgrounds, big car
October 4, 1936, Southern Speedway (Los Angeles), 40 laps, big car
October 25, 1936, Los Angeles Speedway (Mines Field), 200 laps, stock car
April 18, 1937, Southgate Speedway (Los Angeles), 100 laps, big car
May 16, 1937, Clovis Race Speedway (Fresno, CA), 60 laps, big car
May 30, 1937, Oakland Speedway, 300 laps, stock car, Ford Sedan Delivery
June 13, 1937, Oakland Speedway (1/2-mile), 50 laps, big car
August 1, 1937, Southern Speedway, 40 laps, big car
September 6, 1937, San Jose Speedway, 100 laps, big car
February 12, 1939, Southern Ascot Speedway (Los Angeles), 60 laps, big car
September 24, 1939, Oakland Speedway, 500 laps, big car, Gil Pearson
    Miller (co-winner with Tex Peterson)
October 1, 1939, Southern Ascot Speedway, 300 laps, stock car, Citroen

December 3, 1939, Southern Ascot Speedway, 200 laps, big car
March 10, 1940, Madera Speedway (Madera, CA), 25 laps, big car
April 14, 1940, Southern Ascot Speedway, 50 laps, big car
June 16, 1940, Southern Ascot Speedway, 250 laps, stock car, Citroen
June 21, 1940, Southern Ascot Speedway, 40 laps, big car
June 23, 1940, Valley Speedway (Tulare, CA), 30 laps, big car
August 24, 1941, Southern Ascot Speedway, 100 laps, big car
May 12, 1950, Shasta Speedway (Anderson, CA), big car
May 30, 1950, Calistoga Speedway (Calistoga, CA), 15 laps, big car
August 13, 1950, Plumas County Fair (Quincy, CA), 15 laps, big car

ACKNOWLEDGMENTS

A DECADE OR SO AGO I read in a magazine about how a professor of African American literature (as best I remember) at a university in the Midwest was soliciting information for a book he was working on about Rajo Jack. I was ecstatic. I was going to be the first person in line to purchase a copy. But it never happened.

This was a project I didn't intend to write, but I couldn't let the story of Rajo Jack go untold. Undertaking a biography of someone who died sixty years before I dug up one word of research posed challenges. Finding information about incidents that happened a hundred years ago was tedious, but I was determined to tell the life of Rajo Jack as thoroughly as possible. I did everything in my power to be historically accurate in bringing his life to a generation that has likely never heard of him. There were sources with information that conflicted with other sources, and others only provided enough information to make educated guesses. Even with my extensive research, if there are any errors in this book, they are mine and mine alone.

When my father, Jack Poehler, died in 2016, he left behind an enormous collection of books and magazines. His collection became the starting point for my research into the life of Rajo Jack. I didn't write this book for him, but I know he would have been the first to buy a copy.

The rest of my family played huge roles in producing this book. My mother, Marcia Poehler, not only made sure her son who grew up wanting nothing more than to play in the dirt learned how to read and spell, but also was a sounding board for this project. My aunt, Patience Jackson, offered constant encouragement and advice. My sisters, Margaret Poehler and Laura Caulfield, nieces Maya Caulfield and Eva Caulfield, and cousin David Routzon Jr. all made valuable contributions. I must thank Fred and Joan Mickelson for allowing me a venue to turn this from a story about a dead race car driver into something of which I am proud.

Tom Motter told me that at some time every writer of auto racing history wanted to write something on Rajo Jack. I understand why they did, and I understand why no one before accomplished it. I wrote this book and did my own research, but I had much help from those in the racing community including Motter, Don Radbruch, Dennis Mattish, Stan Vermeil, Dick Vermeil (who provided encouragement when I needed it most), Kem Robertson, J. C. Agajanian Jr., Ken Clapp, Bryan Ellis, Hershel McGriff, Chick Lasteri, Bill Lasteri, Gordon White, Brian Pratt, George Hespe and Hal Schlegel of the Golden Wheels Fraternity, Kevin Triplett, the Racing History group on Yahoo, Mike O'Leary, Josh Ashby and Jenny Ambrose at International Motor Racing Research Center, Charlie Yapp, Kelly Petillo Jr., Eddie Anderson Jr., Don Edmunds, Ed Iskenderian, Leonard W. Miller, Jim Miller, Herb Spivey, Freddy Chaparro, and Bobby Unser.

I also must thank Joy Cornin and her family for their help. The great niece of Warren Gatson is the closest living relative of Rajo Jack, and I learned much about the family through her.

Many of my current and former coworkers helped me in many ways, from offering encouragement to facilitating my desire to write this. I must thank Chasity (McCarthy) Colipano, Pete Martini, Gary Horowitz, Bill Kelm, Dick Hughes, and Dana Haynes for their support. When I first started writing about racing, Jerry F. Boone was my competition and mentor and taught me more than he will ever know. I also must thank Robert O'Neill for the motivation, as well as the brilliant legal minds of David Price, Ron Cox, and Mike Shank for their expertise. But it was a Laura Gibson concert that inspired me to write a book.

Being from a family of librarians, I felt comfortable spending many hours in libraries researching this project in Washington, Oregon,

California, and Texas—and many more hours in libraries writing it. Many kindly librarians took pity on me and went out of their way to offer their assistance. In particular, I thank Rebecca Gabert of the Salem Public Library.

My agent, Barbara Collins Rosenberg, was critical in finding a home for this book and provided invaluable encouragement and advice to a neophyte author like me who knew nothing of the book publishing world. My editor at Chicago Review Press, Jerome Pohlen, believed in the project and taught me along the way, and editor Ben Krapohl's keen eyes were instrumental in helping make it a clean work that holds together.

NOTES

Introduction

The kid, large for his age: "Troy Ruttman," Hall of Fame Inductees, 1993, National Sprint Car Hall of Fame & Museum, https://www.sprintcarhof.com/pages/hall-of-fame.aspx.

All the kid knew: Troy Ruttman and Bob Shafer, "Pop 'n' Me," *Speed Age*, May 1952, 18–19.

He got his first view: Urb Stair, *Auto Racing Memories: Stories and Pictures of Racing in the 1930s and 1940s* (Whittier, CA: Kendall Buck & Co., 2001), 75.

The infield of the track: Tom Motter, interview with author, October 8, 2018.

The track appropriated the name: John Lucero, *Legion Ascot Speedway 1920s–1930s: Speed . . . Victory . . . Thrills . . . Spills* (Downey, CA: Orecue, 1982), 164–165.

Rajo cut an imposing figure: Don Radbruch, *Dirt Track Auto Racing, 1919–1941: A Pictorial History* (Jefferson, NC: McFarland & Company, 2004), 50–53.

Indy was a grand: Allan E. Brown, *The History of America's Speedways Past & Present*, 4th ed. (Comstock Park, MI: America's Speedway, 2017), 28.

The racing elite did not: Floyd Clymer, *AAA Official Record Book* (Los Angeles: Floyd Clymer, 1950), 5.

"There were a few": Ruttman and Shafer, "Pop 'n' Me," 19.

Chapter 1: Longing for the Road

When the Emancipation Proclamation: Henry Louis Gates Jr., "What Is Juneteenth?" *Root*, https://www.pbs.org/wnet/african-americans-many-rivers-to-cross/history/what-is-juneteenth/.

The Gaston family rose to prominence: "Col. Robert Kirkpatrick Gaston," *Chronicles of Smith County, Texas*, 5:9.

A young girl named Quilla: Records of the Railroad Retirement Board, Record Group 184, "U.S., Railroad Retirement Pension Index, 1934–1987," National Archives at Atlanta, Ancestry.com, https://www.ancestry.com, 2017.

When Noah and his mother: United States Census, 1910, Tyler (Ward 4), Smith County, Texas, T624, roll 1589, sheet 9A, ED 68, family 192, FamilySearch, https://www.familysearch.org (June 14, 2016).

In the late 1890s: Rodney Lamar Atkins and Endia Robertson Gregory, *Encyclopedia of African American Rural Life in Smith County, 1870–1970* (Tyler, TX: Rodney Lamar Atkins, 2015), 12.

Noah had first met Mattie: Smith County Clerk's Office, *Smith County Marriage Records*, The Book Series ML, 12:179.

Though at the time the Ku Klux Klan: Phil Latham, "The day the Klan came to deep East Texas," *Longview News-Journal*, September 6, 2017, https://www.news-journal.com/opinion/latham-the-day-the-klan-came-to-deep-east-texas/article_f4ca2d7c-d767-5762-a8df-e9144dea49b7.html.

Tyler was the main hub: "St. Louis Southwestern Railway, 1877–1996: The History," Arkansas Railroad Museum, accessed September 24, 2019, http://arkansasrailroadmuseum.org/CBhistory/CBmain.htm#St.%20Louis%20Southwestern%20Railway.

Mattie's job with: *Texas, Death Certificates, 1903–1982*, Texas Department of State Health Services, microfilm, Genealogy Section, Dallas Public Library.

Her name was Frances Scott: Smith County Clerk's Office, *Smith County Marriage Records*, The Book Series ML, 16:201.

Ten months later: United States Census, 1910, T624, roll 1589, sheet 9A, ED 68, family 192.

In the summer of 1907: Donald W. Whisenhunt, *A Chronological History of Smith County* (Tyler, TX: Smith County Historical Society, 1983), 54.

In 1909 Jim Hodge of Tyler: "Lynched Wrong Person," *Arkansas Democrat* (Little Rock, AR), May 3, 1909.

A fellow Texan: Geoffrey C. Ward, *Unforgivable Blackness: The Rise and Fall of Jack Johnson* (New York: Vintage Books, 2006), 238–239.

Barney Oldfield, a cigar: "Berna Eli 'Barney' Oldfield," Hall of Fame Inductees, 1990, National Sprint Car Hall of Fame & Museum, https://www.sprintcarhof.com/pages/hall-of-fame.aspx.

As soon as Johnson: William F. Nalon, *Barney Oldfield: The Life and Times of America's Legendary Speed King*, rev. ed. (Carpinteria, CA: Brown Fox Books, 2002), 155, 204–207.

The American Automobile Association: Rick Knott, "The Jack Johnson v. Barney Oldfield Match Race of 1910; What it says about race in America," Free Library, accessed December 15, 2018, https://www.thefreelibrary.com/The+Jack+Johnson+v.+Barney+Oldfield+match+race+of+1910%3b+What+it+says. . .-a0128705135.

"Of course the contest board": "Race Fake Announced For Publicity Purposes," *Horseless Age*, October 5, 1910.

"You are in error when": Michael L. Berger, "The Great White Hope on Wheels," *Michigan Quarterly Review* 19, no. 4: 479.

"I raced Jack Johnson": "Johnson a Poor Racer," *Wichita Daily Eagle*, October 28, 1910.

Oldfield stuck his neck out: "But Why Bother Suspending Him?" *Buffalo Commercial*, December 27, 1910.

At the time, the five-year-old: United States Census, 1930, Tyler (Ward 4), Smith County, Texas, T626, roll 2390, sheet 1B, ED 13, family 32, FamilySearch, https://www.familysearch.org (November 27, 2018).

Frances Gatson lived in: Larry L. Ball Jr., "Rajo Jack," Hall of Fame Inductees, 2007, National Sprint Car Hall of Fame & Museum, https://www.sprintcarhof.com/pages/hall-of-fame.aspx.

There was a mysterious man: M. B. Marcell, *A Voice from the Grave* (Portland, OR: M. B. Marcell, 1923).

Dewey's family grew: United States Census, 1930, T626, roll 2390, sheet 1B, ED 13, family 32.

Chapter 2: Becoming Rajo Jack

Marcell obtained: "Diploma Sales Charged," *Morning Oregonian* (Portland), November 15, 1924.

Oregon in 1920: Kirk Johnson, "Portland Killings Dredge Up Legacy of Racist Laws in Oregon," *New York Times*, June 4, 2017.

In the 1920 census: *Population of the United States: Census of 1920, by States, Counties, Cities, Towns, Boroughs, and Villages* (Chicago: Rand McNally, 1924), 841.

At the Marcell property: Ball, "Rajo Jack," https://www.sprintcarhof.com/pages/hall-of-fame.aspx.

In early October: "12 Dirt Track Stars in 7 Events This Afternoon." *Morning Oregonian* (Portland), October 4, 1920.

To sanction the races: Addison Bennett, "Wet Track Delays Races at Gresham," *Morning Oregonian* (Portland), October 6, 1920.

J. Alex Sloan and Will Pickens: "J. Alex Sloan," Hall of Fame Inductees, 1990, National Sprint Car Hall of Fame & Museum, https://www.sprintcarhof.com/pages/hall-of-fame.aspx.

Born in Weiner Neustadt, Austria: Kem Robertson, "Joe Jagersberger," Hall of Fame Inductees, 2007, National Sprint Car Hall of Fame & Museum, https://www.sprintcarhof.com/pages/hall-of-fame.aspx.

Marcell had his assignment: Radbruch, *Dirt Track Auto Racing,* 50.

The Tacoma Speedway: "Races at Tacoma Assured," *Morning Oregonian* (Portland), March 4, 1922.

The drive from Portland: "Route to Tacoma Speedway Logged," *Morning Oregonian* (Portland), July 2, 1922.

Walking to the grandstand: "Murphy Is Victor in Tacoma Races," *Morning Oregonian* (Portland), July 5, 1922.

It took time and consolation: "Pilots and Racing Cars Gather for Big Legion Speed Matinee," *Vancouver (WA) Columbian*, May 18, 1923.

Eddie Rickenbacker was born: Edward V. Rickenbacker, *Rickenbacker: An Autobiography* (Englewood Cliffs, NJ: Prentice-Hall, 1967), 182.

As June 24, 1923, dawned: "Bridge Tolls Of $1952.85 Break Record," *Vancouver (WA) Columbian*, May 21, 1923.

In hot laps: "Crowd of 7500 At Motor Races Here," *Columbian* (Vancouver, WA), June 24, 1923.

Promoting a AAA-sanctioned race: Brown, *America's Speedways Past & Present*, 48–49.

And Rajo's position: "Mineral Vendors Clash," *Morning Oregonian* (Portland), August 12, 1923.

In 1924 Marcel pled guilty: "Miracle Man Is Fined," *Morning Oregonian* (Portland), September 6, 1924.

California was a hotbed of racing: Harold Osmer, *Where They Raced* (Los Angeles: Harold L. Osmer Publishing, 1996), 31.

When Rajo Jack found out: "Thirty Pilots Entered," *Los Angeles Times*, June 29, 1924.

It was the last time Rajo: Radbruch, *Dirt Track Auto Racing*, 50.

It was in California: Shav Glick, "The Inside Track; Hot Corner," *Los Angeles Times*, April 29, 2002.

Neither Winfield: "Racing Man Missing," *Los Angeles Times*, August 3, 1924.

The race under AAA sanction: Paul Lowry, "New Culver City Speedway to Be More Spectacular than Beverly," *Los Angeles Times*, October 12, 1924.

Pillsbury was a native: "Art Pillsbury," Hall of Fame Inductees, 1992, National Sprint Car Hall of Fame & Museum, https://www.sprintcarhof.com/pages/hall-of-fame.aspx.

When his gambling in Alaska: Freddy Chaparro, interview with author, September 3, 2018.

After that track: Chris Economacki and Dave Argabright, *Let 'Em All Go! The Story of Auto Racing by the Man Who Was There* (Westfield, IN: Books by Dave Argabright, 2006), 113.

Marcell refused to let his medical license: "Diploma Sales Charged," *Morning Oregonian* (Portland), November 15, 1924.

Rajo Jack tried to enter: "Auto Races Are Enjoyed," *Morning Oregonian* (Portland), June 1, 1925.

By the summer of 1925: "Bear Fights Physician," *Morning Oregonian* (Portland), November 27, 1925.

Rajo Jack was ecstatic: "Record Broken at Bagley Park," *Clark County Sun* (Vancouver, WA), April 5, 1926.

But he was improving: "Racers Fail to Cut Track Mark," *Columbian* (Vancouver, WA), May 2, 1926.

Francis Quinn was far different: Larry L. Ball Jr., "Francis Quinn," Hall of Fame Inductees, 2006, National Sprint Car Hall of Fame & Museum, https://www.sprintcarhof.com/pages/hall-of-fame .aspx.

Quinn returned to his home state: "Racing Auto Burns at Vancouver Meet," *Morning Oregonian* (Portland), July 19, 1926.

For the next race at Bagley: "Driver Strikes Fence," *Morning Oregonian* (Portland), August 2, 1926.

There were a few outlaw races: "Barney Oldfield Tries Out Hudson," *Morning Oregonian* (Portland), June 5, 1927.

Marcell paid $40,000: "Medicine Circus Travels in REOs," *Morning Oregonian* (Portland), July 1, 1928.

Chapter 3: Taking a Step Back to Move Forward

In 1928 Rajo moved: *San Jose City and Santa Clara County Directory 1929*, "U.S. City Directories, 1822–1995," R. L. Polk & Company, Ancestry.com, www.ancestry.com (2011).

Watts had been annexed: Robert J. Lopez, "Watts," *Los Angeles Times*, July 17, 1994.

Francis Quinn had promising results: Ball, "Francis Quinn," https://www.sprintcarhof.com/pages/hall-of-fame.aspx.

Finding a race car driver: Freddy Chaparro, interview with author, September 3, 2018.

With Legion Ascot Speedway on the schedule: Lucero, *Legion Ascot Speedway*, 94–95.

With Quinn distracted: "Quinn Deserts Lucky Mount," *Los Angeles Times*, December 30, 1930.

But a surprise offer arrived: "Russ Garnant," Hall of Fame Inductees, 1999, National Sprint Car Hall of Fame & Museum, https://www.sprintcarhof.com/pages/hall-of-fame.aspx.

The driver who pestered him most: Larry Ball Jr., "Cavino 'Kelly' Petillo," Hall of Fame Inductees, 2009, National Sprint Car Hall of Fame & Museum, https://www.sprintcarhof.com/pages/hall-of-fame.aspx.

Quinn sold his championship car: "Francis Quinn Gets New Car," *Los Angeles Times*, January 23, 1931.

Quinn purchased a new Miller: Gordon Eliot White, *Offenhauser: The Legendary Racing Engine and the Men Who Built It*, 2nd ed. (St. Paul, MN: Motorbooks International, 2004), 42–44.

Francis Quinn left California: "Five More Qualify for 500-Mile Speedway Race," *Richmond (IN) Item*, May 26, 1931.

There was a major change: William F. Sturm, "19th Annual Speedway Event May Bring New Era in Racing," *Indianapolis News*, May 29, 1931.

"Although I see no hope": Rickenbacker, *Rickenbacker: An Autobiography*, 493.

When May 30, 1931, arrived: Charles Dunkley, "Story of Race Told by AP Correspondent," *Kokomo (IN) Tribune*, May 30, 1931.

For the final race of the 1931 season: "Race Driver Killed in Crash; San Jose Motorist Is Held," *Modesto (CA) News-Herald*, December 14, 1931.

Pillsbury urged prosecutors: "Jury Silent on Racer's Death," *Times* (San Mateo, CA), December 15, 1931.

Quinn had put so much time: "Stapp Drives F. Quinn's Car," *Oakland (CA) Tribune*, December 23, 1931.

Rajo Jack's greatest hope: "Speed Pilots Ready Again for Classic," *Oakland (CA) Tribune*, December 31, 1931.

Chapter 4: The Outlaw Emerges

Getting and maintaining a standing: Russ Catlin, *The Life of Ted Horn: American Racing Champion* (Los Angeles: Floyd Clymer, 1949), 23.

He spent five days: "Crowd Thrilled by Speed Races at Stearns Track," *Wichita Beacon*, August 8, 1932.

After the race, a pretty woman: Rajo Jack DeSoto, Appellant, V. Ruth King DeSoto, Respondent, Civ. No. 20638. California Second Dist., Div. Three, May 25, 1955.

Their courtship was fast: Marriage record for Jack DeSoto and Ruth Grace, August 31, 1932, *Oklahoma County Marriage Index, 1889–1951*, Oklahoma Historical Society, Ancestry.com, https://www .ancestry.com.

When a group including Lee Conti: "Ascot Pilots to Appear on Program Here," *San Diego Union*, January 7, 1933.

After the first race at the new Silvergate Speedway: "Local Races Attract New Drivers; 7-Event Bill Booked for Speedway," *Evening Tribune* (San Diego), January 7, 1933.

For the race at Silvergate: "Premier Race Drivers of West to Vie for Honors Today," *San Diego Union*, January 8, 1933.

Everett Balmer drove away: "Race Drivers Will Battle for Further Honors Today," *San Diego Union*, January 15, 1933.

After the first few AAA races: *Tyler Texas City Directory 1933*, U.S. City Directories, 1822–1995, John F. Worley Directory Company, Local History/Genealogy Room, Tyler (TX) Public Library.

Charlie Curryer seized: "Charlie Curryer," Hall of Fame Inductees, 1997, National Sprint Car Hall of Fame & Museum, https://www.sprintcarhof.com/pages/hall-of-fame.aspx.

With outlaw racing picking up: Brown, *America's Speedways Past & Present*, 49.

In the first race: Harry Hache, "Silvergate Card Again Dominated by Curley Mills," *Evening Tribune* (San Diego, California), February 12, 1934.

Rajo had little money: John E. Klann, "Rajo Jack Fast and Furious," *Players*, October 1995.

In the next three races: "Round the Outside and to the Front," *San Diego Union*, March 9, 1934.

Rajo found that his work: Harry Hache, "Rajo Jack Wins Feature at Causeway Auto Oval," *Evening Tribune* (San Diego), March 26, 1934.

"He was not a pushy person": Klann, "Rajo Jack Fast and Furious."

A week later at Silvergate: Harry Hache. "Dog Flirts with Winged Death but Remains Unscathed Though Hit by Racing Car at Speedway," *Evening Tribune* (San Diego), April 11, 1934.

Rajo Jack wasn't embarrassed: Leonard W. Miller, interview with author, August 30, 2018.

Rajo placed second: "Everett Balmer Wins Main Race at Silvergate Track," *San Diego Union*, April 30, 1934.

Rajo's younger brother, Lindsey Gatson: *Texas, Death Certificates, 1903–1982*, Texas Department of State Health Services.

Rajo picked up a different ride: "Outstanding Auto Drivers to Compete at Silvergate," *San Diego Union*, July 1, 1934.

Rajo Jack was off the track: Texas, Death Certificates, 1903–1982, Texas Department of State Health Services.

Instead of returning to California: "Campbell Wins in Automobile Race," *St. Louis Post-Dispatch*, July 30, 1934.

When Rajo returned to Silvergate: Conti, Lee. "Rajo Jack Returns from Eastern Trip," *Coast Auto Racing*, September 1, 1934.

A new driver showed up: Zipp, "Jack Scores Win in Main at Speedway," *Evening Tribune* (San Diego), August 27, 1934.

But the real Barney Oldfield: Nalon, *Barney Oldfield*, 238.

The big car racing at Silvergate: "Record Falls at Flagstaff," *Arizona Republic* (Phoenix), September 4, 1934.

Stock car racing was unheard of: Zipp, "Jack Earns No. 1 Position for Big Race," *Evening Tribune* (San Diego), September 15, 1934.

Most of the twenty drivers: "Rajo Jack Wins Gold Cup Race at Silvergate Track," *San Diego Union*, September 24, 1934.

It wasn't until the big car race: "To Honor Rajo Jack at Speedway Sunday," *Evening Tribune* (San Diego), September 27, 1934.

At the October 14 race: "Oldfield Repeats to Triumph in Silvergate Feature Race," *San Diego Union*, October 15, 1934.

A twenty-seven-year-old man: Zipp, "Cooper Captures Main Auto Test; Thousands See Thrilling Finish," *Evening Tribune* (San Diego), December 3, 1934.

In a cartoon: "Kelly? Floyd? Rajo? You Guess Who It Fits!" *Coast Auto Racing*, September 1, 1934.

A baby-faced driver: Harvey Shapiro, "All Valves Popping for Duke Dinsmore," *Dayton (OH) Daily News*, February 23, 1975.

The December 23 final race: "40-Lap Main to Head Final '34 Race Card," *San Diego Union*, December 27, 1934.

The same day as the Silvergate race: "Kelly Petillo Cruises to Thrilling Victory in 200-Mile Classic," *Los Angeles Times*, December 24, 1934.

"Takio Hirashima, riding mechanic": Bob Ray, "The Sports X-Ray," *Los Angeles Times*, January 3, 1935.

Chapter 5: The Rise to Prominence

Racing with the AAA: Catlin, *Life of Ted Horn*, 222.

After his success at Silvergate Speedway: Brock Yates, *Umbrella Mike: The True Story of the Chicago Gangster Behind the Indy 500* (New York: Thunder's Mouth, 2007), 192.

He loaded up Petillo's Frontenac: Lucero, *Legion Ascot Speedway*, 164–165.

A pair of promoters: "Leverett Wins Race at Colton Sunday," *Coast Auto Racing*, February 15, 1935.

Rajo placed third: "Howard Cox Bests Leverett to Capture Silvergate Main," *San Diego Union*, February 25, 1935.

When San Jose Speedway opened: Dennis Mattish, *History of San Jose Auto Racing 1903–2007*, 2nd ed. (Marceline, MO: Walsworth, 2009), 48–51.

Leverett made Rajo an offer: "10,000 Watch Rajo Jack Win San Jose Race," *San Francisco Chronicle*, March 18, 1935.

And from the start: Bill Feist, "Judges, Pilots Argue 3 Hours over 100-Lap Winner," *San Jose (CA) News,* March 18, 1935.

The reaction to Rajo's win: "Racing Officials Reverse Decision," *San Bernardino (CA) County Sun*, March 18, 1935.

"Rajo Jack, Negro Ace": Bill Feist, "Fans Leave Track in Disgust," *San Jose (CA) News*, March 18, 1935.

When Rajo returned: "Phillips Takes 2nd Straight Headliner at Silvergate Oval," *San Diego Union*, April 1, 1935.

Petillo's results on the track: Ball, "Cavino 'Kelly' Petillo," https://www.sprintcarhof.com/pages /hall-of-fame.aspx.

The month of May: Kelly Petillo Jr., interview with author, December 27, 2017.

Later that afternoon: White, *Offenhauser*, 58–59.

"Just pay attention": Kelly Petillo, "Petillo Gives De Paolo Credit for Race Win," *Los Angeles Times*, May 31, 1935.

Four days after Indy: Joe Custer, "Dinsmore Wins in Auto Races Here; Rajah Jack 2nd," *San Jose (CA) Mercury*, June 3, 1935.

The San Jose promoters: Stan Vermeil, interview with author, November 15, 2016.

San Diego had become a major hub: "Racing Stars to Honor Navy at Speedway," *San Diego Union*, June 14, 1935.

The competition at Silvergate: "Weber Completes Plan for Opening of Silvergate Oval," *San Diego Union*, July 28, 1935.

By late July: "Jack, Cooper Sign for Race," *San Diego Union*, August 7, 1935.

Rajo would have been better served: "Scovell Wins Feature Race of Silvergate Track Card," *San Diego Union*, September 9, 1935.

Weber caught wind of Rajo's argument: "Race Stars to Renew Feuds in 40-Lap Silvergate Main," *San Diego Union*, September 22, 1935.

At another stock car race: "Northerner Captures Weird Silvergate Stock Car Race," *San Diego Union*, October 7, 1935.

In the October 13: "Jensen Wins Speedway Main, but Rose Dominates Program," *San Diego Union*, October 14, 1935.

He raced once more at Goshen: "Mansell Takes Honors at Goshen," *Hanford (CA) Morning Journal*, October 29, 1935.

Chapter 6: The Folly of Negro League Midget Racing

Baseball teams composed solely: Robert Peterson, *Only the Ball Was White: A History of Legendary Black Players and All-Black Professional Teams* (Bexley, OH: Gramercy, 1999), 1–20.

Racing cars was a costly undertaking: Dick Wallen, *Distant Thunder: When Midgets Were Mighty* (Glendale, AZ: Dick Wallen Productions, 2001), 1–8.

The economics of the Depression: Economacki and Argabright, *Let 'Em All Go*, 22.

A baseball stadium: "Speedway Installed at White Sox Park," *Los Angeles Times*, September 5, 1931.

Holding a few exhibition games: "15 Auto Racers Feature Meeting in Los Angeles," *Chicago Defender*, January 27, 1936.

A series of big car races: Todd Gould, *For Gold and Glory: Charlie Wiggins and the African-American Racing Car Circuit* (Bloomington, IN: Indiana University Press, 2002), 33–34.

Neither Rajo Jack: Leonard W. Miller, interview with author, August 30, 2018.

The businessmen involved: Wallen, *Distant Thunder*, 25–26.

And Matlock had something: William F. Sturm, "Arnold Arrives Four Minutes Ahead to Collect Gold, Glory," *Indianapolis News*, May 31, 1930.

The most promising: Leonard W. Miller, interview with author, August 30, 2018.

On January 25: "Gordon, Mechanic Dies," *Oakland (CA) Tribune*, January 27, 1936.

"Automobile racing has outlived": "Automobile Racing Today 'Suicide,' Oldfield Says," *Garrett Clipper*, December 18, 1933.

Glendale American Legion Post 127: Lucero, *Legion Ascot Speedway*, 152.

"I saw Al Gordon and Spider Matlock": Cecilia Rasmussen, "Life—and Death—in Fast Lane at Ascot," *Los Angeles Times*, October 10, 1994.

The person they found was Mel Keneally: "Midget Races at White Sox Park," *Los Angeles Sentinel*, February 6, 1936.

The crowd for the first race: "Rajo Jack Annexes Midget Auto Feature," *Riverside (CA) Daily Press*, February 10, 1936.

Advertising the first race: "Japs, Spanish in Coast Auto Derby," *Chicago Defender*, March 7, 1936.

After a couple rainouts: "Clarence Muse Beats Bill Robinson; It's an Auto Race," *Chicago Defender*, March 14, 1936.

He wrangled a ride: "Jack Captures 25-Lap Battle at Silvergate," *San Diego Union*, March 30, 1936.

Charlie Curryer was always: Tom Motter, *A History of the Oakland Speedway 1931–1941* (Rancho Cordova, CA: Vintage Images, 2002), 62–63.

Curryer played up Rajo Jack: "L.A. Race Ace to Drive Here," *Oakland (CA) Tribune*, April 14, 1936.

"They would turn over in their graves": Klann, "Rajo Jack Fast and Furious."

Working long, hot days: "Police Asked to Catch Balloon in Stratosphere," *Oakland (CA) Tribune*, May 26, 1936.

On race day, Rajo was running: "Ordinary Stock Cars They Go Like Dickens," *San Francisco Chronicle*, June 1, 1936.

Curryer arranged for Rajo: "Negro Auto Ace Signs Up Here," *Seattle Daily Times*, May 27, 1936.

Rajo's next race: Motter, *History of the Oakland Speedway*, 125.

By 1931, boxer Jim Jeffries: "Burbank Speedway to Reopen Sunday," *Los Angeles Times*, June 16, 1933.

The Robson brothers: Norm Bogan, "Hal Robson," Hall of Fame Inductees, 2010, National Sprint Car Hall of Fame & Museum, https://www.sprintcarhof.com/pages/hall-of-fame.aspx.

Alex Podurgiel owned a crummy: Tom Motter, interview with author, October 8, 2018.

The group dug a half-mile: "Speedway Program on Tap Today," *Los Angeles Times*, June 7, 1936.

Rajo's mind was elsewhere: Alan Ward, "17 Drivers to Clash on Speedway Today," *Oakland (CA) Tribune*, June 14, 1936.

A five-eighths-mile dirt oval: Jeff Zurschmeide, *Portland Speedway* (Charleston, SC: Arcadia, 2014), 9.

"Rajo Jack, a colored driver": "Wilburn Annexes Feature Race at Portland Track," *Morning Oregonian* (Portland), June 22, 1936.

Instead of going to Oakland: "Midget Race Pilots Meet," *Los Angeles Times*, June 28, 1936.

followed by a big car race: "High-Powered Racing Cars to Afford Thrills Tomorrow in Show at Capitola Airport," *Santa Cruz Evening News*, July 3, 1936.

a fifty-mile race: "Leading Racers in State Clash Today," *San Bernardino (CA) County Sun*, July 5, 1936.

and another midget race: "Slim Mathis in Midget Win at Southern Oval," *Los Angeles Times*, July 13, 1936.

Then he raced in the July 19: "Rose Wins Goshen Automobile Races," *Fresno (CA) Bee*, July 20, 1936.

Rajo showed up too late: "Crack-Up, New Record Liven Goshen Races," *Tulare (CA) Advance-Register*, July 20, 1936.

Where Rajo did go: "Flagstaff Improves Track for Annual Auto Classic," *Arizona Republic* (Phoenix), July 26, 1936.

He followed that with a: "George Robson Leads Racers," *Los Angeles Times*, August 10, 1936.

A promoter in Yakima: "Racer Escapes Harm When Car Crashes Fence," *Yakima (WA) Herald-Republic*, September 15, 1936.

After months of disagreement: Alan Ward, "Neutral Corner," *Oakland (CA) Tribune*, September 20, 1936.

On September 27, Rajo placed: "Cunningham Wins at South Gate," *Los Angeles Times*, September 28, 1936.

then won the big car: "Rajo Jack Leads South Gate Drivers," *Los Angeles Times*, October 5, 1936.

Chapter 7: From Obscurity to National Champion

The popularity and concentration: Osmer, *Where They Raced*, 1–3.

When the Los Angeles Motordrome: Brown, *America's Speedways Past & Present*, 146.

In 1930 a new airport: Cecillia Rasmussen, "L.A. Then and Now; For Auto Racers and Fans, It Was the Roaring '30s; Dirt-Track Driver Had True Grit, and Some of It Landed on Spectators at Mines Field Near LAX." *Los Angeles Times*, February 26, 2006.

One man saw the potential: "Pickens's Death Recalls Famous Sports Ventures," *Los Angeles Times*, June 21, 1934.

After the success: "Kelly Petillo Cruises to Thrilling Victory in 200-Mile Classic," *Los Angeles Times*, December 24, 1934.

Once Curryer was involved: "Mel Keneally Enters 250-Mile Stock Car Race," *Los Angeles Times*, October 17, 1936.

On the day of the race: "Rain Washes Out Stock Car Classic Today," *Los Angeles Times*, October 18, 1936.

When the drivers first got on track: "Stock Car Race Today Lures Thrill Lovers," *Los Angeles Times*, October 25, 1936.

The number 4 Ford: "Local Race Drivers Will Vie with Famed Speed Demons Here Sunday," *Petaluma (CA) Argus-Courier*, October 25, 1936.

As the twenty-four cars: "Rajo Jack Winner as Crashes Mar Race," *Los Angeles Times*, October 26, 1936.

The track was brutal: "11 Injured in 200-Mile Auto Race on Coast," *St. Louis Post-Dispatch*, October 26, 1936.

And every story noted Rajo Jack: "Negro Pilot Wins Stock Car Event," *Indianapolis Star*, October 26, 1936.

"probably one of the outstanding Negro": "11 Injured in 200-Mile Auto Race on Coast," *St. Louis Post-Dispatch*, October 26, 1936.

And for the first time: "Royal Giants Meet White Kings Sunday," *Los Angeles Sentinel*, October 29, 1936.

Southern Speedway was holding: "Jimmy Wilburn Wins Race Feature," *Los Angeles Times*, November 2, 1936.

Rajo showed up: "Rajo Jack to Be on Hand Sunday for Auto Races," *Los Angeles Times*, November 5, 1936.

And Curryer was putting on: Dick Friendlich, "Midget Racers Steal Show at Oakland Speedway," *San Francisco Chronicle*, November 9, 1936.

He had three weeks: Charles Curtis, "Jimmy Miller Annexes Los Angeles Speedway Race," *Los Angeles Times*, November 30, 1936.

Rajo's car broke: "Baby Cars Top in Auto Grind," *Oakland (CA) Tribune*, December 18, 1936.

Chapter 8: Independence and Reaching a New Height

Harry Eisele became enraptured: Jack Curnow, "By Another Name, Bud Rose of Gasoline Alley Smells Just as Sweet," *Los Angeles Times*, February 25, 1948.

Eisele's friends already called him: Motter, *History of the Oakland Speedway*, 63.

Bud Rose so resembled Clark Gable: "Gable 'Twin' in Race Here," *Des Moines Register*, June 29, 1946.

The manager came to the table: Klann, "Rajo Jack Fast and Furious."

After years of work and planning: "Rajo Jack Races Sunday," *San Francisco Chronicle*, January 8, 1937.

By the time Rajo's new car: "George Robson Wins South Gate Race," *Los Angeles Times*, February 22, 1937.

The one advantage Rajo's car had: Stair, *Auto Racing Memories*, 125.

Rajo had many problems: "Oakland Auto Race Card Is Completed," *San Francisco Chronicle*, March 11, 1937.

Rajo needed a good run: "Rajo Jack Wins Auto Race," *Los Angeles Times*, April 19, 1937.

"I've carried that piece of fur and bone": "Race Entries Close Tonight," *Oakland (CA) Tribune*, April 23, 1937.

And at the April 25 fifty-lapper: Alan Ward, "Bud Rose Wins 50-Lap Race," *Oakland (CA) Tribune*, April 26, 1937.

"I've never heard of such a thing": "Drivers Plan to Use Wives as Mechanics," *Oakland (CA) Tribune*, May 14, 1937.

The other race the same day: "Jack Captures Race at Clovis," *Fresno (CA) Bee*, May 17, 1937.

The rained-out, three-hundred-lap: "Jack Victor in Stock Car Jaunt," *San Francisco Examiner*, May 31, 1937.

"It should be called the Altamont": Alan Ward, "Rajo Jack Wins 300 Mile Speed Test," *Oakland (CA) Tribune*, May 31, 1937.

Rajo longed for the setup: Radbruch, *Dirt Track Auto Racing*, 300.

With the new truck: Joe Scalzo, "Rajo Jack Part III," *Secrets of Speed Society*, October 1999, 34.

But the first race: "Racing Driver Killed at South Gate," *Los Angeles Times*, June 7, 1937.

And then Rajo made a triumphant return: "Jack Captures 50-Lap Race," *Oakland (CA) Tribune*, June 14, 1937.

But the next race at Oakland: Alan Ward, "Race Flop!" *Oakland (CA) Tribune*, June 28, 1937.

Rajo Jack had little experience: "Spider Webb Race Winner," *Los Angeles Times*, July 12, 1937.

With the AAA gone: "Four-Way Speed Duel in Offing," *Los Angeles Times*, July 31, 1937.

At the next race at Southgate: "Jack Takes Auto Race," *Fresno (CA) Bee*, August 2, 1937.

Rajo was running fourth: "Spider Webb Squeezes Way to Victory in Forth-Lap Race," *Los Angeles Times*, August 16, 1937.

The promoters at Flagstaff: "Californian Wins Flagstaff Race," *Arizona Republic* (Phoenix), August 30, 1937.

Rajo desperately wanted his race car: "Hal Robson Race Winner," *Los Angeles Times*, September 6, 1937.

There was a race in San Jose: "Takes Race at San Jose," *Fresno (CA) Bee*, September 7, 1937.

Qualifying for the hundred-lap race: "Rajo Speeds to Victory," *San Francisco Chronicle*, September 7, 1937.

For the main event: Miller, Gilbert S. "San Jose Auto Racing Events Well Attended," *Santa Cruz (CA) Sentinel*, September 7, 1937.

But Rajo had reason to step up: "Hal Robson Triumphs in Fifty-Lap Race," *Los Angeles Times*, October 25, 1937.

Word got out: "Driver Faces Fine Before Sunday Race," *Los Angeles Times*, November 11, 1937.

Southgate had arranged: "George Robson Noses Out Kin in South Gate Race," *Los Angeles Times*, November 15, 1937.

Once his hurt feelings: "George Robson Captures Holiday Sweepstakes," *Los Angeles Times*, December 20, 1937.

Rajo Jack won the championship: Joe Scalzo, "Making His Own Music," *Open Wheel*, November 1994, 57–64.

Chapter 9: Lucky Charms Fail to Deliver

When Rajo Jack first started traveling: "Alan R. Ward, longtime Oakland Tribune sports editor and . . ." UPI Archives, United Press International, originally published November 30, 1982, accessed September 25, 2019, https://www.upi.com/Archives/1982/11/30/Alan-R-Ward-longtime-Oakland-Tribune-sports-editor-and/4484407480400/.

While some southern California: "Spider Webb Takes State Auto Race Championship," *Riverside (CA) Daily Press*, February 14, 1938.

George "Joie" Chitwood was born: "Joie Chitwood (Sr.)," Hall of Fame Inductees, 1993, National Sprint Car Hall of Fame & Museum, https://www.sprintcarhof.com/pages/hall-of-fame.aspx.

A bright spot for all drivers: T. Benson Hoy, "Flying Junkman," *Saturday Evening Post*, April 13, 1940, 27.

Rajo expected a lot: Alan Ward, "Rose Wins 10-Mile Race; Fire, Crash Enliven Events," *Oakland Tribune*, May 9, 1938.

"Polish the trophy": Alan Ward, "Rajo Jack Enters Race," *Oakland (CA) Tribune*, June 1, 1938.

But on Rajo's drive: Alan Ward, "Fred Agabashian Takes 250-Mile Stock Car Race," *Oakland (CA) Tribune*, June 6, 1938.

Rajo's performance improved slightly: "Bud Rose Captures Feature Ascot Auto Race," *Los Angeles Times*, June 20, 1938.

His on-track fortunes: "Rajo Jack Signs to Enter Speedway Test," *San Francisco Chronicle*, August 5, 1938.

Two days later, on August 9: Texas, *Death Certificates, 1903–1982*, Texas Department of State Health Services.

Rajo didn't return: "Rajo Jack Wins Pole Spot for 500-Mile Auto Classic," *Oakland (CA) Tribune*, September 19, 1938.

Rajo's superstitions had grown: Alan Ward, "On Second Thought," *Oakland (CA) Tribune*, September 21, 1938.

When Rajo started on the pole: Alan Ward, "Bud Rose Takes First in 500-Mile Auto Race," *Oakland (CA) Tribune*, September 26, 1938.

In his next race: "Tex Peterson Gold Cup Ascot Speedway Victor," *Riverside (CA) Daily Press*, October 10, 1938.

No one needed to remind: "Hal Robson Victor in Ascot Feature," *Los Angeles Times*, November 28, 1938.

After one race at Southern Ascot: Chick Lasteri, interview with author, March 23, 2017.

J.C. Agajanian was born in California: Ben Foote, "J. C. 'Aggie' Agajanian," Hall of Fame Inductees, 1990, National Sprint Car Hall of Fame & Museum, https://www.sprintcarhof.com/pages/hall-of-fame.aspx.

Rajo Jack's disappointing conclusion: "Peterson Wins Ascot Laurels," *Los Angeles Times*, January 2, 1939.

"The rabbit foot": Alan Ward, "Ray Gardner to Race Here," *Oakland (CA) Tribune*, March 24, 1939.

Rajo never liked racing midgets: "Perry Grimm in Midget Win," *Los Angeles Times*, January 9, 1939.

He was confident he could be competitive: "Ellyson Keeps Going to Annex Ascot Race," *Los Angeles Times*, January 30, 1939.

Midget racing was splintered: "Midget Group Joins A.A.A.," *Los Angeles Times*, January 24, 1939.

For the sixty-lap: "Rajo Jack Wins Sweepstakes at Southern Ascot Speedway," *Los Angeles Times*, February 13, 1939.

A new manufacturer: "Challenger Citroen Sets New Gas Economy Mark," *Los Angeles Times*, February 26, 1939.

J. C. Agajanian devised a four-hundred-lap: "Bud Rose Victor as Jinx Hinders Rivals," *San Bernardino (CA) Sun*, February 27, 1939.

Agajanian brought in three-time: "Ascot Cards 101-Lap Race," *Los Angeles Times*, March 12, 1939.

In the rain-postponed: Alan Ward, "Ray Gardiner Wins Speed Test; David Escapes Injury as Car Burns," *Oakland (CA) Tribune*, April 3, 1939.

He didn't listen: Alan Ward, "On Second Thought," *Oakland (CA) Tribune*, April 4, 1939.

The following week he pulled: Scalzo, "Rajo Jack Part III," 34.

The other southern California boys: "Schock Captures 100-Mile Grind," *San Francisco Chronicle*, May 1, 1939.

Rajo placed second: "Ranny Idne Victor in Midget Feature," *Oregonian* (Portland), July 15, 1939.

and fifth in a 250-lap: "Scoville Wins Race Event," *Oregonian* (Portland), July 17, 1939.

The promoters at Langford Speedway: "California Driver Finally Booked to Race at Langford," *Victoria (BC) Daily Colonist*, Saturday, July 22, 1939.

Rajo left his truck in Washington: Radbruch, *Dirt Track Auto Racing*, 50.

"I'll be back again": "Sutton Wins at Lanford Races," *Racing Wheels*: July 25, 1939.

And when Rajo got his car fixed: "Bud Rose First in Ascot Event," *Los Angeles Times*, July 31, 1939.

Chapter 10: The Super-Sub Wins the Other 500

Charlie Curryer dreamt of making: "Charlie Curryer," National Sprint Car Hall of Fame & Museum.

In 1939, Curryer scraped together: Motter, *History of the Oakland Speedway*, 65.

There were many fast cars: "Drivers Stage Trials Today," *Oakland (CA) Tribune*, September 17, 1939.

In the first round of qualifying: "Agabashian Wins Pole Spot in Race," *Oakland (CA) Tribune*, September 18, 1939.

Showing up two days before the race: "Rajo's 105 M.P.H. Tops Speed Trials," *San Francisco Chronicle*, September 23, 1939.

Officially, forty-two cars entered: Alan Ward, "Gene Figone to Drive Douglas Car in 500-Mile Race Here Tomorrow," *Oakland (CA) Tribune*, September 23, 1939.

One of the cars: Alan Ward, "Thirty-Three Speed Stars Battle Today for Honors in Oakland's 500-Mile Test," *Oakland (CA) Tribune*, September 24, 1939.

The race was scheduled to begin: "Peterson Wins 500-Mile Oakland Race," *Riverside (CA) Daily Press*, September 25, 1939.

When the racers finally put a clean start: "Rajo Jack Wrecks Car, Wins Anyway," *Santa Ana (CA) Register*, September 25, 1939.

"Get that guy out of there": "What a Relief! Rajo Jack Wins Speed Test for Tex Peterson," *San Francisco Chronicle*, September 25, 1939.

"Keep 'er on the track and win": Alan Ward, "Peterson Started Something, but Jack Finished It," *Oakland (CA) Tribune*, September 25, 1939.

Dozens of newspapers: Alan Ward, "On Second Thought," *Oakland (CA) Tribune*, September 25, 1939.

On October 1, Rajo Jack: "Rajo Jack Drives to Close Victory," *Los Angeles Times*, October 2, 1939.

Rajo first met Frame: Alan Ward, "Thanks A Million," *Oakland (CA) Tribune*, October 11, 1939.

Rajo Jack never liked racing the tiny cars: "Midgets Race Today for Frame Trophy," *San Francisco Chronicle*, November 12, 1939.

After months of rained-out races: "Bud Rose Speeds to Victory in Opening Ascot Feature," *Los Angeles Times*, March 4, 1940.

The promise of a big race: "Jack Wins Feature," *Madera (CA) Tribune*, March 11, 1940.

For many years: "Auto Racing Speedster Mel Leighton Is Top Money Winner on Los Angeles Track," *Ebony*, August 1948, 36-39.

Big car fields were waning: "Bud Rose Victor in Ascot Feature," *Los Angeles Times*, March 18, 1940.

He drove Vince Podurgiel's midget: Tom Motter, interview with author, October 8, 2018.

And then Rajo broke through: "Bill Brereton Race Favorite," *Los Angeles Times*, April 14, 1940.

He followed that by placing third: "Bud Rose Winner in Ascot Feature," *Los Angeles Times*, April 22, 1940.

The promoters of Los Angeles' Atlantic: "Farmer and Lindskog Loom as Midget Threats Tonight," *Los Angeles Times*, April 16, 1940.

Rajo also brought his big car: Scalzo, "Rajo Jack Part III," 34.

The new surface: Prescott Sullivan, "The Low Down," *San Francisco Examiner*, May 9, 1940.

An astounding field: "Schock Wins; Four Drivers Hurt," *Oakland (CA) Tribune*, May 13, 1940.

Over the years, Rajo and Bud Rose: "Rose Takes Main Event at Ascot," *Los Angeles Times*, May 20, 1940.

For years, Fred Frame's desire: "Fred Frame in Critical Shape After Crackup," *Riverside (CA) Daily Press*, June 3, 1940.

A bomb was detonated: "Northern Driver Cops 250-Mile Race," *Los Angeles Times*, June 2, 1940.

"Boy, oh boy, what a lucky break": Alan Ward, "C'Mon You Citroen!" *Oakland (CA) Tribune*, June 7, 1940.

Two weeks later, in the same car: "Rajo Jack Victor in Ascot Feature," *Los Angeles Times*, June 17, 1940.

When the four leaders: "Four Drivers Hurt in Ascot Crackup," *Los Angeles Times*, June 22, 1940.

Then Rajo made it three: Rajo Jack Wins Goshen Car Race," *Fresno (CA) Bee*, June 24, 1940.

He placed second in a two-hundred-lap: "Pilots Drive for Red Cross," *Los Angeles Times*, June 28, 1940.

third in a hundred-lap jalopy: "Angelino Driver Wins Speedway Test at Oakland," *Klamath News* (Klamath Falls, OR), July 6, 1941.

"Where was Rajo Jack": "Race Drivers Arrive at Riverside Track," *Los Angeles Times*, July 13, 1940.

Chapter 11: The Big Crash and Road to Obscurity

The bright center of the racing universe: Brown, *America's Speedways Past & Present*, 28–31.

Bayless Levrett was one of the first: Don Radbruch, "Bayliss Levrett," Hall of Fame Inductees, 2007, National Sprint Car Hall of Fame, https://www.sprintcarhof.com/pages/hall-of-fame.aspx.

Throughout the 1930s: Robert Franklin, "Outlaw King of the Dirt Track . . . Gus Schrader," *Speed Age*, November 1950, 24-27.

John A. Sloan wanted to bring in new drivers: "John Sloan," Hall of Fame Inductees, 1996, National Sprint Car Hall of Fame & Museum, https://www.sprintcarhof.com/pages/hall-of-fame.aspx.

As soon as Rajo agreed: "California Comer and Portuguese Racer File," *Argus-Leader* (Sioux Falls, SD), August 9, 1940.

The schedule Sloan put together: "Labor Day Races Attract Classy Talent to Huron," *Daily Plainsman* (Huron, SD), August 27, 1940.

The general public: Radbruch, *Dirt Track Auto Racing*, 53.

Rajo had to update the story: "A Refugee from War Torn Europe," *Daily Plainsman* (Huron, SD), August 27, 1940.

The half-mile dirt oval: "At Warren County Fair . . . Auto Racers Seriously Hurt." *Des Moines Register*, August 9, 1940.

A third ambulance arrived: Stan Vermeil, interview with author, November 15, 2016.

Over the next few days: "Speed Kings at Algona," *Estherville (IA) Daily News*, August 15, 1940.

Rajo wasn't going to be earning: "Rajo Jack Gets Garnant Special," *Oakland (CA) Tribune*, August 28, 1940.

Rajo barely got his number 33 car: Alan Ward, "Rajo Favorite in 500 Miler," *Oakland (CA) Tribune*, August 30, 1940.

On October 20, he came to the ARA: "Shock Annexes Race in Clovis," *Fresno (CA) Bee*, October 21, 1940.

Rajo tried to race again: "Speed Kings Vie at Fair Track Today," *Arizona Republic* (Phoenix), November 11, 1940.

Rajo finally healed enough: "Leads Stock Car Race for 100 Miles, Then Radiator Goes Hot on Sepia Driver," *Chicago Defender*, January 25, 1941.

Rajo repainted his big car: "Hal Cole Wins 100-Mile Auto Race," *Oakland (CA) Tribune*, April 21, 1941.

Shortly after Rajo returned: "Peterson Snags Ascot Auto Race," *Los Angeles Times*, June 9, 1941.

He showed up almost a week early: "Rajo Jack in Oakland Race," *San Francisco Examiner*, June 28, 1941.

"I don't believe there will be any racing": Alan Ward, "On Second Thought," *Oakland (CA) Tribune*, August 31, 1941.

Going into the final: Alan Ward, "Thirty Pilots File Entries For 500-Mile Auto Classic," *Oakland (CA) Tribune*, August 28, 1941.

Hal Cole and Wally Schock: Clyde Giraldo, "Oakland Auto Racer Killed," *San Francisco Examiner*, September 2, 1941.

Rajo returned to Southern Ascot: "Scheffler Sets Ascot Record in Drizzle," *Los Angeles Times*, October 13, 1941.

J. C. Agajanian—taking a page: "Phoenix Pilot Enters Fair Auto Events," *Arizona Republic* (Phoenix), November 6, 1941.

He passed Dave Champeau: "Phoenix Bid Big for Black," *Billboard*, November 29, 1941.

For the remainder of his life: Foote, "J. C. 'Aggie' Agajanian," https://www.sprintcarhof.com /pages/hall-of-fame.aspx.

On December 21, AAA Contest Board president: Rickenbacker, *Rickenbacker: An Autobiography*, 185.

Southern Ascot held its first race: "Scheffler Speeds to Victory in 100-Lap Race at Ascot," *Los Angeles Times*, January 5, 1942.

Rajo placed seventh: "Bill Sheffler Monopolizes Honors at Ascot Speedway," *Los Angeles Times*, February 16, 1942.

Rajo raced April 25: "Bill Sheffler Nabs Ascot Race," *Los Angeles Times*, April 27, 1942.

Then the US government banned: Wallen, *Distant Thunder*, 53.

Rajo registered for the draft: "U.S. WWII Draft Cards Young Men, 1940–1947," National Archives and Records Administration, Ancestry.com, https://www.ancestry.com (2011).

Two of Rajo's brothers: Joy Cornin, interview with author, April 15, 2017.

And Noah Gatson died in 1943: "U.S., Railroad Retirement Pension Index, 1934–1987," National Archives and Records Administration, Ancestry.com, https://www.ancestry.com (2017).

While Rajo had always been religious: Scalzo, "Rajo Jack Part III," 34.

Though racing was banned: Wallen, *Distant Thunder*, 54.

Chapter 12: Racing Around the Fringes

None of the Gatson: Joy Cornin, interview with author, February 8, 2017.

Ruth's younger brother: United States Census, 1940, Tyler (Ward 4), Smith County, Texas, T627, roll 4137, sheet 7A, ED 212-13, family 144, FamilySearch, https://www.familysearch.org (August 20, 2019).

Before Rajo and Ruth: Rajo Jack DeSoto v. Ruth King DeSoto, Civ. No. 20638.

When a floorboard on the back: Art Stewart, "Rajo Jack—Biography," *National Speed Sport News*, June 1944.

The one thing Rajo maintained: Scalzo, "Rajo Jack Part III," 34.

There were hundreds of race car owners: "Auto Race Booked for Imperial Oval," *San Diego Union*, October 17, 1945.

Most of the former southern California: "Bud Rose Cops El Centro Race," *Los Angeles Times*, October 28, 1945.

Eddie Rickenbacker still owned: Rickenbacker, *Rickenbacker: An Autobiography*, 185–186.

Of the seventy entries filed: Klann, "Rajo Jack Fast and Furious."

"In case they got their back up": Herb Spivey, interview with author, August 23, 2018.

Kelly Petillo also filed an entry: "Petillo in Suit Against Speedway," *Palladium-Item* (Richmond, IN), May 24, 1946.

When George Robson took the lead: W. Blaine Patton, "Robson Wins as 8 Finish," *Indianapolis Star*, May 31, 1946.

Chickie Hirashima, Robson's engine builder: Curt Cavin, "Long Time Coming: Japanese Automakers Have Shown an Interest in Indy Since the '60s," *Autoweek*, May 4, 2003.

Oakland Speedway had closed: Tom Motter, *A History of the Oakland Stadium 1946–1955* (Rancho Cordova, CA: Vintage Images, 2001), 1–4.

"Rajo ought to be calling": Herb Spivey, interview with author, August 9, 2018.

"This is standard": Herb Spivey, interview with author, August 9, 2018.

When Rajo finally saw the new track": Alan Ward, "Whitmer Cops 3rd Straight at Speedway," *Oakland (CA) Tribune*, July 8, 1946.

Rajo returned: Alan Ward, "Leverett, Rose Tie in First Dead Heat of Local Racing," *Oakland (CA) Tribune*, September 2, 1946.

What made things worse: "Driver Killed, Three Hurt in Dirt Track Crackup," *Los Angeles Times*, September 3, 1946.

After Kelly Petillo gave up: Ball, "Cavino 'Kelly' Petillo," https://www.sprintcarhof.com/pages/hall-of-fame.aspx.

Despite all the horrible things: Kelly Petillo Jr., interview with author, December 27, 2017.

The first plot of land: "Orange County Bosses Reject Race Track Plan," *Santa Maria (CA) Times*, February 7, 1946.

He told the press: Ken Bojens, "Off the Main Line," *San Diego Union*, August 24, 1946.

Days before his new track: "Auto Speed King Puts Up $750 to Obtain Release," *San Bernardino County Sun*, December 12, 1946.

The San Diego Motor Speedway: "Race Driver Injured as Car Smashes Rail," *San Diego Union*, January 2, 1947.

Even if Rajo were in any shape: "Big Cars in Debut Here Today," *San Diego Union*, January 5, 1947.

Charlie Curryer had always been a good mark: Alan Ward, "On Second Thought," *Oakland (CA) Tribune*, June 2, 1947.

Rajo eventually found a pair: Jack Williamson, "Veteran Tex Peterson Enters Races," *Daily Review* (Hayward, CA), July 15, 1947.

Rajo also worked: Jack Currow, "Big Cars Race Today at Carrell Speedway," *Los Angeles Times*, April 25, 1948.

He put on weight: Jim Miller, interview with author, August 31, 2018.

Chapter 13: Rising from the Ashes

When Louis Vermeil bought: "Louis Vermeil," Hall of Fame Inductees, 1995, National Sprint Car Hall of Fame & Museum, https://www.sprintcarhof.com/pages/hall-of-fame.aspx.

The shop would become known: Dick Vermeil, interview with author, February 16, 2017.

While travelling through San Mateo: Stan Vermeil, interview with author, November 15, 2016.

Vermeil was instrumental: Stan Vermeil, interview with author, April 18, 2017.

"He was very sort of warm": Dick Vermeil, interview with author, February 16, 2017.

Rajo Jack held a lingering, romantic notion: Clymer, *AAA Official Record Book*, 5.

The American Racing Association had: Stan Vermeil, personal interview, December 27, 2017.

For the first race of his comeback: "Reilly Wins Meadows Race," *Oregonian* (Portland), September 19, 1949.

While some would have been devastated: "Benoit Is Winner," *Times* (San Mateo, CA) October 1, 1949.

In what was scheduled to be: "Bob McLean Wins Calistoga Auto Race," *San Francisco Chronicle*, November 14, 1949.

But at the last minute: "S.F. Driver Takes Race at Stockton," *San Francisco Examiner*, December 5, 1949.

In the early years of J.C. Agajanian's career: Foote, "J. C. 'Aggie' Agajanian," https://www.sprint carhof.com/pages/hall-of-fame.aspx.

In 1949, 1950 and 1951: Stephen Michael Cullen, *Fanatical Fay Taylour: Her Sporting and Political Life at Speed, 1904–1983* (Warwick: Allotment Hut, 2015), 212–214.

For the opening race of the 1950 season: "Something New Added to Racing," *Oakland (CA) Tribune*, April 26, 1950.

Rajo Jack arrived fashionably: "S.F. Race Driver Wins Feature," *San Francisco Examiner*, April 24, 1950.

"These are the only tires I have": Stan Vermeil, interview with author, November 15, 2016.

At the Stockton Fairgrounds: "L.A. Driver Wins Stockton Race," *San Francisco Chronicle*, May 8, 1950.

There was another new track: "Memorial Day Races Planned," *Press Democrat* (Santa Rosa, CA), May 26, 1950.

Rajo returned to Calistoga: "Rajo Jack Drives Calistoga Winner," *Press Democrat* (Santa Rosa, CA), May 31, 1950.

By that time, Rajo was telling: Stan Vermeil, interview with author, April 18, 2017.

To follow up his win: "Reilly, B.C. Pilot, Wins Big Car Race," *Times* (San Mateo, CA), June 5, 1950.

Rajo and Reilly: Dick Vermeil, interview with author, February 16, 2017.

When the California contingent: "Carter Victor at Meadows," *Oregonian* (Portland), June 12, 1950.

He raced at the resurrected fairgrounds: "Bob Willis Snags Napa Big Car Race," *San Francisco Chronicle*, July 4, 1950.

then followed it with a fifth-place: "Bob Willis Wins Main Event Race," *Nevada State Journal* (Reno), July 5, 1950.

After the races ended the first night: Stan Vermeil, interview with author, November 15, 2016.

"This is my house": Stan Vermeil, interview with author, November 15, 2016.

"Rajo, let's test the compression": Stan Vermeil, interview with author, November 15, 2016.

Rajo won the fifteen-lap main event: "Rajo Jack Captures Quincy Auto Race," *San Francisco Chronicle*, August 14, 1950.

placed third in the August 26: Jack Menges, "The Checkered Flag," *Oakland (CA) Tribune*, August 29, 1950.

then struggled the next week: "Big Car Racing at Calistoga Track September 2," *Healdsburg (CA) Tribune, Enterprise and Scimitar*, August 31, 1950.

Two days later at Stockton: "Top Drivers Will Race Big Cars in Stockton," *Sacramento Bee*, September 1, 1950.

There were several races: Stan Vermeil, interview with author, April 18, 2017.

But Rajo, along with Reilly: "Big Cars Set for Meadows," *Oregonian* (Portland), September 10, 1950.

For Rajo to race in 1951: Radbruch, *Dirt Track Auto Racing*, 53.

The many-time IMCA champion: Franklin, "Outlaw King of the Dirt Track," 24–27.

Though the segregated grandstands: Gordon White, "Breaking the Barrier," *Vintage Oval Racing*, February 2003, 9–10.

Rajo Jack finally raced: "25-Car Field Set for Downs Run," *Dallas Morning News*, June 24, 1951.

In late August, Rajo traveled: Brad Wilson, "23,000 See Grim Stave Off Luptow in Fair Race," *Des Moines Register*, August 27, 1951.

For the September 1 race: Brad Wilson, "Fatality Mars Races as Luptow Wins," *Des Moines Register*, September 2, 1951.

Chapter 14: The Indy 500 Dream

With Anderson's distinct: "Rochester Radio Star Finds Long Greens Buy Lots of Comfort and Ease," *Ebony*, November 1945, 13–18.

"You babies come down": Stan Vermeil, interview with author, April 18, 2017.

He was the skipper: Eddie Anderson Jr., interview with author, December 11, 2016.

Rajo convinced Anderson: "Auto Kings Hold Tests in Oakland," *San Francisco Examiner*, April 13, 1941.

Nearly every race car builder: Mark Vaughn, "'Legends of Los Angeles' Exhibit at the Petersen Opens with a Tribute Night to Parnelli Jones," *Autoweek*, November 12, 2018.

In 1948 Diedt started: "1950 Diedt/Rochester Special," Sold, Fantasy Junction, accessed September 25, 2019, https://www.fantasyjunction.com/sold/1950-diedt-rochester-special-n-a/overview.

"The only thing that might stop me": "Auto Racing Speedster Mel Leighton is Top Money Winner on Los Angeles Track," *Ebony*, August 1948, 36–40.

Rajo still didn't like Leighton: Leonard W. Miller, interview with author, August 30, 2018.

One of the drivers: Patrick Sullivan, *Brick by Brick: The Story of Auto Racing Pioneer Joie Ray* (Fishers, IN: American Scene, 2008), 71.

He was recruited to race: "Big Cars Roll at De Anza Park in Tomorrow's Inaugural Races," *Riverside (CA) Daily Press*, May 17, 1952.

Many of the cars brought: Joe Wimer, "1400 Race Fans Turn Up for Opening at De Anza," *Riverside (CA) Daily Press*, May 19, 1952.

Eddie Anderson, Andy Granatelli: Robert Cromie, "A.A.A. Refuses Bill Holland's License Plea," *Chicago Tribune*, November 20, 1952.

Joie Ray didn't develop: Sullivan, *Brick by Brick*, 170.

Chapter 15: Hawaiian Interlude

By the mid-1950s: Scalzo, "Rajo Jack Part III," 34.

Three days before the race: "Divorces Granted," *Los Angeles Times*, March 18, 1953.

At the end of the 1947 season: H. A. Branham, *Big Bill: The Life and Times of NASCAR Founder Bill France Sr.* (Toronto: FENN-M&S, 2015), 25–34.

A baseball and football stadium: "Stocks to Wind Up 1952 Racing Season Tonight," *Honolulu Advertiser*, March 28, 1952.

Lou Abrams received NASCAR sanctioning: Gene Wilhelm, "Auto Races Definitely Scheduled for Tonight," *Honolulu Star-Bulletin*, December 18, 1953.

Jerry Unser, Jr. was an upstart: Bobby Unser, interview with author, September 20, 2018.

Ward and Johnson arranged a ship: Gene Wilhelm, "15 Racing Cars Scheduled to Arrive Tuesday for Quartermile Track Championship at Stadium," *Honolulu Star-Bulletin*, January 9, 1954.

Alan Ward did everything he could: Joe Anzivino, "New Sport in Local Debut Friday," *Honolulu Advertiser*, January 20, 1954.

One of the media outlets: "Colored Cal. Driver in Hawaiian Car Races," *Jet*, January 21, 1954, 53.

The flight to Hawaii: "15 Mainland Drivers to Arrive Thursday," *Honolulu Advertiser*, January 19, 1954.

There had been significant rain: "Sprint Cars to Race for Title Tonight," *Honolulu Star-Bulletin*, January 22, 1954.

"We had a tough time": Bill Miller, "Jack Flaherty Cops Auto Race," *Honolulu Advertiser*, January 23, 1954.

The January 29 race: "Palmer Wins Main Event at Stadium," *Honolulu Advertiser*, January 30, 1954.

Johnson lost money: Alan Ward, "On Second Thought," *Oakland (CA) Tribune*, February 2, 1954.

After returning to the mainland: "Negro Driver Wins 2 Hawaiian Auto Races," *Jet*, February 18, 1954, 51.

Not long after he returned: Rajo Jack DeSoto v. Ruth King DeSoto, Civ. No. 20638.

Chapter 16: A New Dream

Bob Barkheimer got out of driving: Jane M. Yasukawa, *Tales of the Oval: The Short Stories and Memories of Robert "Barky" Barkhimer* (Albuquerque, NM: RJ Communications, 2002), 56.

NASCAR held a race: Greg Fielden, *Forty Years of Stock Car Racing: The Beginning 1949–1958* (Ormond Beach, FL: Galfield, 1987), 157.

"He was pretty iconic": Kenn Clapp, interview with author, March 20, 2017.

This wasn't some small race: Hershel McGriff, interview with author, December 20, 2016.

On May 25, 1955, the Second District: Rajo Jack DeSoto v. Ruth King DeSoto, Civ. No. 20638.

He knew a person: "Amick Triumphs in 200-Lapper," *Los Angeles Times*, May 30, 1955.

"I never heard him swear": Herb Spivey, interview with author, August 9, 2018.

Rajo finally would have had a legitimate: Ray Silvius, "Fair Race Crash Kills Driver," *Arizona Republic* (Phoenix), November 7, 1955.

On February 27, 1956, Rajo and Warren: Death record for Rajo Jack, February 27, 1956, "California Death Index, 1940–1997," California Department of Public Health – Vital Records, FamilySearch, https://familysearch.org: 2016.

"He drove in hundreds": "Heart Attack Claims Life of Rajo Jack," *Los Angeles Times*, February 29, 1956.

Rajo Jack's funeral: "Rites Arranged for Rajo Jack," *Los Angeles Times*, March 4, 1956.

Ed Winfield was named the executor: Bob Blake, "They Called Him Rajo Jack," *Secrets of Speed Society*, July 1999, 30–31.

Epilogue: Rajo Jack as a Work of Art

Salvatore Scarpitta arrived: Joe Scalzo, "Making His Own Music," *Open Wheel*, November 1994, 57–64.

Scarpitta was born: Salvatore Scarpitta, oral history interview, Archives of American Art, Smithsonian Institution, January 31–February 3, 1975, https://www.aaa.si.edu/collections/interviews/oral-history-interview-salvatore-scarpitta-12727#overview.

When Italy entered: Robert M. Edsel, *Saving Italy: The Race to Rescue a Nation's Treasures from the Nazis* (New York: W.W. Norton, 2014), 6–7.

Scarpitta went to every dirt track: James Harithas, "Dirt-Track Sculpture Salvatore Scarpitta," *Sculpture*, March 2006, 46–49.

"This man was so eloquent": Beth Faban, "Scarpitta's Show Exciting Artistry," *Oregonian* (Portland), March 23, 1979.

A group called the Black American Racers Association: Ev Gardner, "Marylander Wins the Rajo Jack DeSoto Award," *Evening Star* (Washington, DC), February 27, 1976.

When Miller approached STP executives: Miller, interview with author, August 30, 2018.

The BARA held a convention: Leonard W. Miller, *Silent Thunder: Breaking Through Cultural, Racial, and Class Barriers in Motorsports* (Trenton, NJ: Red Sea, 2004), 18.

In 2002 Leonard Miller's: Miller and Kenneth Shropshire, *Racing While Black: How an African-American Stock Car Team Made Its Mark on NASCAR* (New York: Seven Stories, 2010), 18, 23–25, 297, 308.

The 2003 ESPN documentary: ESPN, *The Forgotten Race: Where the Finish Line Crosses the Color Line*, (Bristol, CT: 2003).

In 2017, Freewheelers and Company of Japan: "Rajo Jack," blog archives, Freewheelers and Company, June 19, 2017, http://freewheelers.co.jp/blog/archives/19981.

When the West Coast Stock: "Hall of Fame," West Coast Stock Car Hall of Fame, accessed September 25, 2019, http://westcoaststockcarhalloffame.com/hall-of-fame/.

Gerald Gatson died in 1970: *Texas, Death Certificates, 1903–1982*, Texas Department of State Health Services.

Warren Gatson died in 1976: Joy Cornin, interview with author, April 15, 2017.

Geneva Gatson died in Kern County: Death record for Geneva Gatson, June 17, 1995, "California Death Index, 1940–1997," California Department of Public Health – Vital Records, FamilySearch, https://familysearch.org: 2016.

The restored number 18: Amphora Art & Antiques, "Indy Racecar American Miller Schoenfield Engine Body Clyde Adams Offenhauser," eBay, updated March 20, 2019, https://www.ebay .com.

There was one place Rajo Jack: Radbruch, *Dirt Track Auto Racing*, 50–53.

In 2007 Rajo Jack was inducted: Ball, "Rajo Jack," https://www.sprintcarhof.com/pages/hall-of -fame.aspx.

BIBLIOGRAPHY

Books

Ashe, Arthur R., Jr. *A Hard Road to Glory*. New York: Warner Books, 1988.

Brown, Allan E. *The History of America's Speedways: Past & Present*. 4th ed. Comstock Park, MI: America's Speedway, 2017.

Catlin, Russ. *The Life of Ted Horn: American Racing Champion*. Los Angeles: Floyd Clymer, 1949.

Cullen, Stephen Michael. *Fanatical Fay Taylour: Her Sporting and Political Life at Speed, 1904–1983*. Warwick, UK: Allotment Hut, 2015.

Donovan, Brian. *Hard Driving: The Wendell Scott Story*. Hanover, NH: Steerforth, 2008.

Economacki, Chris, and Dave Argabright. *Let 'Em All Go! The Story of Auto Racing by the Man Who Was There*. Westfield, IN: Books by Dave Argabright, 2006.

Edsel, Robert M. *Saving Italy: The Race to Rescue a Nation's Treasures from the Nazis*. New York: W. W. Norton, 2014.

Fielden, Greg. *Forty Years of Stock Car Racing: The Beginning 1949–1958*. Ormond Beach, FL: Galfield, 1987.

Fox, Jack C. *The Mighty Midgets*. Madison, IN: Carl Hungness, 2004.

Gould, Todd. *For Gold and Glory: Charlie Wiggins and the African-American Racing Car Circuit*. Bloomington, IN: Indiana University Press, 2002.

Jeffers, H. Paul. *Ace of Aces: The Life of Captain Eddie Rickenbacker*. New York City: Random House, 2003.

Kehoe, Bob. *Art Pollard: The Life and Legacy of a Gentleman Racer*. Scotts Valley, CA: CreateSpace Independent, 2016.

Lucero, John. *Legion Ascot Speedway 1920s–1930s: Speed . . . Victory . . . Thrills . . . Spills*. Downey, CA: Orecue, 1982.

Mattish, Dennis. *History of San Jose Auto Racing 1903–2007*. 2nd ed. Marceline, MO: Walsworth, 2009.

Mattish, Dennis. *History of San Jose Racing Part 2*. Marceline, MO: Walsworth, 2016.

McDonald, Johnny. *San Diego Motorsports: 100 Racing Years.* Scotts Valley, CA: CreateSpace Independent, 2015.

Miller, Leonard T., and Kenneth Shropshire. *Racing While Black: How an African-American Stock Car Team Made Its Mark on NASCAR.* New York: Seven Stories, 2010.

Miller, Leonard W. *Silent Thunder: Breaking Through Cultural, Racial, and Class Barriers in Motorsports.* Trenton, NJ: Red Sea, 2004.

Motter, Tom. *A History of the Oakland Speedway 1931–1941.* Rancho Cordova, CA: Vintage Images, 2002.

Motter, Tom. *A History of the Oakland Stadium 1946–1955.* Rancho Cordova, CA: Vintage Images, 2001.

Motter, Tom. *Sacramento: Dirt Capital of the West.* Rancho Cordova, CA: Vintage Images, 2009.

Nalon, William F. *Barney Oldfield: The Life and Times of America's Legendary Speed King,* rev. ed. Carpinteria, CA: Brown Fox Books, 2002.

Rand McNally & Company. *Population of the United States: Census of 1920; By States, Counties, Cities, Towns, Boroughs, and Villages.* Chicago: Rand McNally, 1924.

Radbruch, Don. *Dirt Track Auto Racing, 1919–1941: A Pictorial History.* Jefferson, NC: McFarland, 2004.

Radbruch, Don. *Roaring Roadsters.* Ypsilanti, MI: Cartech, 1994.

Radbruch, Don. *Roaring Roadsters #2: The Exciting World History of Track Roadster Racing.* Washington, UT: Hot Rod Library, 2000.

Rickenbacker, Edward V. *Rickenbacker: An Autobiography.* Englewood Cliffs, NJ: Prentice-Hall, 1967.

Rose, Buzz. *Show Biz Auto Racing: IMCA Big Cars 1915-1977.* Tempe, AZ: Rose Racing Productions, 2001.

Schilling, Bob. *Pole Position Rex Mays: The Life of America's Most Popular Race Driver and a Long Look Back at American Auto Racing and Life Circa 1931-1949.* South Pasadena, CA: Race Data Press, 2011.

Seymour, Miranda. *The Bugatti Queen.* London: Simon & Schuster, 2004.

Stair, Urb. *Auto Racing Memories: Stories and Pictures of Racing in the 1930s and 1940s.* Whittier, CA: Kendall Buck, 2001.

Sullivan, Patrick. *Brick by Brick: The Story of Auto Racing Pioneer Joie Ray.* Fishers, IN: American Scene, 2008.

Wallen, Dick. *Distant Thunder: When Midgets Were Mighty.* Glendale, AZ: Dick Wallen Productions, 2001.

Ward, Geoffrey C. *Unforgivable Blackness: The Rise and Fall of Jack Johnson.* New York: Vintage Books, 2006.

Whisenhunt, Donald W, *A Chronological History of Smith County.* Tyler, TX: Smith County Historical Society, 1983.

White, Gordon Eliot. *Offenhauser: The Legendary Racing Engine and the Men Who Built It.* 2nd ed. St. Paul, MN: Motorbooks International, 2004.

Wiggins, David K., ed. *African Americans in Sports.* 2 vols. Armonk, New York: Sharpe Reference, 2004.

Yasukawa, Jane M. *Tales of the Oval: The Short Stories and Memories of Robert "Barky" Barkhimer.* Albuquerque, NM: RJ Communications, 2002.

Yates, Brock. *Against Death and Time: One Fatal Season in Racing's Glory Years.* Cambridge, MA: De Capo Press, 2005.

Yates, Brock. *Umbrella Mike: The True Story of the Chicago Gangster Behind the Indy 500*. New York: Thunder's Mouth, 2007.

Yunick, Smokey. *Best Damn Garage in Town: My Life & Adventures*. Fort Myers, FL: Carbon Press, 2003.

Zurschmeide, Jeff. *Portland Speedway*. Charleston, SC: Arcadia Publishing, 2014.

Magazines

"Auto Racing Speedster Mel Leighton Is Top Money Winner on Los Angeles Track," *Ebony*, August 1948.

Blake, Bob. "They Called Him Rajo Jack." *Secrets of Speed Society*. July 1999.

Carter, Duane, and Bob Shafer. "Racing Is My Business." *Speed Age*, August 1952.

Catlin, Russ. "The Rickenbacker Saga." *Speed Age*, May 1955.

"Colored Cal. Driver In Hawaiian Car Races." *Jet Magazine*, January 21, 1954.

Corkery, Mike, and Tim Corkery. "Johnny Parsons The New Champ." *Speed Age*, February 1950.

Franklin, Robert. "Outlaw King of the Dirt Track . . . Gus Schrader." *Speed Age*, November 1950.

Harithas, James. "Dirt-Track Sculpture Salvatore Scarpitta." *Sculpture*, March 2006.

Klann, John E. "Rajo Jack Fast and Furious." *Players*, October 1995.

Marcell, Doc Marcus. "Pitchmen vs. Pitchmen," *Billboard*, August 26, 1936.

Miller, Leonard T., and Leonard W. Miller. "Black Motor-Racing History: The Golden Era of Motorsports, 1910-1978." *Boule Journal*, Summer 2013.

"Negro Driver Wins 2 Hawaiian Auto Races." *Jet Magazine*, February 18, 1954.

Profrock, Wally, and Les Radbruch. "Racing's Minor League." *Speed Age*, May 1952.

Radbruch, Don. "The Fabulous Fred Frame." *Speed Age*, August 1956.

Radbruch, Don. "Mystery Man Rajo Jack." *Secrets of Speed Society*, April 1999.

Rivetti, Ermanno, "Market Revs Up for Racing Car Artist Salvatore Scarpitta." *Art Newspaper*, October 16, 2016.

"Rochester Radio Star Finds Long Greens Buy Lots of Comfort and Ease," *Ebony*, November 1945.

Ruttman, Troy, and Bob Shafer. "Pop 'n' Me." *Speed Age*, May 1952.

Scalzo, Joe. "Making His Own Music." *Open Wheel*, November 1994.

Scalzo, Joe. "Rajo Jack Part III." *Secrets of Speed Society*, October 1999.

White, Gordon. "Breaking the Barrier." *Vintage Oval Racing*, February 2003.

Newspapers

Argus-Leader (Sioux Falls, SD), 1940.

Arizona Capitol Times (Phoenix), 2017.

Arizona Republic (Phoenix), 1934–1946.

Bakersfield Californian, 1936–1949.

Beaumont (TX) Journal, 1938–1939.

Bergen (NJ) Herald, 1937.

Billboard, 1941.

Boston Herald, 1976.

Calgary (AB) Herald, 2012.

Charleston (SC) News and Courier, 1938.

Chicago Defender, 1936–1941.

Chicago Tribune, 1952.

Clark County Sun (Vancouver, WA), 1926.

Coast Auto Racing, 1934–1935.

Columbian (Vancouver, WA), 1923–1926

Courier (Waterloo, IA), 1940.

Covina (CA) Argus, 1934.

Daily Independent Journal (San Rafael, CA), 1949.

Daily Oklahoman (Oklahoma City), 1937–1939.

Daily Plainsman (Huron, SD), 1940.

Daily Review (Hayward, CA), 1946–1947.

Dallas Morning News, 1951.

Danville (PA) Morning News, 1936.

Des Moines Register, 1940–1951.

Detroit Times, 1937–1939.

El Paso Times, 1936.

Estherville (IA) Daily News, 1940.

Eugene (OR) Guard, 1936–1939.

Evening News (Harrisburg, PA), 1939.

Evening Star (Washington, DC), 1976.

Evening Tribune (San Diego, CA), 1933–1936.

Feather River Bulletin (Quincy, CA), 1950.

Fort Worth (TX) Star-Telegram, 1951–1997.

Fresno (CA) Bee, 1934–1941.

Globe-Gazette (Mason City, IA), 1940.

Great Falls (MT) Tribune, 1939.

Healdsburg (CA) Tribune, Enterprise and Scimitar, 1950.

Honolulu Advertiser, 1951–1954.

Honolulu Star-Bulletin, 1937-1954.

Houston Chronicle, 1937.

Indian Valley Record (Greenville, CA), 1950.

Indianapolis Star, 1936-1951.

Kane (PA) Republican, 1938.

Lewiston (ID) Tribune, 1937–1938.

Los Angeles Sentinel, 1936.

Los Angeles Times, 1924–2006.

Madera (CA) Tribune, 1940

Milwaukee Journal Sentinel, 1936.

Minneapolis (MN) Star, 1940.

Modesto (CA) Bee, 1941.

Modesto (CA) News-Herald, 1931.

Morning Herald (Klamath Falls, OR), 1938.

Morning Olympian (Olympia, WA), 1937.

Morning Oregonian (Portland), 1920–1936.

National Speed Sport News, 1944.

Nevada State Journal (Reno), 1950.

New York Age, 1940.

New York Amsterdam News, 1936.

Oakland (CA) Tribune, 1931–1954.

Omaha World-Herald, 1937.

Oregon Daily Journal (Portland), 1923.

Oregon Journal (Portland), 1936–1946.

Oregon Statesman (Salem), 1949.

Oregonian (Portland), 1937–1979.

Petaluma (CA) Argus-Courier, 1936–1949.

Philadelphia Tribune, 2007.

Pittsburgh Courier, 1941.

Portola (CA) Reporter, 1950.

Press Democrat (Santa Rosa, CA), 1941–1951.

Racing Wheels, 1939.

Reno (NV) Gazette-Journal, 1944–1950.

Riverside (CA) Daily Press, 1935–1952.

Riverside (CA) Independent Enterprise, 1950.

Sacramento Bee, 1937–1969.

Salt Lake Telegram (Salt Lake City), 1939.

San Bernardino Sun (CA), 1935–1947.

San Diego Tribune, 1934.

San Diego Union, 1933–1950.

San Francisco Chronicle, 1934–1954.

San Francisco Examiner, 1936–1951.

San Jose (CA) Mercury, 1935–1936.

San Jose (CA) News, 1935–1938.

San Luis Obispo (CA) Telegram-Tribune, 1939–1941.

Santa Ana (CA) Register, 1939.

Santa Cruz (CA) Evening News, 1936–1940.

Santa Maria (CA) Times, 1934.

Seattle Daily Times, 1935–1939.

St. Louis Post-Dispatch, 1934–1936.

St. Petersburg (FL) Times, 1999.

Tacoma (WA) Daily Ledger, 1956.

Tampa (FL) Times, 1980.

Tampa (FL) Tribune, 1941.

Times (San Mateo, CA), 1931–1955.

Ukiah (CA) Daily Journal, 1951.

Vancouver (WA) Columbian, 1923.

Victoria (TX) Advocate, 1937.

Victoria (BC) Daily Colonist, 1939.

Victoria (BC) Daily Times, 1939.

Washington Post, 1937.

Wichita Beacon, 1932.

Wilmington (CA) Daily Press Journal, 1934–1948.

Hall of Fame Biographies

Agan, Craig. "Eddie Rickenbacker." Hall of Fame Inductees, 1992. National Sprint Car Hall of Fame & Museum. https://www.sprintcarhof.com/pages/hall-of-fame.aspx.

"Art Pillsbury." Hall of Fame Inductees, 1992. National Sprint Car Hall of Fame & Museum. https://www.sprintcarhof.com/pages/hall-of-fame.aspx.

Ball, Larry, Jr. "Cavino 'Kelly' Petillo." Hall of Fame Inductees, 2009. National Sprint Car Hall of Fame & Museum. https://www.sprintcarhof.com/pages/hall-of-fame.aspx.

Ball, Larry, Jr. "Charlie Wiggins." Hall of Fame Inductees, 2015. National Sprint Car Hall of Fame & Museum. https://www.sprintcarhof.com/pages/hall-of-fame.aspx.

Ball, Larry L., Jr. "Francis Quinn." Hall of Fame Inductees, 2006. National Sprint Car Hall of Fame & Museum. https://www.sprintcarhof.com/pages/hall-of-fame.aspx.

Ball, Larry L., Jr. "Rajo Jack." Hall of Fame Inductees, 2007. National Sprint Car Hall of Fame & Museum. https://www.sprintcarhof.com/pages/hall-of-fame.aspx.

"Berna Eli 'Barney' Oldfield." Hall of Fame Inductees, 1990. National Sprint Car Hall of Fame & Museum. https://www.sprintcarhof.com/pages/hall-of-fame.aspx.

Blumer, Bill, Jr. "Anthony 'Andy' Granatelli." Hall of Fame Inductees, 2011. National Sprint Car Hall of Fame & Museum. https://www.sprintcarhof.com/pages/hall-of-fame.aspx.

Bogan, Norm. "Hal Robson." Hall of Fame Inductees, 2010. National Sprint Car Hall of Fame & Museum. https://www.sprintcarhof.com/pages/hall-of-fame.aspx.

"Duane 'Pappy' Carter (Sr.)." Hall of Fame Inductees, 1993. National Sprint Car Hall of Fame & Museum. https://www.sprintcarhof.com/pages/hall-of-fame.aspx.

Foote, Ben. "J. C. 'Aggie' Agajanian." Hall of Fame Inductees, 1990. National Sprint Car Hall of Fame & Museum. https://www.sprintcarhof.com/pages/hall-of-fame.aspx.

"Frank Kurtis." Hall of Fame Inductees, 1994. National Sprint Car Hall of Fame & Museum. https://www.sprintcarhof.com/pages/hall-of-fame.aspx.

"Fred Offenhauser." Hall of Fame Inductees, 1994. National Sprint Car Hall of Fame & Museum. https://www.sprintcarhof.com/pages/hall-of-fame.aspx.

"Gus Schrader." Hall of Fame Inductees, 1990. National Sprint Car Hall of Fame & Museum. https://www.sprintcarhof.com/pages/hall-of-fame.aspx.

"Harry A. Miller." Hall of Fame Inductees, 1990. National Sprint Car Hall of Fame & Museum. https://www.sprintcarhof.com/pages/hall-of-fame.aspx.

"J. Alex Sloan." Hall of Fame Inductees, 1990. National Sprint Car Hall of Fame & Museum. https://www.sprintcarhof.com/pages/hall-of-fame.aspx.

"John Sloan." Hall of Fame Inductees, 1996. National Sprint Car Hall of Fame & Museum. https://www.sprintcarhof.com/pages/hall-of-fame.aspx.

"Joie Chitwood (Sr.)." Hall of Fame Inductees, 1993. National Sprint Car Hall of Fame & Museum. https://www.sprintcarhof.com/pages/hall-of-fame.aspx.

Kennedy, Doug. "Johnnie Parsons." Hall of Fame Inductees, 2008. National Sprint Car Hall of Fame & Museum. https://www.sprintcarhof.com/pages/hall-of-fame.aspx.

"Louis Vermeil." Hall of Fame Inductees, 1995. National Sprint Car Hall of Fame & Museum. https://www.sprintcarhof.com/pages/hall-of-fame.aspx.

Peters, George, and Henri Greuter. "W. C. 'Bud' and Edward Winfield." Hall of Fame Inductees, 1991. National Sprint Car Hall of Fame & Museum. https://www.sprintcarhof.com/pages/hall-of-fame.aspx.

Radbruch, Don. "Bayliss Levrett." Hall of Fame Inductees, 2007. National Sprint Car Hall of Fame & Museum. https://www.sprintcarhof.com/pages/hall-of-fame.aspx.

Robertson, Kem. "Joe Jagersberger." Hall of Fame Inductees, 2007. National Sprint Car Hall of Fame & Museum. https://www.sprintcarhof.com/pages/hall-of-fame.aspx.

Sims, Carol. "Ted Horn." Hall of Fame Inductees, 1991. National Sprint Car Hall of Fame & Museum. https://www.sprintcarhof.com/pages/hall-of-fame.aspx.

Sullivan, Pat. "J. Gordon Betz." Hall of Fame Inductees, 2002. National Sprint Car Hall of Fame & Museum. https://www.sprintcarhof.com/pages/hall-of-fame.aspx.

"Troy Ruttman." Hall of Fame Inductees, 1993. National Sprint Car Hall of Fame & Museum. https://www.sprintcarhof.com/pages/hall-of-fame.aspx.

"Travis 'Spider' Webb." Hall of Fame Inductees, 1997. National Sprint Car Hall of Fame & Museum. https://www.sprintcarhof.com/pages/hall-of-fame.aspx.

Public Records

Death record for Geneva Gatson, June 17, 1995. "California Death Index, 1940–1997." California Department of Public Health – Vital Records. Digital images. FamilySearch. https://family search.org: 2016.

Death record for Rajo Jack, February 27, 1956. "California Death Index, 1940–1997." California Department of Public Health – Vital Records. Digital images. FamilySearch. https://www .familysearch.org: 2016.

Death record for Warren Gatson, 1976. "California Death Index, 1940–1997." California Department of Public Health – Vital Records. Digital images. FamilySearch. https://www.familysearch .org: 2016.

Marriage record for Jack DeSoto and Ruth Grace, August 31, 1932. *Oklahoma County Marriage Records Index, 1889–1951.* Oklahoma Historical Society. Ancestry.com. https://ancestry .com.

Rajo Jack DeSoto, Appellant, V. Ruth King DeSoto, Respondent. Civ. No. 20638. California Second Dist., Div. Three. May 25, 1955.

Records of the Railroad Retirement Board, Record Group 184. "U.S., Railroad Retirement Pension Index, 1934–1987." National Archives at Atlanta. Ancestry.com. https://www.ancestry .com: 2017.

San Jose City and Santa Clara County Directory 1929. "U.S. City Directories, 1822–1995." R. L. Polk & Company. Digital images. Ancestry.com. https://ancestry.com.

Smith County Marriage Records, The Book Series ML, 12:179. Smith County Clerk's Office. Local History/Genealogy Room, Tyler (TX) Public Library.

Smith County Marriage Records, The Book Series ML, 16:201. Smith County Clerk's Office. Local History/Genealogy Room, Tyler (TX) Public Library.

"Texas, County Marriage Index, 1837–1977." Texas county courthouses. Digital images. FamilySearch. https://www.familysearch.org: 2018.

Texas, Death Certificates, 1903–1982. Texas Department of State Health Services. Microfilm. Genealogy Section, Dallas Public Library.

Texas, Death Index, 1903–2000. Texas Department of State Health Services. Microfilm. Local History/Genealogy Room, Tyler (TX) Public Library.

Tyler Texas City Directory 1933. U.S. City Directories, 1822–1995. John F. Worley Directory Company. Local History/Genealogy Room, Tyler (TX) Public Library.

United States Census, 1910. Tyler (Ward 4), Enumeration District 68, Smith County, Texas. Bureau of the Census. Digital images. FamilySearch. https://www.familysearch.org: June 14, 2016.

United States Census, 1930. Tyler (Ward 4), Enumeration District 13, Smith County, Texas. Bureau of the Census. Digital images. FamilySearch. https://www.familysearch.org: November 27, 2018.

United States Census, 1940. Tyler (Ward 4), Enumeration District 212-13, Smith County, Texas. Bureau of the Census. Digital Images. FamilySearch. https://www.familysearch.org: August 20, 2019.

"U.S., Social Security Applications and Claims Index, 1936–2007." Ancestry.com. https://www.ancestry.com: 2015.

"U.S. WWII Draft Cards Young Men, 1940–1947." National Archives and Records Administration. Digital images. Ancestry.com. https://ancestry.com: 2011.

Race Programs

Bay Meadows Race Course. Race program, August 22, 1954.

Legion Ascot Speedway. Race program, January 27, 1935.

Southern Speedway. Race program, August 23, 1936.

Thesis

Ellis, Bryan. "A Historical Materialist Analysis of the Labor of Black Males in Professional Sport in the United States: From Chattel Slavery to Globalization." PhD diss., Howard University, 2009.

Journal Article

Hall, Randal L. "Carnival of Speed: The Auto Racing Business in the Emerging South, 1930-1950." *North Carolina Historical Review* 84, no. 3 (July 2007): 245–275. https://www.jstor.org/stable/23523062?seq=7#metadata_info_tab_contents.

Interviews

Chaparro, Freddy. Interview with author, September 3, 2018.

Clapp, Ken. Interview with author, March 20, 2017.

Cornin, Joy. Interview with author, February 8, 2017.

Cornin, Joy. Interview with author, April 15, 2017.

Edmunds, Don. Interview with author, December 21, 2016.

Lasteri, Chick. Interview with author, March 23, 2017.

McGriff, Hershel. Interview with author, December 20, 2016.

Miller, Jim. Interview with author, August 31, 2018.

Miller, Leonard W. Interview with author, August 30, 2018.

Motter, Tom. Interview with author, October 8, 2018.

Petillo, Kelly Jr. Interview with author, December 27, 2017.

Spivey, Herb. Interview with author, August 9, 2018.

Spivey, Herb. Interview with author, August 23, 2018.

Spivey, Herb. Interview with author, September 1, 2018.

Vermeil, Dick. Interview with author, February 16, 2017.

Vermeil, Stan. Interview with author, November 15, 2016.

Vermeil, Stan. Interview with author, April 18, 2017.

Vermeil, Stan. Interview with author, December 27, 2017.

INDEX

Page numbers in italics refer to images.